A NEW LOOK AT
THE SACRAMENTS

A NEW LOOK AT
THE SACRAMENTS

William J. Bausch

TWENTY-THIRD PUBLICATIONS
P.O. Box 180   West Mystic, CT 06388

Fifth printing 1980

Take Sky, copyright # 1961, 1962 by David McCord, used with permission of Little, Brown and Co.

Library of Congress Cataloging in Publication Data

Bausch, William J.
  A new look at the sacraments.

  Includes bibliographical references.
  1. Sacraments—Cahtolic Church. I. Title.
BX2200.B37   264'.02   77-2975
ISBN   0-89622-139-3

In Memoriam

REV. THOMAS NOLAN

"He who can preserve gentleness amid pains,
and peace amid worry
and multitude of affairs,
is almost perfect"
                    —St. Francis de Sales

Contents

Introduction

It started with a standard letter from the bishop's office. For the first time as a pastor I was to have confirmation in my parish in the spring. It seemed that a routine preparation was at hand. Still, I knew I had better brush up on my background and check the newer catechisms so as to present a well rounded program to those who shared the religious education of the parish with me. However, even a casual check of the textbooks told me that there was more to confirmation than meets the eye. There had been some changes in emphasis and enough diversity of approach and context to throw my understanding out of focus rather quickly. It was at this point that I knew I would have to delve deeper into the history and the theology of this sacrament.

I soon found out what the professional educators already knew. Confirmation was but a link in the sacramental chain. I could not, try as I might, see it or understand it apart from the whole process of initiation which included, as I found out, baptism and the eucharist. I was soon off on these intimate connections and, in time, onto the extrinsic connection with penance which in its turn could not be entirely discussed apart from the sacrament of the sick with which its history is somewhat intertwined.

In any case, the result of what should have been a routine preparation for confirmation is this book about the five sacraments of baptism, confirmation, eucharist, penance, and the sick. (Because these five are peculiarly and historically related I have confined myself to them and have omitted the social sac-

1

raments of holy orders and matrimony.) I have tried to combine the history, theology, and modern revisions of the sacramental rituals into a coherent meaning for the simple reason that one element is totally dependent on the other. I hope the results will provide the reader with a sense of the deeper meaning and even excitement that are a part of Christ's sacraments. Especially I hope that it will aid teachers and parents in assessing the new moods and programs concerning the sacraments that are apparent today.

As always, I wish to thank the people who first heard these chapters in unfinished form as a part of an adult class. I wish also to thank Ann DeVizia whose expert fingers typed the manuscript and whose keen eye saw to sensible corrections.

1

Removing Motes...

1

Before we take a look at the five sacraments which form the topic of this book, we must clear away as many obstacles, the "motes" in our eyes that keep us from seeing what the sacraments are all about. Originally, the word sacrament referred to the old Roman custom of making an oath of allegiance. A soldier made his "sacrament" or avowal of allegiance to pledge his services to the empire. The word never lost this meaning entirely, especially in reference to baptism which was seen as a pledge of allegiance to Christ. In the scripture, however, the word *sacrament* translates the word *mystery*. Here it has a quite broad meaning referring to God's plan and activity, revealed in Christ, for our salvation. It is a wide-ranging word embracing all the ways that God has and does reach out to us in the world and particularly that world as revealed in Christ. Any object, any person, any thing which somehow brought God and man into contact, which revealed his saving love could be called a sacrament. Sacrament meaning mystery was therefore quite open-ended, flexible and, desirably, imprecise.

Judaism had its sacraments and it is quite correct to speak of Jewish sacraments. We read in the bible that there were all kinds of blessings, the imposition of hands, oil, bread, wine, water, washings, kisses, greetings, the notion of a ritual meal (Passover), sacrificial offerings—all of which were part of broad, contextualized happenings which in some way showed forth God's saving presence and special power. Sometimes we forget that the Jews had baptism. Recall that the Jew, John the Baptizer, was baptizing along the Jordan before Jesus came. There was an official confession of sins since Solomon's time. Rabbis wrote of an anointing of the sick with oil. So, the first Christians, all Jews, inherited a vast complex of sacred signs and rituals, which conveyed in some way the mystery of God. But what happened was that among all of the ancient signs and rituals, blessings and gestures, seven in time became the most important and the most authentic because they had within themselves Christ's own dynamism. The church, under the Spirit, came to recognize this and so drew out of its tradition those elements which best described and evoked the work of Jesus.

This was not arbitrary. All of the basic grace-filled actions which we came to call the sacraments can be found in the New Testament, but they are not there in precise form and exact ritual, for the sacraments are not inventions but conclusions from what was found in the church's tradition and scripture. Jesus did not invent each and every one in blueprint form. Even the number seven is not quite accurate because, as we shall see, several sacraments are really ritual aspects of a single sacrament which became "subdivided." The number seven may be more akin to the fondness for seven as a mystical number and memory aid in the age before universal reading and writing. We see this reflected in the seven works of mercy, the seven petitions in the Lord's prayer, the seven capital sins, and the seven gifts of the Holy Spirit. On the other hand, we do not want to be casual with that number seven either. It is one of those mystic numbers which has a meaning beyond its count. It carries with it the notion of fullness, perfection, completeness. Therefore the sacraments could be numbered seven, regardless of whatever unity or subdivisions there might be, to denote that the mystery they embrace does in fact encompass the fullness of the life and love that God wills for us. In any case, what we want to understand is that the seven sacraments were not handed down as-is personally from Jesus himself. They have a derivation from and association with the so-called Jewish sacraments, they are to be found in spirit in the scripture, but their exact numbering and defining were to be left to the church of a later, more analytical age. This will help us when we come to look at the revision of the rites in our time and explain how the sacraments could be revised to begin with. The answer, we now see, is that from the beginning the church has always had charge of the style and approaches to the essential "mysteries" of salvation left by Jesus.

A more analytical age. Here we come to our first obstacle that prevents us from seeing the sacraments as they truly are. Recall that we said that formerly the sacraments referred to those over-all mysteries of salvation, those complex celebrations of what God was doing through Jesus. Sacramental celebration, as we may properly term it, is a communal response to God's call in Christ—a response which involves words and gestures, vocal and silent. It was not this or that particular item which was important or even vital. Rather what counted in celebrating the sacrament, the mystery, was the whole, overarching activity, atmosphere, movement, and context within the community of what was taking place in faith. Individual details did not matter. They were incidental to what was *happening.* This explains, for instance, why in many of the scriptural symbols of the Holy Eucharist one or other element is omitted. In the story of Cana, only the wine is mentioned. Nothing about bread. On the other hand, in the meeting of Jesus with the two disciples after his resurrection at Emmaus only the "breaking of the bread" is mentioned. No reference to the wine. In pre-Nicene times (before the fourth century) some of the eucharistic rites did not even contain the actual words which we call today the necessary words of consecration. Such words were only slowly introduced into the church as it gradually came to be felt that such words were the best articulation of what the congregation was *doing* when it met for the eucharist.

What started to happen, however, to pull the focus away from the overall "mystery," the complex sacramental ritual, was the legitimate desire by some to explain things more precisely. Through various circumstances, such as fighting heresies, more attempts were made to narrow down the mystery to certain words and actions. In the attempt to get at the "substance" of the mystery, to find out what exactly was necessary to make it really "there" (validity), the search was on for some specific words or actions which told the whole story. Such discovered words or actions, of course, were not the whole story and ultimately they did not really say very much when separated from the overall celebrating pattern of the worshiping community. But the trend was started.

So, slowly but inevitably the in-depth mystery, the whole complex celebration of the community became reduced to the "basic" elements. A mere simple rubbing with oil, overlaid with endless rubrics, was substituted for the marvelous tapestry of community prayer, praise, scripture, and ritual regarding the sick. A simple hand blessing substituted to delineate many a complex and involved rite. The whole pristine symbolism of sharing food and therefore one's life's sustenance, one's fellowship and fraternal love—the celebrating intricacies of eating, drinking, singing, praying, praising, sharing—all were summed up in a thin, pure white round wafer which eventually was not even eaten but looked at from a distance!

What is happening here? What is happening is the foundation of the first obstacle we have to overcome in order to appreciate the sacraments. We have to overcome a long history of reductionism; that is, of reducing an encounter with God in Christ to a momentary time or isolated element alone and by ourselves. We have to regain the context of the sacraments, and a context which includes the community. Perhaps an example will help. Suppose someone of prosaic mind tried to get at the meaning of our national Thanksgiving Day. He worked at it until at last he declared that the whole "essence" of this holiday could be captured in the turkey wing. That told it all. But, of course, what a fantastic reductionism! What a poor substitute for the whole turkey itself, the whole range of long-term preparations, family gatherings, reunions, old friendships, familial visitations, renewed emotions, old joys and a meaningful spirit of what families and individuals had to be thankful for. It is conceivable that the reduced turkey wing *might* mean all of this, but surely it is a terribly reduced symbol of all that the ritual of Thanksgiving has come to mean for the American family. In fact, to carry the example one step further, it is conceivable that in due time the turkey wing might become the only symbol of the interlacing, celebrating patterns of Thanksgiving Day. Future generations might well be perplexed as to what it was all about. Worse. A future generation might be content to go through some brief motion with the turkey wing in order to get on with the "real" business of life.

Something like this actually happened to the sacraments (as we shall see). In the process of analyzing them, the mystery was stripped to what some thought were the bare essentials. Then these essentials were put in the concrete of laws and rubrics. Now there was a quick and easy measurement of their validity. It was made easier for everyone to say, "*This* is a sacrament. *That* is not." It was easier to figure out precisely where grace resided and what to do to get it. Every person with rubrical savvy could call it forth. The step to magic was a short one.

Because we shall meet this problem of reductionism so often we must emphasize it with another example. Think of a great National Symphony Orchestra, masterfully rendering a beautiful piece of music. By nature there is the complexity of the instruments working together to produce the tonalities, shades, harmony, and art that are involved in the splendid whole. What a difference between being caught up in the symphonic music of a great orchestra and having the conductor tap out the main "tune" of the music on the piano with one finger. To have reduced an intricate piece of music to a simple, one-finger tune is precisely what happened to the sacramental system. Shades and complexities, life and celebration, community and ritual, were reduced to a bare minimum in an attempt to get at what was really "valid" and essential in a sacrament. In this manner the sacraments were gradually narrowed to isolated moments, closed off from the general community music which is the Christian life.

If the sacraments were looked upon no longer as celebrating actions between God and man, but as isolated and reduced rites, then it was easy for people to feel that they could capture them. Once this happened, then the sacraments came to be looked upon as possessions rather than gifts. As possessions, the sacraments were called the causes of grace, causes which we could manipulate and activate by the proper use of the basic ritual gesture and words. It was only a matter of time that such sophisticated causes should be put exclusively into the hands of specialists: the clergy. No longer the property of the celebrating Christian community at large, the sacraments became the preserve of the sacred specialist who dispensed them. We still use a vocabulary which reflects this. We say, "The priest or bishop *dispenses* the sacraments"; or, "The sacrament of confirmation will be *administered* by the most reverend bishop," "The priest *gives* communion, the priest *hears* confessions, *baptizes*, *anoints*, etc." The sacraments are something he gives out, not mysteries celebrated by the community over which he presides.

The next step is the evolution of a liturgical etiquette needed to obtain the sacraments from the clergy. Again, to go back to our example of the orchestra, it is as if the members of the orchestra were no longer presided over by the conductor (bishop, priest), but now all the music had been put on tapes. If any individual wanted to passively listen to them, he must go to the conductor to be serviced. The conductor would "administer" or dispense the tapes privately. None of this means, of course, that there is no room for the ministerial priesthood. Not at all. Rather the examples tell us how the priesthood can slip from being ministerial to becoming a caste system, how a servant can become a master and how a celebrant can become a dispenser. This can only happen when our community rituals which celebrate the mystery of our encounter with a God who first loved us are reduced to minimal objects. We, in our turn, act accordingly: how much of the Mass can I miss before it's a sin, how many ounces of meat break the fast, and all I want to hear are those words of absolution.

All that we have written so far means that the sacraments gradually became separated from life. The separation quickened as society lost its close-to-earth sense. Natural earthy actions and materials were rerouted into more sophisticated and cerebral mental ideals. Bread and wine and rubbing with oil, nudity, hand laying, kissing, embracing and dancing—all these homely, community rituals were sidetracked into brain waves rather than body English. This process, as we shall see, was completed by the arrival of technological society. As people learned more and more to read and write they tended to verbalize rather than to *do*. Sacramental liturgies in time became something you watch, not something you get up and celebrate (Mass was "said," for instance, before a passive audience). Our basic body instincts were over-intellectualized. We see the trouble many people have with the handshake or kiss of peace at Mass. For them it comes across as an uncalled for, low-class vulgarity interrupting their Mass-watching. It is likewise interesting to observe the strong reaction to centuries of denying physical elements. The reaction is in such movements as Cursillo and Marriage Encounter where much body contact and touching and kissing have been once more legitimized; a reaction long practiced for centuries in endless processions and cults of the more energetic Latin Catholic peoples. Catholics have had their emotions ritually and liturgically starved for too long. Yet, sacraments are mysteries to be celebrated by a people. It was a mistake that they have come to be seen as private, individual devotions. The newly revised rites called for by Vatican II are trying to reverse the trend.

So, at some length and perhaps with some exaggeration, we have examined the first obstacle to appreciating the sacraments. Perhaps the time spent might be worth it if it causes us to sit back and reflect; if it makes us impatient with any simple word or gesture or ceremony reduced in order to get at the "essentials." We must instead learn to see the sacraments as complex rituals, with fantastic biblical roots and overlaid traditions and as indications and signs of the larger mystery of God's encountering us in the here and now. The sacraments, as we were taught, are truly outward signs of an invisible grace, but signs that bristle with meanings and which demand many deeper and complex community associations. They are *not* bare-boned, "matter-and-form" objects. They are community celebrations of the mysteries of salvation.

2

We have already mentioned that the Christian sacraments are derived from the Jewish symbols of the Old Testament. However, since the Jewish symbols and rites are symbols and rites of *something,* then that "something" must be included in Christianity as well. In other words, the great themes of the Old Testament which gave rise to the Jewish rites must be understood if we are to comprehend the derivative Christian sacraments. If the sacraments are celebrations of the marvelous works of God in Jesus, then those marvelous works, foreshadowed and given content in the Old Testament themes, must be known to us. If, for example, the Christian Mass is rooted in the Jewish thanksgiving meal or the Passover, then it must celebrate basically the same thing as the Passover does. So, to get to the Mass we must first get to the Old Testament and there reflect upon and discover what *it* was saying.

In other words, for the average person, the sacraments are like crushed roses in an old book. We admire them, but really don't know who put them there, why they are at this particular page, what significance it all has, what is the background of the book, where did it come from, who owned it, and a host of other background questions. So this is the second obstacle we meet in talking about the sacraments. We no longer have a context for them in our minds. We no longer (for the most part) have the biblical background to understand them, the Old Testament keys that are essential to unlock them. Yet the sacraments and their liturgies are shot through with Old Testament themes, allusions, references, and meanings. The notions that appear so simple to us—the use of water, for example—have biblical overtones that are truly staggering. But, again, this is our problem. If the sacraments are really embedded in Old Testament lore, how can we master them? Long ago we have left bible lands and bible times and bible ways of thinking and seeing reality. Those old biblical allusions and old rites say nothing to modern, technological man. All of the deep Old Testament resonances connected with the New Testament sacraments go over our heads. That is why some have suggested that we simply jettison the biblical language, history, and symbols and convert them all to modern idioms in an effort to make the sacraments relevant.

The trouble with this suggestion is twofold. First of all, for any symbol to acquire a deep meaning, it has to be around for a while. It has to be honed and deepened by human experience. Shared experiences are at the heart of symbol meaning. They must be built up layer by layer. To go back to our old example, it has taken many years to overtone Thanksgiving dinner with the many leveled meanings and associations that we know today. We cannot just willy-nilly change symbols or invent new themes on the spot. (On-the-spot "symbols" are advertisers gimmicks called fads.) Time alone gives them significance and so to opt for new symbols is to wait around constantly for shared experiences to make them meaningful, and that might mean living without them at all for too many years. Likewise, whatever new themes or symbols we might devise these days would be in constant danger of being trivialized by the mass media. Modern symbols are too quickly made consumer items. Consider that we remember the father of our country by having gigantic store-wide sales on his birthday. (Some multinational corporations tried to do this with local national heroes in other countries and offended the people gravely.) The mystique is simply subverted when George Washington sells writing tables on television, Abe Lincoln hawks cars, and Paul Revere races to tell us that the latest product is coming. So many of our basic life symbols are already skewed by consumerism. Perhaps the traditional biblical ones stand a better chance of surviving than any new ones we might invent. We had better stick with the bible and its themes.

The second reason we cannot jettison the bible is that, for better or for worse, the bible is normative for God's revelation in Israel and in Jesus. It is God's chosen vehicle of self-disclosure. As such, it is of such a nature that it can and does speak to all people of all times and places. So, it seems that rather than try to invent new themes and symbols to express revelation and the sacraments, it is far better for us moderns to clear away this second obstacle—our ignorance of scripture—and go back and understand the bible and its themes. Every sacrament is an echo of something in the Old Testament. Our task is to go back and listen to the original sound.

These then, are the first two obstacles to clear away in our thinking about the sacraments. We must put them back in a far larger context than we ever thought and we must take the trouble to become acquainted with the bible and the history of salvation. If we can achieve these objectives, then we will be ready to clear away the other motes from our vision. Those "other motes" are the subject of the next chapter.

2

...That We Might See

1

A third obstacle we face in understanding the sacraments is that we have a wrong notion (or no notion) of how they "work." If we are heirs of the first obstacle we spoke about and so are familiar with the bare minimal word, gesture, or object, then we probably feel that the answer is easy: one uses the proper materials, says the proper words, and, like cause and effect, out comes grace. But the sacraments are not at all like that. They are not what the old phrase called "instruments of grace." They are more properly "mysteries of salvation." What is more, they are mysteries foreshadowed in Israel's history, brought to fulfillment in Jesus (who is the New Israel), and effected *here and now* in the church.

A father looks down on his newborn son and in a precious moment he is caught up in the wonder of this small miracle. He catches a whole sudden insight into birth and life, harmony and meaning, and his own godlike creative powers. He knows that something greater than himself has been at work. A girl looks at a sunset and is pulled out of herself as it were. She suddenly grasps (or is grasped by) a sense of another dimension of reality and senses the mystery of a divine presence. There are experiences like this in the lives of many. In these special moments individuals and a whole people can look back. On reflection they sense that they had witnessed or felt or experienced in some way a golden moment; that in this or that experience they truly came alive, saw reality in a different way and felt a love born and a growth take place. In their minds there was no doubt that something especially beautiful and meaningful happened. A Power was felt, experienced.

Israel's whole history is like that. In fact, the Old Testament is a record of some wondrous things that happened to a small, nomadic people that could only be interpreted (by them at least) as interventions of a higher power and the revelation of a mighty and caring God. The Old Testament is one large reflection of a people who knew that Yahweh-God had intervened in their history and that therefore, without any merit of their own, they had been graced. The Old Testament is summed up in Moses' experience when God said that although he (Moses) could not look at his face and live, any more than any man could really see God face-to-face as he is, nevertheless, if Moses hid behind the rock God would pass before him and call out his name: "I will pronounce before you the name Yahweh. I have compassion on whom I will, and I show pity to whom I please" (Exodus 33:19). After that, Moses would see God from behind, from the back. The meaning of this episode is precisely what we have been saying. The Israelites could not perceive God directly in the present moment, but if they thought about it, they did experience compassion and pity in many unexpected ways in the past, such as when, against all odds, they were delivered from Egypt and escaped Pharaoh's soldiers and were fed in the desert. Looking *back* on these things, they would perceive the hand of a loving and caring God. That is the meaning of Moses looking at God from *behind;* that is, from all that has happened to the Israelites he could see where God had been and where he had been with uncalled-for compassion and undeserved pity.

All this meant, once more, that God had indeed entered their history and the Israelites were glad. The memory of this they would cherish and celebrate for all time. And not just the memory as one might dwell on the past joys. No, they knew that once they had sensed God in his mighty deeds of compassionate deliverance, once, so to speak, he had committed himself to them, insignificant as they were, then such a God would *continue* to give that same deliverance, for it was evident that he was faithful. That is why they came to speak in terms of a "covenant." Clearly once God had intervened, a love-bond was forged. From now on, Israel could rely on an ever faithful God who first loved them.

The Israelites, therefore, must have ritual and ritual with a twofold purpose: to celebrate what God *had* done for them and, next, *by a clear and faith-filled implication,* what he is doing for them right now. Their ritual, in other words, would not only conjure up a happy memory of deliverance, but invite and bring about that same deliverance into their lives right here and now. So, for example, they invented the Passover meal. This special meal celebrated perhaps the most famous of all God's interventions: the exodus from slavery and the deliverance into freedom. However, in that careful ritual of unleavened bread, wine, and bitter herbs—in these old Jewish sacraments as we might say— they were evoking the past but also *they were thinking of the present.* The Passover meal in effect was saying, "Yes, Yahweh-God, you delivered us in the past. Now bring that same love and concern, that same saving call to freedom to us now. We know you are here. Your arm has not lost its power to deliver. Therefore, in what we are doing now, you are as much present and acting. Be praised and thanked forever!" The ritual sign of the Passover, then, carried in itself both the calling to mind of the past and the special power to evoke the mighty God now into a special saving encounter with the believing community. The whole mystery of Israel's *continuing* salvation was called into being.

This is the way the Christian sign-sacraments "work." They work by being a potent sign of God's saving acts in Jesus brought into being for us here and now by the same here and now God. All the shadowed themes of love, care, deliverance, and freedom of the Old Testament were brought into clarity and perfection for all mankind in Jesus. And now mankind—at least Christian mankind—celebrates and evokes such realities in its sacraments. The sacraments say that not only has God called all human beings into everlasting freedom, but these sacraments celebrate and apply that reality in the present. They make present the saving actions of the Now-God in Christ. The sacraments are community celebrations of the church which encounter in this moment Christ and his special activity which we know by the name of grace. The sacraments do not "give" grace in the sense of handing over a product. Rather the sacraments bring about the activity of God and man and it is this activity which is the grace. Grace is a divine action, an encounter, not a divine product packaged and delivered on demand in the sacraments. On the contrary, the sacraments are signs, "rhythms" by which God "graces" us. They are those mysteries of salvation by which God's loving action in Christ is made to encounter us through signs evoking past glories (deliverance, freedom, salvation) and calling forth *present* love.

So the sacraments work, not in the sense of "pull the lever and out comes grace." They work to the extent that they are signs which "activate" the past and present saving actions of God in Jesus, *but such powerful, Spirit-filled signs that they actually effect here and now for us the very thing they are celebrating.* The baptism of a person, for example, not only makes him remember Jesus' own burial in the waters of the Jordan, his own anointing by the Spirit, but also brings those events here and now to him. This person is encountered by the living, dying, rising Christ who here and now pours forth his Spirit and enables that person also to call God Abba, Father. All that was involved in those great mysteries are, as it were, reinvolved in this person. A gracious encounter is taking place. Perhaps it might help if we think of the sacraments as activating signs in three tenses: they build on the past, invoke the active and present God in ritual actions, and are orientated to future fulfillment and glory. Once more, sacraments work by being encountering signs, rooted in the confidence of the past, that celebrate, effect, and cause those same mysteries of salvation now.[1]

If we grasp all this then we must immediately move to another point when we speak of how the sacraments work. Negatively, we might say that they do not work "supernaturally" in the sense that they are somehow geared to a world other than this one in which we live. On the contrary, all biblical signs and symbols speak to the world. They are related to *human* experience. They are meant, intended, and designed for secular living. They are secular gestures and deal with secular activity. In fact, to put it strongly, the sacraments are meant to enrich the human experience and *that* is their special grace. Actually, this should be neither novel nor confusing, not when we remember that we have always honored one of the greatest events of history, the incarnation. And what is the incarnation but the fact that God definitively entered human life and affairs? He came into the human condition where eating, drinking, buying and selling, ailing and dying, God and Caesar resided. He came, not to destroy these things, but to promote them to their fullest. Jesus did not try to set up a world separate from the human condition. Rather he insisted that God's will was, in the last analysis, that we be *fully* human and that consequently, sin is being less than human. Sin is the greed of taking to oneself instead of the more human sharing. Sin is the lust of using people instead of the more human caring. Sin is the avarice that makes people brittle instead of promoting them as more fully human and compassionate. Sacraments, then, are meant to bring about our genuine humanness, a humanness that is only adequately modeled on the human Christ.

So we can talk about "supernatural" and "grace" all we want. They are the words of the technicians (theologians) who must analyze the faith and produce some understanding. But we ought not to let these necessary terms fool us into thinking that religion in general and the sacraments in particular deal with some otherworldly realm. They do not deal with some new kind of human experience. They deal with making human reality *truly* human by anchoring it to God and bringing humanity to its full potential in Christ. C. S. Lewis caught the spirit when he reminded us that it is precisely those whose eyes were not fixed on heaven who did most for the earth. He meant that those people we call saints were not dedicated to doing "their own thing," but rather they expended so much energy founding hospitals, orphanages, schools, and clinics precisely because they knew that only by developing the genuinely human, by caring for the human, by helping people to rise out of the less-than-human degrading poverty, hunger, sickness, and ignorance they would wind up more human and *therefore* more divine.

Our concern, then, is to not make religion or the sacraments something for an elite group to dabble in while the rest of the "real" world goes by. No, the sacraments, even though surrounded with some pretty technical and biblical terminology, have at their roots a relationship to, a concern for, a bringing to perfection, this old world of ours. The old adage is true, "Sacraments are for people." Indeed they are. They are designed to make people more human, liberated; and when you have a genuinely human and liberated being, you have a saint. It is in line with these thoughts that theologian Karl Rahner describes grace as "simply the final depth and radical meaning of all that the created person experiences, enacts, and suffers in the process of developing and realizing himself as a person. . . . Whenever someone lived as he would like to live, combatting his own egotism and the continual temptation to inner despair—there is the event of God's self-communication."[2] Sacraments are signs which encounter us with Jesus, whose activity (grace) is to make us like himself, which is to say, fully human.

A final word is in order here. The sacraments are signs of God's ever-present activity in Jesus not only for those celebrating them, but also for those beyond the group. This is to say, that the sacraments celebrate in the concrete what God has in mind for all. It is not that God does not give his grace-filled love to others, for he is master of his gifts and is not bound by his own sacraments. Rather, the sacraments are outward signs of what is indeed promised to all who live a full human life of love, forgiveness, and service. The sacraments are, in one writer's words, the italicized words of the language that the Lord speaks to all men all of the time. They are the concrete celebrations of the liberation held out to all. They are the rituals of those who know (the church) and as such advertise God's gracious goodness in Christ for those who don't.

2

The fourth obstacle to our understanding of the sacraments is the failure to see them as related to the church. Or, perhaps more accurately put, it is our failure to understand the nature of the church. The church is not that institution which is the keeper of the sacraments as a palace contains the royal jewels. Rather the church is itself a sacrament. It is a sign of Jesus himself. If we would draw a mental schema, we would see that the Father outpours himself totally into the Son's humanity. That humanity—Jesus—is therefore the Father's outward sign. What more could the Father do than to become tangible for our sakes, to be an outward, living sign (sacrament) of his inward, invisible love? "God *so* loved the world," says St. John, "that he sent his only begotten Son so that those who believe may not perish but have life everlasting." Jesus is the external valentine from the Father,- an outward sign, a sacrament. Augustine summed it up by saying, "There is no other mystery of God except Christ." So again, St. John:

> This is what we proclaim to you:
> What was from the beginning,
> what we have heard,
> what we have seen with our eyes,
> what we have looked upon
> and our hands have touched—
> we speak of the word of life.
> This life became visible;
> we have seen and bear witness to it
> and we proclaim to you the eternal life
> that was present to the Father
> and became visible to us (1 John 1:3).

Now, when Jesus who was the Father's visible self-disclosure left us in this form he assumed another: he remained in his body, the church. The church is his sacrament, his continuation in time and space. Or, put simply, Jesus is the human face of God and the church is the historical face of Jesus. About fifty years ago, a great spiritual writer wrote a classic called *Christ the Life of the Soul,* and he sums it up well:

> Such is then in its majestic range and merciful simplicity, God's plan for us. *God wills our holiness.* . . . He wills to make us saints in making us participate in his very life, and for that end, he adopts us as his children and the heirs of his infinite glory and eternal beatitude. *Grace* is the principle of this holiness, supernatural in its source, in its acts, and in its fruits. But God only gives us this adoption *through his Son Jesus Christ.* . . . Thus God communicates the fullness of his divine life to the humanity of Christ and through it, to all souls in the measure of their predestination in Jesus Christ . . . [But] Christ came on earth, not only for those who lived at that time in Palestine, but for men of all times. When he deprived men of his sensible presence, He gave them the Church. . . . It is in the church that we can find him. No one goes to the Father except through Christ. But remember well this no less important truth; no one goes to Christ except through the church. . . . It is only in the unity of the church that we can live the life of Christ.[3]

The sacraments are the actions of such a church. The sacraments are the actions of the church which is the action of Christ who is the act of the Father's love. Again, the Father pours himself into the humanity of Christ and so becomes visible (sacramental). The Son's humanity by this same principle of the incarnation is extended to the church and the church then acts visibly in the continuing incarnations of the sacraments. Our United States bishops accordingly have called the sacraments "the principle action through which Christ gives his Spirit to Christians and makes them a holy people. He has entrusted the sacraments to the church but they are always to be thought of as actions of Christ himself from whom they get their power."[4] The Dutch catechism is even more clear, "When we consider the place taken by these signs in the work of salvation, we may sum up by saying that in Christ God became visible and tangible. That in the church Christ, and hence God, remains visible and tangible among us. And that the church in turn becomes visible and tangible in the seven signs. They are Christ's hands which now touch us and Christ's words which now ring in our ears. They are his way of being palatable today."[5]

So the church is a sign (sacrament) of Christ among us and the sacraments are the way he encounters us in his church. The church then is a gathering which celebrates the Lord's saving actions. Each time someone celebrates baptism or confirmation or the eucharist or reconciliation the event is a church affair and Christ through that church is in action, encountering and gracing the person.

Of course we will never come to this understanding if we have overly stressed the church as a building which dispenses services. If to us the church is an administrative center that pays the bills and runs the organizations, then the sacraments are pious interruptions to its daily and more practical routines. If the church is represented by a parish plant, dedicated to paying off its mortgage and running money-making affairs solely to achieve this end, then the sacraments are incidents to this major business. But if we see the church as a gathering of the baptized in faith striving to "be" Christ in the world, then we have a community. We have a sign of Jesus himself. Then the sacramental signs are truly evocative: they are displaying the church which displays Christ who is the herald of that God who from the beginning of time has called all men to himself. The sacraments are signs in ritual form which are the actions of a Christ who is visible in his church body.

This leads us to the final point in this section. For many centuries there was a rather false line of demarcation between Protestants and Catholics on the use of scripture. It started when the reformers began to react against a very mechanical and almost magical use of the sacramental signs. The reaction took the form of turning to the bible and saying that it is this scriptural word, heard and received in faith, that truly sanctifies. Rote signs are meaningless. As a result, which really came about more by default and practice rather than by reasoned theory, reacting Catholics tended to emphasize the external sacraments as grace-giving while the Protestants tended to rely heavily on the read or preached scriptural word. In the end the Catholics wound up neglecting the bible and the Protestants wound up neglecting the ritual signs. They even reduced the number of the sacraments and seldom celebrated the eucharist or communion services.

Today we see more clearly that there is not and never has been any real conflict. The bible is not an autonomous force. It is rather a part of that mysterious presence by which God reveals himself in Jesus in a believing community. "The scriptures exist as saving word of God when and because they are spoken by the Spirit-filled believing community and are therefore word of Christ who is sacramentally operative through that community."[6] This translates to mean that the sacraments are, if you will, the scriptural words in pantomime, italicized words as we said before. "Scripture and liturgical ceremony form, then, one conjoined reality of the church giving expression to its own sacramental function of making Christ redemptively present to men and women throughout history. The ritual actions that have come to be named 'sacraments' because they speak in special fashion of the mystery of Christ continuing to transform human experience by his death and resurrection are 'word of God' in the fullest sense."[7]

Actually, the spoken words of scripture have always been associated with sacramental ritual (even though at times omitted in practice). And they were spoken, not as some kind of needed clarification, but as words of power, as words of the risen Christ integral to what was going on. Word and ritual still remain as two sides of the same sacramental coin. However, to be sure that the misunderstanding does not occur again, the church has gone out of its way in all of the sacramental revisions to fill the pages with many scriptural readings and with many other scriptural options. There is no sacramental occasion when scripture is absent. The church wants us to understand completely that scripture and sacramental ritual are one piece and that Jesus, in his living community, is once more speaking and acting prophetically in this word-act we call sacrament.

3

Many times we have remarked that the sacraments are ritual signs. We come back to this now as we explore this final difficulty we have about the sacraments. The difficulty centers around that whole notion of ritual and its use of words, symbols, gestures, movements, and objects. As many writers have been reminding us these past years, the sacramental job is harder. The reason is that we are no longer a ritual people. Well, that is not exactly true. Just by being human we are and always will be a ritual people. Rather what is meant is that the rituals and symbols themselves no longer mean anything to us for we have lost common understanding and agreement as to their meaning; and, what is more, we find ourselves incapable of seeing *through* them to the mystery beyond. The reasons are not hard to find: technology and the media. Technology removes us more and more from the natural feel of and appreciation for such things as oil and water and touch and bread and wine. We mediate everything through plastic. On its part the media constantly devalues what is natural by selling its products and undermining language. Oil means Penzoil, water might mean pollution; bread is a thin anemic, bleached, tasteless slice; wine is a sign of sophistication and the proper label and year are important. The media is a world that sells imitation artificial margarine, synthetic eggs, and endless solids and liquids designed to destroy any trace of aromas (especially ethnic ones such as Kielbasa or garlic) which might please the sense of smell. The nitty-gritty touch and feel of things are gone. And with it, the sense of mystery.

Our scientific mentalities always want to explore, decipher and ultimately "use" things. Things are valued for what they can do for us, produce and turn a profit. We no longer wonder at the world. We want to know how we can make it work for us. The mystery of the world is not to be experienced or even worshiped, but examined and laid bare. If we have lost the sense of wonder and mystery in our ordinary, daily lives and our senses have been dulled, how can we expect to approach the stuffs of the sacraments—oil, water, bread—and experience through them the special mystery of God in Christ mediated through the church? How can our actions, gestures, songs, words, in short, our sacramental rituals, evoke Mystery with an upper case *M* when we have been conditioned not even to perceive mystery in the lower case? We can't put our hands to the earth or our face to the wind and experience life and spirit. We have become the "white man" as in this Indian's lament:

> The white people never cared for land or deer or bear. When we Indians kill meat, we eat it all up. When we dig roots, we make little holes. . . . We shake down acorns and pinenuts. We don't chop down the trees. We only use dead wood. But the white people plow up the ground, pull up the trees, kill everything. The tree says, "Don't, I am sore. Don't hurt me." But they chop it down and cut it up. The spirit of the land hates them. . . . The Indian never hurt anything, but the white people destroy all. They blast rocks and scatter them on the ground. The rock says, "Don't! You're hurting me." But the white man pays no attention. When the Indians use rocks, they take the little round ones for their cooking. . . . How can the spirit of the earth like the white man? . . . Everywhere the white man has touched it, it is sore.[8]

We find it difficult if not impossible to think of the rocks or land as "sore" or any kind of "spirit" of the earth. Therefore we find it difficult and perhaps impossible to sense in ritual in general and sacramental ritual in particular any kind of touchstone with God. If there is no touchstone, then there is no encounter, and participation in baptism or penance or the eucharist does not move us to sense anything different. Theodore Roszak has some relevant words we might ponder:

> The essence of good magic—magic as it is practiced by the shaman [a combination of guru, spiritual leader, priest] and the artist—is that it seeks always to make available to all the full power of the magician's experience. While the shaman may be one especially elected and empowered, his role is to introduce his people to the sacramental presences that have found him out and transformed him into their agent. His peculiar gift confers responsibility, not privilege. Similarly, the artist lays his work before the community in the hope that through it, as through a window, the reality he has fathomed will be witnessed by all who give attention. For the shaman, ritual performs the same function. By participating in the ritual the community comes to know what the shaman has discovered. Ritual is the shaman's way of broadcasting his vision; it is his instructive offering. If the artist's work is successful, if the shaman's ritual is effective, the community's sense of reality will become expansive; something of the dark powers will penetrate his experience.[9]

So it is—or should be—in our sacramental celebrations. The ritual should reveal. We should be brought into contact with the Power which is God himself. We should experience an unfolding of the Mystery to some degree. But, of course, this does not often happen for we are no longer a ritual people or think symbolically or even *expect* any revelation. The objects and minerals and elements of this planet are to give up their molecular components to be used and rearranged for our use. They must be passive before our science. We simply do not expect them to be active in revealing.

And yet, if religion is to "succeed," if we are to have a sense about the sacraments, its rituals must possess the power to shake the individual in his deepest insides and pull him into the mys-

tery of God's presence in the world. It may be therefore, that
before we can ever really enter into the mysteries of salvation
which are the sacraments; if we are ever to find in the sacramental rituals touchstones with God in Christ through the church,
then we may have to spend sometime in getting sensitized to the
basic mystery of life in *all* its forms. Before the sacraments can
succeed in the modern world we may have to spend some time
assimilating the sensitivities of David McCord's poem:

> Now think of words. Take *sky*
> And ask yourself just why—
> Like sun, moon, star, and cloud—
> It sounds so well out loud,
> And please so the sight
> When printed black on white.
> Take syllable and thimble:
> The sound of *them* is nimble.
> Take bucket, spring, and dip
> Cold water to your lip.
> Take balsam, fir, and pine:
> Your woodland smell and mine.
> Take kindle, blaze, and flicker—
> What lights the hearth fire quicker?
>
> Three words we fear but form:
> Gale, twister, thunderstorm;
> Others that simply shake
> Are tremble, temblor, quake.
> But granite, stone, and rock:
> Too solid, they, to shock.
> Put honey, bee, and flower
> With sunny, shade, and shower;
> Put *wild* with bird and wing,
> Put *bird* with song and sing.
> Aren't paddle, trail, and camp
> The cabin and the lamp?
> Now look at words of rest—
> Sleep, quiet, calm, and blest;
>
> At words we learn in youth—
> Grace, skill, ambition, truth;

At words of lifelong need—
Grit, courage, strength, and deed;
Deep-rooted words that say
Love, hope, dream, yearn, and pray;
Light-hearted words—girl, boy,
Live, laugh, play, share, enjoy.
October, April, June—
Come late and gone too soon.
Remember, words are life:
Child, husband, mother, wife;
Remember, and I'm done:
Words taken one by one
Are poems as they stand—
Shore, beacon, harbor, land;
Brook, river, mountain, vale,
Crow, rabbit, otter, quail;
Faith, freedom, water, snow,
Wind, weather, flood, and floe.

Like light across the lawn
Are morning, sea, and dawn;
Words of the green earth growing—
Seed, soil, and farmer sowing.
Like wind upon the mouth
Sad, summer, rain, and south.
Amen. Put not asunder
Man's *first* word: wonder . . . wonder . . . [10]

Wonder is both the basis and the beginning of sacramental celebration. It may be a long time before we with our jaded senses
can appreciate this, but we must try. If we are ever to praise God
properly we must begin to get a sense of wonder.

These have been long thoughts in our approach to the five
sacraments we shall examine, but they have been necessary. Let
us restate them.[11] First, the sacraments are not mere matter and
form in the restrictive sense. They belong to a larger context of
community, celebration, ritual. They demand preparation, publicity, people—an assembly or church. To be satisfied with a bare
isolated, individual gesture or word is to flirt with magic. Secondly, all of the sacraments are but the final realization of the

great biblical themes of liberation and freedom, but brought to fulfillment in Jesus. Therefore, to understand what we do and in what we are sharing in baptism or the eucharist or any of the other sacraments does require some background familiarity with the bible. Thirdly, the sacraments do not automatically produce grace as water from a faucet. They are evocative. That is, they play on the themes of the past in Jesus, and they make present his saving actions (grace) now. The ritual celebration of the sacramental rituals, done in faith, actually effect what they are celebrating. Therefore we must not be passive. We must be active with a strong faith and an understanding readiness to participate. Fourthly, the sacraments are but acts of the church which in its turn is the outward sign (sacrament) of Christ himself. Sacraments therefore are what we call ecclesial actions. They are incarnations of the Mystical Body, the church. Finally, since the sacraments involve symbols and signs and rituals, it would seem that we must first be educated to an understanding and appreciation of ritual itself. We moderns must recapture a sense of wonder, a sense of mystery, if we are to celebrate the sacraments fruitfully.[12]

NOTES FOR CHAPTER 2

1. Theologian Michael Schmaus expresses this idea more soberly: " . . . When the sign is performed, God is making known his hidden, saving presence. The sign is the manifestation and the image of the divine communication of salvation. This statement must not be confused with the opinion sometimes expressed in early scholastic theology (e.g., Hugh of St. Victor) that grace itself is contained in the sign—for example, in the water—as in a vessel. Such thoroughgoing sacramentalism runs the risk of acquiring the connotations of magic. It does, however, contain one element that is correct: namely, that the sign indicates the saving presence of God, and when the sign is made here and now God's self-communication is made historically tangible in the form of the sign" (Michael Schmaus, *Dogma 5: The*

Church as Sacrament [Sheed and Ward, 1975], p. 33). St. Thomas Aquinas gives the additional reminder that the precise saving action evoked in the sacraments is Christ's passion: "From the side of Christ dying on the cross sprang the sacraments through which the church is saved. Thus it appears that the sacraments derive their virtue from the passion of Christ" (*Summa Theologica* III, q. 60, Introduction).

2. Quoted by Mary Perkins Ryan in "Sacraments in Context," *Pace 5* (St. Mary's College Press, 1974), p. 3. Bernard Häring expresses it by saying that "The New Testament admits a distinction but no separation between supernatural revelation and natural events. The disjunction appears when comparing the outlook of the believer with that of the unbeliever or superficial man. For those who konw Christ in his mission, the material world is not speechless. The created universe transcends the mere terms of causality and utility. Once the full light of Christ has shone, the believer perceives the whole of creation and the ongoing history of mankind in the perspective of God's self-disclosure, of an unfolding manifestation of God's loving design for man" (*The Sacraments and Your Everyday Life* [Liguori Publications, 1976], p. 18). In this quotation and in what we have written in this section there is no intention to suggest that God's grace and the sacraments are mere "horizontal" happenings and that therefore man's ultimate salvation is to be found in man. Rather what is being emphasized is the truly transcendent God who nevertheless meets us all incarnationally. Whatever (Spirit-prompted) self improvements there are simply form the ground on which God can meet and touch us. Becoming more fully human means, in the last analysis, becoming more open to the "Wholly Other."

3. D. Columba Marmion, *Christ the Life of the Soul* (B. Herder Book Co., 1922), pp. 23 and 91.

4. "Basic Teachings for Catholic Religious Education" (United States Catholic Conference, 1973), p. 11.

5. *A New Catechism* (Seabury Press, 1969), p. 253.

6. Bernard Cooke, *Ministry to Word and Sacraments,* (Fortress Press, 1976), p. 323.

7. Ibid.

8. Quoted in *The Making of a Counter Culture,* by Theodore Roszak (Doubleday, 1968), p. 245.

9. Ibid., p. 260.

10. *Take Sky,* by David McCord (Little Brown and Co., 1961).

11. Theologian Bernard Häring sums up what we have been saying in the following outline:

To avoid any misunderstanding, it seems well to state the following premises:

1. Even in speaking of the seven sacraments, the point of view remains always the *unique sacramentality of Christ,* the Word Incarnate, in his dynamic presence in the church as sign of his presence among us and symbol of his benevolence. The sacraments will be considered in their *capacity to open us to a broader view of the saving presence of Christ in history and in the daily events of our lives and of our times.*

2. The sacraments are privileged and efficacious signs of grace. They are true symbols of God's gracious presence instituted by Christ and dispensed by the church in obedience to him. This does not mean, however, that the sacraments hold a *monopoly* on grace.

It is true that man has to submit himself humbly to the will of Christ who gave his church some visible signs of grace; but the fact that Christ has given these special signs, in which he manifests his graciousness and invites man to open himself visibly to this grace, cannot be interpreted to mean that Christ himself or the Holy Spirit is bound to these signs in such a way as to be unable or unwilling to convey salvation in other ways. The opposite is true. As privileged signs of salvation, the sacraments open us and direct our attention to all the other ways in which God shows men his graciousness. The sacraments do not allow any form of evasion or alienation, but demand vigilance to the "signs of the times" and great respect and reverence for the wonderful ways in which God works and manifests himself outside of the sacramental life of the church.

3. It may not be easy to find the happy medium which on the one hand considers the sacraments of the church as the *privileged key* which provides an understanding of the economy of salvation, and on the other hand does *not assert a monopoly* of the sacraments on God's grace. I think, however, that a theology of the world, centered on the sacramental character of creation in the light of redemption, will be able to grasp the dynamics and vitality of the seven sacraments. This broader vision of sacramentality will also help to overcome any tendency toward mere ritualism.

4. We must not forget that for many centuries the church stood as the sacrament of salvation and celebrated the sacraments without exactly determining their number.

Eagerly concerned not to diminish the value of any of the seven sacraments, we shall seek to avoid in our discussion a too technical concept of them. The direction set by Vatican II in the theology and in the life of the church is reflected also in its vision of the sacraments. One cannot forget that in the sacramental theology of past centuries an overemphasis on the role of the minister and great stress on ritual and rubrics resulted in a certain degree of underdevelopment in the doctrine of the universal priesthood of the people. This authoritarian aspect found expression in a variety of forms. The church of today is more conscious of her freedom with respect to the way she proclaims salvation by means of actions, words and symbols through which she realizes it. Today much more attention is given to the active participation of the faithful. (*The Sacraments and Your Everyday Life* [Liguori Publications, 1976], p.p. 71 and 72.)

12. In making the points of this and the previous chapter we do not wish to patronize the remote or immediate past. Many a parish had a high community sense and many a sacramental celebration was both moving and satisfying. It's just that the problems we have mentioned lent themselves more easily to misuse and manipulation by the minimal Catholic. The devout of any era in history have always had that special grace to do and see and realize more than is there.

3

Water and the Spirit

1

In the chapters that follow we shall see more at length that in ancient times a person became a Christian by submitting himself to Christian initiation. This initiation was one single but elaborate ceremony which a much later age would divide into baptism, confirmation, and the eucharist. But at the very beginning, the time of the apostles, there was very likely only the simple act of water-baptism. This water-baptism was meant to be (like all the other sacraments) a repetition of the original Pentecostal experience of the Spirit. In fact, the water and the Spirit figure so prominently both in the theology and practice of baptism (and confirmation) that it will be worth our while to see its origins in the thinking patterns of the Jews and its application by the Christians.

First, a little game of word association. Take the word "water" and ask the person nearest you to tell you all the things he or she associates with water. Here are some actual associations given by adults and children: pollution, bath, chlorine, pool. Obviously such associations very much depend on what part of the country or the world you are in. If you have just had floods, water means terror; if you are in northern Africa, water means life. But for most Americans water is something that comes out of a faucet and has some of those associations given above. This is a far cry from the ancients' concept of water, miles from their associations. So we must go back to the bible and see the resonances tied in with the meaning of water, because these meanings are precisely what Jesus had in mind when he was baptized and gave us the value we call Christian baptism.

There was the beginning of time. Of this beginning the bible instantly speaks of water in a double way. Water is seen in the bible's first page as carrying a twofold meaning: that of life and that of death. First, death. To catch a sense of the almost overwhelming power of death inherent in water, modern people can recall such popular movies of the past years as the *Posidon Adventure* or *Jaws*. There, through the trickery of the camera, the audience could get some feel of the sheer terror of water whether it took the form of a massive, drowning tidal wave or the form as the natural habitat of a primitive evil force (the shark). If one has ever witnessed a flood, he knows the havoc and destruction water can cause. No wonder the opening verses of the bible speak of the waters of chaos. No wonder that in so many biblical episodes water is so threatening: it covers the whole earth and only Noah escapes. It parts for the Israelites but rushes back in terrible revenge on the pursuing Egyptians. Water, then, carried with it for the bible writers high overtones of the end of an era, destruction, death, and burial.

But water carried with it the notion of fruitful life also. For, after all, from this primeval chaos of water comes life. Modern science itself is busy in the laboratories creating the primitive earth's atmosphere in which the simple molecules and amino acids can be formed to produce life. Life from the waters is a scientific axiom as well as a biblical one. The rivers of the Garden of Eden are life-giving. Water, even if it killed the Egyptians, did give life to the Israelites. In crossing the barren desert they were refreshed with water from the rock. In their final trek they crossed the river Jordan to pass into the Promised Land "flowing with milk and honey." It was very much by design that John the Baptizer baptized in those Jordan waters. It symbolized that those who came to him were also to leave a land of slavery (sin) and pass over to a new Promised Land. The Syrian Naaman was cleansed of his leprosy in the waters of the Jordan. The prophet

Ezekiel describes a new life coming in terms of water, "For I will take you from the nations and gather you from all the countries and bring you back to your own land. I will sprinkle clean water upon you, and you shall be clean . . . And you shall be my people and I will be your God. And I will deliver you from all your uncleanness" (Ezekiel 36: 24ff). The prophet Isaiah says, "I will pour out water on the thirsty plain, streams over the land that once was dry" (Isaiah 44:3). We are all familiar with the favorite twenty-second psalm which speaks of being brought out to the cool refreshing water. And even as late as the last book of the bible, St. John has a vision which describes "a river whose waters give life; it flows, crystal clear, from the throne of God" (Revelations 22:1). So water had many associations for the biblical Jews. Water carried the double message of life and death. But what made the difference between the two is enormously important and significant: the difference was the Spirit.

Let us go back to that bible beginning. What is the force that takes the watery chaos and makes out of it order? It is, in Hebrew, the *ruah*—the breath, the wind, the Spirit. The Spirit makes the difference between life and death. It is not difficult to see how the *ruah*—the breath, the wind, the Spirit—came to do so. The old Hebrews, nomads as they were in a harsh country, knew by experience what our TV weathermen know by their satelites: wind brings water or wind dries up water. So if the wind is a land breeze it brings no water at all: it brings dryness, heat, and the ruination of crops (death). If the wind (*ruah*) is an ocean breeze, it brings water and with it coolness, refreshment, and welcome rain (life). So the wind and water, the *ruah*, the breath, (the *spiritus* in Latin) became a general symbol of life giving or death dealing as the case might be. The notions of the breath of the living and the winds were joined, spiritualized, and developed into the concept which best portrayed the life-giving Spirit of God. That is why God's Spirit is spoken of as bringing life, as being poured out, changing things around, renewing the face of the earth. Moreover, from now on (life-giving) water will always imply the activity of the *Ruah*, the Spirit. That is why St.

Peter's first public sermon on Pentecost day quotes the prophet who spoke of the Spirit. Peter says, "Listen to what I have to say . . . it is what Joel the prophet spoke of: It shall come to pass in the last days, says God, that I will pour out a portion of my spirit on all mankind . . . then everyone shall be saved who calls on the name of the Lord" (Acts 2:14ff). And after all of this Spirit-talk, the people were baptized in water. In this Peter was only echoing Jesus who told Nicodemus that unless a man was born again of water and the Spirit he could not be saved. Through the water (baptism) Jesus' Spirit would be poured forth. So water and Spirit are interchangeable symbols. To be baptized, to be plunged into the waters, is to open oneself to the Spirit of Jesus. To be baptized is to have the Spirit make order out of chaos (forgiveness of sin), to cross over to the Promised Land (the church), to have the leprosy of evil washed away, to be sprinkled anew, cleansed of all impurities, to become truly alive. To be baptized is to undergo Pentecost.

2

With all of these associations of water and spirit in the minds of the Jews it was but natural that they used water rather frequently in their rituals. The Torah prescribed baths for the removal of various kinds of impurities just as in paganism water purifications figured predominately in the mystery religions of the East. When there were Gentile converts to Judaism they were baptized in Jordan's waters. The obvious symbolism was that since, unlike born Jews, they had never crossed the waters of the Jordan into the freedom of the Promised Land in *their* ancestors, they had to do it themselves in symbol. They had to repeat ritually the experience of the Israelites. From the middle of the second century B.C. on there was a great deal of baptismal activity in the upper Jordan. One group whose type of baptism influenced John the Baptizer was the monastic group known as the Essenes. Their baptism, however, consisted of a series of ritual washings. But John's was different and in fact so different that he above all others earned the nickname of the Baptizer. What made the difference?

First of all, John's baptism was a once-and-for-all call to repentance, not just a series of rituals. Secondly, he gave baptism immediately to whoever asked for it sincerely, Jew and Gentile alike. His baptism was not reserved, like the others, to members of a special group. Thirdly, John's baptism had quite rigorous ethical demands attached to it as we read in the gospels. Finally, and most importantly, John's baptism was consciously ushering in the "last times," that is, those new and final days of the Messiah's reign. The Jews, we should remember, had the notion that when the final beginning of the new messianic age would begin, it would begin with water, purification. (Recall Ezekiel: "I will sprinkle clean water upon you . . . and you shall be my people and I shall be your God.") If the old Israel had its beginnings in water from the passage through the Red Sea to the crossing of the River Jordan then the new Israel would also have water as a sign of its new age. So John the Baptizer was announcing that his water-baptism was indeed ushering in that new age. He was the last of the old to point to the new. He was the last prophet to "look for another" and to prepare the way for another.

Now we can understand why Jesus came to be baptized by John. The early Christian church was at first embarrassed by this because some of them tended to think of baptism exclusively as forgiving sin and how could this be true of Jesus? But on reflection they saw the importance and the meaning of what Jesus did. He was baptized by John as a sign that he *was* the new age. He was himself the inaugurator of the new times. In his own life he repeated all that went before in Israel: his baptism was Israel's Red Sea crossing, his forty day fast was Israel's forty years' wandering in the desert, his three temptations were exactly those proposed and surrendered to by Israel but resisted by him—but now he gives new dimensions to all that was foreshadowed. Where Israel failed, he succeeded. Where Israel grumbled, he was obedient. Where Israel doubted, he put his trust in the Father. Where Israel turned to idols, he worshiped none other than God. Where Israel was the figure of all that God would do for the Jews, Jesus was the reality of all that God would do for all. Jesus was the old times fulfilled. He brought a new era. And, as we might now expect, this new era was ushered in by water and the Spirit.

So Jesus was baptized in the waters. Then the Spirit descended on him like a dove; not necessarily in the form of a dove, but, true to the wind-concept, like the flutter that a dove makes when it is landing. Water and Spirit once more converged. Then, immediately after his baptism Jesus goes "in the power of the Spirit" as Luke puts it, to Nazareth. There he is invited to speak at the local synagogue. He goes in, takes the scripture scroll and opens up to the book of Isaiah, the forty-second chapter. He reads these words to the congregation: "The Spirit of the Lord is upon me; therefore he has anointed me. He has sent me to bring good tidings to the poor, to proclaim liberty to captives, recovery of sight to the blind and release to prisoners, to announce a year of favor from the Lord." Then, still fresh from his Spirit-filled water baptism, he looks the congregation square in the eye—that congregation who knew well enough that this Isaian prophecy was about the messiah—and said directly, "Today this scripture passage is fulfilled in your hearing" (Luke 4:18–21).

So Jesus verified what John's baptism was all about as far as he was concerned. It was not a baptism of repentance. It was that baptism inaugurating the new age, the time and the hour which is "already here, when authentic worshipers will worship the Father in Spirit and truth" (John 4:28). So it was, at the moment of his baptism, that Jesus received his mandate. He "knew he was in the grasp of the Spirit. God was taking him into his service, equipping him and authorizing him to be his messenger and the inaugurator of the time of salvation. At his baptism, Jesus experiences his call."[1] Once more the water-Spirit had ended an old age and started a new one. Once more chaos, under the power of the Spirit, receded and order was brought forth.

3

But there is more—and here we move beyond any natural symbol to an interpretation (theology) given by St. Paul. According to Paul there is an essential element that made Jesus' baptism unique, gave meaning to our baptism and made the new age truly a new age. For according to Paul what happened to Jesus at the Jordan, what he was doing symbolically, was so profound that it became the basis of what we call the sacrament of baptism. It is not without reason that Christian art has endlessly depicted Jesus' baptism or that in the Coptic church their word for the baptismal font is al-Urdunn, the Jordan. In any case, we have seen that water is the ancient double symbol: death and life. Jesus took advantage of this double meaning. When he went down into the waters of the Jordan, he was symbolically going down into the grave. In ritual he was going down into his death. He was acting out those profound words of his, "Unless the grain of wheat falls to the earth and dies, it remains just a grain of wheat. But if it dies, it produces much fruit. The man who loves his life loses it, while the man who hates his life in this world preserves it to life eternal" (John 12:24ff). So Jesus was the grain of wheat. His love for us would lead him to give his all, to surrender himself to the Father. Jesus would die to self and so unleash a whole new Spirit. He would hand over his whole person to the mystery of a merciful and loving Father.

But, notice, when Jesus emerged from his baptism—that symbolic descent into Jordan's watery grave—immediately the Spirit became apparent. By this anticipated dying to self in surrender to the Father's will, a whole new Spirit is let go upon mankind. From this terrible chaos of death the Spirit brings the order of a new age to love and salvation. In a word, the baptism of Jesus is a ritual enactment of his passion, death, and resurrection. This is the heart of what it meant. He shall now fulfill all those slavery-freedom themes of the Old Testament. Now in his person all mankind is released from slavery, brought through the waters, led to freedom, and anointed with a whole new Spirit under whose impulse they can cry out "Abba, Father!" Again, baptism is associated with Jesus' central acts of passion, death, and resurrection. That is why he used the baptismal figure of speech in talking about these acts. He said, "There is a baptism I must needs be baptized with and how impatient I am for its accomplishment!" (Luke 12:50). That is why, when asking James and John if they were really ready to share in his death, he remarked, "You do not know what it is you ask. Have you the strength to drink of the cup I am to drink of, to be baptized with the baptism I am to be baptized with?" (Mark 10:38). Baptism must be understood in the context of Calvary.

What, then, is Jesus saying in identifying his passion and death with the word baptism? He is telling us that the old symbols of the bible hold. The waters *are* death-dealing and life-giving. They are like a watery grave. However, just as he emerged from Jordan's waters and was filled with the Spirit, so too he would rise from Joseph of Arimathea's grave and give that Spirit. It would be this Spirit that would enable people to live by a different tempo, urging them to also die to self and live for others. By baptism, people would enter into the rhythm of his death and resurrected life. In other words, to be baptized is to go into those waters which signify that we have died to evil and are risen with Jesus and have been anointed with his Spirit. To put it another way, one who is baptized is undergoing conversion, a genuine "turn about," a decisive leaving of the old and a public and sincere adoption of the new. Therefore, with such a radical decision, once more, as at the beginning of time, the Spirit has triumphed. Paul, who had worked all this out, summarized the experience of baptism by saying, "Are you not aware that we who were baptized into Christ Jesus were baptized into his death? Through baptism into his death we were buried with him so that, just as Christ was raised from the dead by the glory of the Father, we too might live a new life" (Romans 6:3). In other words, we were Israel enslaved and now set free, thirsty and now nourished by water, wandering and now delivered through the water passage, threatened by the flood waters, now rescued by the baptismal waters, dead to self and now alive to Christ in the Spirit. Baptism conforms us to the crucified and risen Christ. Baptism in principle plunges us into his death on Calvary and inserts us into his Spirit-filled, resurrected life. We are made new. We are by adoption what Jesus is by nature: truly children of the Father. We have been inserted into the last times of history and brought into a community of "Easter" people, the Spirit-filled community of believers.

We carefully said that we are plunged into Jesus "in principle." This is meant to get across that baptism is basically a future-oriented thing. Baptism is the embrace of God who first loved us. It is an uncalled-for pouring out of his Spirit when we did not and cannot deserve it. Now it remains for us to grow into what we are. The rest of our earthly existence is to become morally what we are "objectively" through baptism: sons and daughters of God, an Easter people of the Spirit. The baptismal life remains for us a progressive laying hold of and the deliberate appropriation of what was made accessible to us in baptism. We are, of course, free to make a shambles of our adoption and turn away from our Father. We are free to choose slavery over freedom. About the only thing we are not free about is the Father's love for us in Jesus. We cannot control that. We can control only our response in faith.

4

By way of conclusion let us make some brief random remarks. First, the liturgy of Lent and Holy Week. As we shall see in the next chapter, Lent started out as the church's official preparation for baptism which was celebrated on the vigil of Easter (and later Pentecost). Naturally the biblical references all during Lent would be heavily Old Testament. Then when we came to the vigil itself, there would be (in the old days, before the revision of Holy Week) those twelve readings which never meant much to us. Our comment here is that those readings were heavily filled with allusions to water. Now we know why.

Secondly, we see why baptisms, as we know them, are almost always celebrated on Sundays. The "first" Sunday was, of course, Easter, the great and only feast in the church for centuries. It was precisely on this once-a-year Easter Sunday, as we have just noted, that baptisms were held. When in time it was not practical to hold them on this "primary" Sunday (Easter), then they moved to the "secondary" Easters or Sundays of the year.

Thirdly, with all of the water-Spirit connections we have just examined, it is not surprising that many variations on this theme appeared quickly in the church. The New Testament took many facets of baptism and presented them to the people. For example:

1. Baptism is a change of allegiance. We are no longer slaves to sin but now slaves to God (Romans 6). This is the new era theme that water brings. As we shall see, some liturgies were most descriptive about this end-of-the-old and the beginning-of-the new. They had their baptismal candidates turn to the west to renounce Satan and turn to the east to accept Christ.

2. Baptism was putting off the old man and putting on the new (Colossians 3:9). Again, old-times, new-times theme. This would find expression in the undressing before entering the baptismal waters and dressing again afterwards in a white robe.

3. Baptism was a new birth (John 3:5). The shape of some of the early baptismal fonts was highly suggestive of the womb.

4. Baptism enlightens (Hebrews 6:4). Again, the chaos theme: darkness and light. Some day the lighted candle would spell this out.

5. Baptism makes a person a sharer in Christ (1 Peter 2) and therefore he is, like Christ, anointed priest and king. The anointings that came to be associated with baptism would underscore this theme.

However, in whatever way the New Testament writers presented baptism, and no matter how developed the whole ceremony eventually became we shall always sense how normative the biblical themes of water, chaos, Spirit and burial will remain. In a word, we shall always have to come back to what Jesus' own baptism meant to him to see what it means for Christians. And the one sure thing that emerges over and over again is that baptism means a quite radical change of life. In fact, it made many a candidate for baptism pause. To plunge oneself into Jesus, to be that committed for the rest of one's life, to receive the Spirit and live by his impulses, was not to be done lightly. No wonder the church eventually demanded that baptism be preceded by a long catechesis of instruction, prayer, and fasting. Baptism was to be for all what it was for Jesus: an event as decisive as death and as final as everlasting life.

NOTE FOR CHAPTER 3

1. Joachim Jeremias, *New Testament Theology* (Charles Scribners and Son, 1971), p. 55. See also the article, "Luke 3: 21–22, Baptism or Anointing" by Raymond F. Collins in *The Bible Today* 84, (April 1976), pp. 821 ff. Father Collins says, "The descent of the Spirit is not only the Father's response to the prayer of Jesus; it is also his response to the messianic expectations of the people. . . . In a word, Luke 3: 21–22 does not so much state that Jesus has been baptized by John the Baptist as it proclaims that Jesus has received a messianic anointing from the Father through the gift of the Spirit."

4

Christian Initiation

1

The very first Christians were an exception. Since, as we have seen, baptism is that unity of water-Spirit, then they were directly baptized in the Spirit minus the water symbol at Pentecost. They were baptized, so to speak, by the whole Christ event itself. The apostles and others in that upper room were the first members of the new age, the new "last times" foretold by the prophets. St. Peter makes reference to this on the very day of his baptism-Pentecost by reminding his bible-steeped listeners of the promise of the prophet Joel: "Listen . . . it is what the prophet Joel spoke of, 'It shall come to pass in the last days, says God, that I will pour out a portion of my spirit on all mankind . . . '" (Acts 2:15). Peter was obviously anxious to share with them what he and his fellow apostles had experienced, the outpouring of the Holy Spirit. Only now, for the rest of the people, this outpouring would be in the nature of the old unity of water and Spirit. By this we mean, of course, baptism. The Pentecostal outpouring would come in the baptismal waters. In fact, it is true to remark here again that baptism in particular and the sacraments in general are basically nothing more or less than the attempt to "effectively reproduce, for subsequent generations of believers, the pentecostal experiences of the first disciples."[1] Therefore St. Peter's first sermon urging that "you must reform and be baptized, each one of you, in the name of Jesus Christ, that your sins may be forgiven; then you will receive the gift of the Holy Spirit" (Acts 2:38)—this urging was to be expected. In the normal psychology of good news it was but logical that Peter would want to share the water-Spirit, that he should naturally and forcibly speak in terms of baptism. We have here, then, the first introduction to baptism: no catechism, no instruction, no long preparation—just the basic proclamation about Jesus to Jews already steeped in biblical water-Spirit lore, already anticipating the "last times."

What did the apostles actually do in baptism? The New Testament does not give us details. Most probably the candidates for baptism were immersed in the water; that is, they stood knee deep or waist deep in the river or pool or one of the public baths of those days and water was poured over their heads. This approach would linger on until the fourteenth century. How about being baptized "in the name of Jesus"? This most likely means that the candidate accepted Jesus, took his ways to himself and was acting under his impulse and command much the same way that the Romans would act "in the name of Caesar." It might also mean that, during the actual baptism, the candidate himself spoke the name of Jesus as his act of faith. Later on, by the time Matthew gets around to writing his gospel, the Trinitarian formula is given and it is pronounced by the one giving the baptism rather than the one receiving it. (A transition from pronouncing the name of Jesus to the Trinitarian formula can be seen in Acts 18:25 and 19: 2–6.)

But even this Trinitarian formula was not necessarily a declarative sentence as we know it today. Rather, since the main basis for baptism was faith-conversion, then the candidate was asked to express that faith in a threefold question and answer format: "Do you believe in the Father? Do you believe in the Son? Do you believe in the Spirit?" And each time as the candidate answered in the affirmative he was immersed into the water. By the fifth century in the eastern section of Christianity, the threefold immersion was reduced to one immersion and the threefold questioning was reduced to the simple declarative statement, "I baptize you in the name of the Father and of the Son and of the

Holy Spirit." In the western section of Christianity this evolution took about three centuries more. So, for the first centuries there were the essentials of water and words but much flexibility in approach, leaving room for the many ceremonies and additions that would shortly come. However, this flexibility and many-faceted emphases concerning baptism were not to endure and in fact were to change quite dramatically.

What caused a new, stricter interpretation and practice of baptism was the quarrel that arose in the early persecution-time centuries. Forced on the Christian community was the question of people who were baptized by heretics. We must remember that Christianity, right from the beginning, suffered the fate of all movements: deviation, disagreement, and splintering. Were baptisms, given by Christian heretics, true and genuine (valid)? Then what about those Christians who in time of persecution denied the Christian faith and wanted now to get back in? Did they have to be rebaptized? Well, as soon as the questions were asked, they demanded answers and, as always, answers tended to be restrictive. Norms were sought and given on these matters and they were to influence baptism for all times.

The controversies and the norms need not detain us here, except to recall something we referred to in the last chapter. There was a beginning of a sacramental materialism. That is, the preoccupation was starting with the "basics" of the sacraments. What made baptism baptism was going to be analyzed someday. The sacrament was going to be tied down to a once-and-for-all event of water and words. It would slip away from its role as initiation, a beginning of the Christian life in desperate need of development, fulfillment, and ongoing faith. Someday baptism would be seen as almost an official registering of a child into society without the implication that what was begun needed to be continued. In other words, Christian registration would replace Christian living. Secondly, as time went on the old "look-to-the-last times" approach faded. People really did expect Jesus to come again quickly on the clouds of majesty. (Read Paul's epistles to the Thessalonians.) Baptism was to enroll them into the kingdom which would bring them salvation. But time softened such expectations and baptism came to be seen, not as insertion into the kingdom of God, but increasingly as insertion into the church itself. Getting into church membership (especially when the church became the state religion) was the goal and purpose of baptism rather than getting into the kingdom on its way to fulfillment. Again, the precisions about baptism tended to urge one to join a churchy club rather than to embark on the pilgrimage in the kingdom. In any case, the time of the simple proclamation of water, Spirit, conversion was over. A new approach was about to begin.

2

The apostles are all dead. What went on after them? How did baptism fare? Our earliest description of what went on comes from a man named Justin Martyr who lived in the year 150. Writing in Rome he gives us this outline:

The candidate prays and fasts
The church community prays and fasts with him
The candidate enters the water
The minister asks him the three Trinitarian questions
The candidate now is introduced into the assembly
Common prayers are said by all
The kiss of peace is given
The eucharist is celebrated.

Fifty years later another writer named Tertullian adds more details. He speaks of an anointing, a signing of the cross, a prayer and an outstretched hand over the candidate and a distinct mention, omitted in Justin Martyr's outline, of the Holy Spirit who descends on the water so that sins may be forgiven and who descends on the candidate as well. We are not sure whether Justin—who did not want to confuse the Romans to whom he was explaining all this or provoke suspicions of magic—just gave the bare outline of the real (Tertullian's) version or if Tertullian's account is Justin's version with edifying additions. In any case, we have here the beginning of a terrible confusion, unresolved to this day, in the rites and in the variations of the traditions of Eastern and Western Christianity. The problem centers around the anointing, the hand-laying, and the Holy Spirit. In modern terminology, the problem centers around the existence and practice of what we have come to call confirmation. Is the Holy Spirit given at baptism, or at the anointing, or at the hand-laying, or what? Is confirmation really a baptismal ceremony, or is it a distinct rite of conferring the Spirit? What do all those anointings mean? These and a host of other complex questions we shall explore in another chapter. For the moment, now that Tertullian has brought it up, we want merely to mention that a large and difficult problem awaits our discussion.

But to continue the development of Christian initiation. More and more non-Jews were entering the faith. That meant more and more people not at all familiar with the old biblical themes which we have seen as necessary to understand the sacraments. Obviously something had to be done. As Tertullian himself had remarked, Christians are made, not born. So the church invented the catechumenate. It was invented to meet this deep pastoral need of preparation into Christianity among those with no or little biblical roots. It was started around the second century and reached its flourishing point in the fourth and fifth centuries. Almost all of the great names who laid the foundations for our first real theologies flourished at this period and between the years from 330 to 460 almost every major Church Father (except Origen) was alive and active and dealing in a very practical and pastoral way with the vast numbers coming into the church; and all but one (Jerome) was a bishop of a local church. During Augustine's own lifetime (354–430) some of the greatest were at work: Ambrose, Jerome, Gregory from Nyssa and the Gregory from Nazianzen, Basil, John Chrysostom, Cyril of Jerusalem, Cyril of Alexandria, and Athanasius. These are strange names to most of us, these Africans, Greeks, and Romans, but we are still nourished by their writings and insights.

To these Fathers of the Church we also owe another debt. Not only did they invent the catechumenate and use their pastoral genius to make the ceremonies real and meaningful, but they also guided the church through an embarrassing transition. You see, before the "Peace of Constantine" in the fourth century, the church was illegal, underground, persecuted. It was a civil crime to be a Christian and the possibility of being hauled off to torture and death was quite real. In this context, baptism necessarily had very deep and personal overtones of commitment and martyrdom. One did not get baptized lightly. When the step was taken the candidate knew in his heart that this was a final and irrevocable commitment with the full expectation of martyrdom and everlasting life in heaven. Baptism was a serious step done at great cost; it placed one at radical odds against contemporary society. It is not surprising that some remained catechumens and delayed their baptisms. They were just too much a part of their world, and their routine lives could not easily be set aside since baptism demanded the cessation of certain jobs such as being a soldier or circus performer or idol maker, and so on. They compromised by remaining catechumens, hoping to receive baptism on their deathbeds. This provided them with the grand opportunity to have their sins forgiven (which, as we shall see, could be forgiven only in baptism at this time) and necessarily preempted any radical change in their lifestyles or commitments since they were so near death. This was something of a scandal. At any rate, the point we wish to make is that baptism was very orientated to segregation, radical commitment, martyrdom, the after life.

Then all this changed. Christianity became legal and it became somewhat politic to be a Christian. *Then* being baptized no longer meant being all that different, separating oneself from society. Baptism, in other words, lost a great deal of its radical decisiveness, elitism, martyrdom, and ready-for-heaven complexion. It let one loose in a now congenial world. But that was the question. How did one, radically baptized, fit into the world here and now? How did a formerly underground Christian cope above ground without compromising his Christianity? Many again postponed baptism in order not to deal with the tension and still kept it reduced to an entrance-into-heaven rite. It was the genius of the Fathers, as we shall see, which guided the transition to a here and now, in-the-world Christianity. In their theology they shifted the emphasis of baptism from being only a final forgiveness for sin and a preparation for heaven to being the sacrament that conforms one here and now to the passion, death, and resurrection of Jesus. In principle, all the baptized are pulled into Jesus' saving actions and are redeemed. Their lives are to be but an unfolding of the salvation in the Christ they encountered in their baptisms. In other words, here was a rationale to be baptized now (not later or at deathbed time), live in this world and penetrate it with the mission of Christ. "By emphasizing baptism not only as the saving bath which purified from all sin and threw open the gates of heaven, but showing the relationship of this salvation to the salvific action of the life, death, and resurrection of Christ, and the candidates' conformity to this through faith, and the expression of this faith in the act of baptism, then a major step had been taken towards providing the candidate with a spirituality for a Christian life in this world, central focus of which is his dynamic union with the humanity of Christ."[2] In short, we owe it to the Fathers that baptism was no longer to be seen as the final act of the remission of sins and the passage into heaven which set one *against* this world, but as the *beginning* of the candidate's life in Christ here and now *in* this world.

3

But let us now examine this catechumenate. The catechumenate was something very special. It is not to be confused with catechism in its narrow sense. Rather the catechumenate referred to that long, probational process by which a candidate for Christianity practiced and grew into that virtue which would make him worthy and prepared to make his great dedication for a new life in Christ. The catechumenate was a long training period of instruction, prayer, fasting, and conversion. It was a learning how to live as a Christian, a spiritual internship. Here is how it worked. Someone from the Christian community would sponsor a candidate. This sponsoring is akin to our modern practice of sponsoring someone for membership in an organization or private golf club. The sponsor puts his own name on the line and testifies to the worthy character of the candidate and assumes responsibility for him. So in the early church. The Christian put in the name of an interested candidate with the bishop. Bishops had to be careful in those days lest they unwittingly take in a Roman spy who would eventually turn them all in. The sponsor testified to the bishop about the candidate's worthiness and then, over the next years, worked, prayed, and fasted along with the candidate until the moment of initiation. It takes little imagination to see how emasculated today's notion is about our sponsors or godparents for the sacraments.

The catechumenate had two phases. One was the rather remote phase, the time of spiritual preparation which lasted about three years. Then came the immediate, proximate preparation. To catch something of the spirit of this preparation right through to the completion of the Christian initiation rites, let us take an imaginary candidate, Mark, and follow him through the steps.[3] Mark is twenty-six now. He had for a long time been distressed at the empty paganism in which he was brought up. Times were changing, the multiple gods of the empire never seemed more remote or unreal. Like many a young man of the twentieth century Mark was looking for meaning to life. Three years ago he had heard about the new Christian religion. Carefully he has ascertained the person to whom he could speak. After much caution he at last found a sponsor to come forth to instruct, guide, and pray with him. For the last three years, therefore, Mark has gone through a serious routine of prayer, scrutinies, exorcisms. Now he has arrived at the time he desired. It is the beginning of Lent. Mark has to decide whether he will go through with it all, whether or not to hand in his name and thereby request baptism. After much prayer, he decides to do just that. He is now ready for forty days of intensive learning, prayer, meditation, and fasting. Almost daily he and the other candidates are led before the bishop who questions them as to the sincerity of their motives and the worthiness of their characters. These interrogations—scrutinies, as they were called, impressed Mark. Later on, he would write of his experience to a friend,

> I think I also ought to tell you how instruction is given to those who are baptized at Easter. Those who give in their names do so the day before Lent begins; the presbyter writes down the names of all. This takes place before the eight weeks during which, as I told you, Lent is observed here. When the presbyter has made a note of all the names, later on another day in Lent, the day on which the eight weeks begin, the bishop's chair is set up in the middle of the great church. . . . The presbyters sit on either side on chairs and all the clerics stand. Then the candidates are brought in one by one, the men with their "fathers", the women with their "mothers" (sponsors). Then the bishop one by one asks their neighbors, "Is he a good living man? Does he respect his parents? Is he a drunkard or untrustworthy?" He asks them like this about every vice, at least the more serious ones. If the bishop finds that the candidate is free from all these faults about which he has questioned the witnesses, he writes down the candidate's name with his own hand.[4]

Mark now sees the bishop do just that: write his name—and his heart gives a jump. He knows full well that in these times of persecution, should this book be found, it would be his death warrant. To have his name written down in the baptismal register was a most serious commitment and the risk of his life. This baptismal book was therefore a source of anxiety and a source of pride for the Christian community. Anxiety lest it fall into the wrong hands; pride because it was truly the "book of life." What another age would do so casually in writing down a name in a baptismal register or casually handing out a baptismal certificate was done seriously in Mark's time.

Then there were the exorcisms. They happened daily during Lent, during Mark's proximate preparation to become a Christian. We moderns have much difficulty in relating to this. Even though our consciousness has been heightened somewhat (and even distorted) by such movies as *The Exorcist* and the revival of the occult, still we feel no sympathy for daily exorcisms of good people like Mark applying to enter the Christian community. But the ancients, like St. Paul, knew that our struggle was not with flesh and blood but with the principalities and the powers. The spirit of evil was no abstraction to the ancients. Evil was there then as now in the form of hatred and war and famine and injustice and corruption. Man is born into a network of evil. It impinges on him at his first breath. One can catch what we mean if he thinks for a moment of what it was like to be born ten years ago in Mississippi—black. The gospels themselves lose no time in introducing Satan in his struggle with Jesus and his activity in Judas' heart at the end. Satan and evil were realities for a people not used to verbalizing away the basic symbols of life. It was for this reason that the Satan-Christ temptation gospel is still placed at the first Sunday of Lent, the time, in the old days, when candidates began their immediate preparations for enrollment. So Mark and the others were exorcised daily, but let us hasten to add in the light of what we have just written, this did not imply devil possession. It implied rather that the candidates were in the bondage of sin and that is a big difference. The exorcisms were designed to help them break away from sinfulness, to dramatize their determination to "put on Christ."

It was also during this Lenten time that further instruction was given to Mark and the other candidates. For instance, on the third Sunday of Lent he would hear the gospel story of the Samaritan woman at Jacob's well and how Jesus promised her "living water," a clear reference to his forthcoming baptism. On the fourth Sunday of Lent the gospel would be about the man born blind and so the theme was the light that baptism would bring. On the fifth Sunday of Lent the gospel was about Lazarus and therefore how Mark would die to self but have a new resurrected life in Christ through his baptism. (These gospels still form part of the Lenten "A" cycle Sunday readings.) Then, too, Mark and the others learned for the first time the "Christian secrets." Up to this time Mark had learned some things, but not all. After all, he had been dismissed after the liturgy of the Word at Mass, so there were some things he did not yet know. Gradually it was revealed to him more and more. For instance, he was allowed to hear the Creed and the Our Father. In fact, he had to memorize them in order to give them back by rote to the bishop and the congregation. He was not the greatest scholar and was nervous about this, but his teacher tried to reassure him. He said to Mark, "You will have to repeat what you have learnt today. Your godparents are responsible for teaching you... [but] no need to be nervous and so fail to repeat the words. Do not worry, I am your father. I do not carry a strap or a cane like a schoolmaster!"[5] If Mark was reassured by his kindly teacher, later on, when all was revealed to him at Mass and the joy of it all became apparent, he would be heartened by the loud applause of the congregation. But that lay in the future. Right now, Mark was still in the process of scrutinies, exorcisms, instruction, penances, the confession of his sins, and daily attendance at the Lenten liturgies. At last came the culmination of all this preparation, the great week, Holy Week. At its end, on the Saturday night Easter vigil, the candidates would actually be baptized. The joyful tension is mounting.

On Holy Thursday, as he had been instructed, Mark took a bath. Not an ordinary bath, but one done consciously as a sign of ritual purification. Then on Good Friday and Holy Saturday Mark fasted and prayed. Now it was Holy Saturday night, about ten o'clock. Mark has gone to the preappointed place. There, along with about seventy-five other young boys and men (the women are meeting elsewhere) he is brought into a large room.

The sponsors are there—and the bishop. The room is darkened to give the sense of what Mark and the others are indeed about to experience: not a mere, passive watching, but a genuine religious drama. The ceremony begins. As a body the seventy-five men all face west. Mark knew why. His teacher had told him that the west was the symbol of darkness. After all, did not the sun set there and let darkness in? It was considered therefore the abode of Satan, the place of evil. In another month, Mark in his post-baptismal instructions, would hear these words from his teacher, "I wish to say why you stood facing the west, for it is necessary. Since the west is the region of sensible darkness, and he being darkness has his dominion also in darkness, you therefore, looking with a symbolic meaning towards the west, renounce that dark and gloomy potentate."[6]

Mark and the others did not really need that reminder. They were children of their time and understood and believed in the reality of evil spirits. In fact, even now the evil spirits were present among them, fighting, as it were, over the candidates, trying to prevent their "folly" of becoming Christians. The seventy-five candidates understood why they were told that they were like the Israelites of old after the exodus, for as the Israelites were on their way to freedom through the waters of the Red Sea, the cunning and wicked Pharaoh was in hot pursuit. So too Satan is right on the heels of them all right up to the Red Sea of the baptismal waters. Mark realized this and became more conscious of the presence of the evil spirits. Then the quiet was broken as one of the deacons shouted, "Stretch out your hands!" This they all did. They stretched out their hands in the dark almost trying to feel the evil spirits and ward them off. Then they expelled their breath in an effort to blow the spirits away. Mark shuddered. Then, on cue, all the candidates spoke firmly out loud with one voice, "I detach myself from you, Satan, from your pomp, your worship, and your angels." There was a collective sigh of relief at that bold declaration. Mark felt it. He knew all about those "pomps." They were the pagan games, the pagan idols, the pagan devil worship he had come close to dabbling in. No more of that.

Then the group suddenly made an about-face. They turned noisily to the east and said with even more firmness and volume, "And I attach myself to you, Oh Christ!" Their faces were brighter now for they all knew that the east was a sign of life and therefore a sign of Christ. In the east the Garden of Eden had been planted, that place of original innocence to which they all inspired. In the east the sun rises bringing newness, life, brightness, the very things which would be the fruits of their baptism. In the east Christ would come again. They all knew the verse of scripture which read, "As the lightening appears from the east, so shall the Son of man appear."

This turning away from the west (Satan) and towards the east (Christ) was a dramatic addition to the original demand of the first apostles. Mark and the others liked this "spelling out" of what Peter and the other apostles had demanded. They had called the people of their time to conversion. They asked the people to opt for Christ. Of course, if people set their choice *for* Christ then they automatically placed their choice *against* whatever was hostile to him. When the apostles called for *metanoia*, a conversion, they meant what they said: the people were to convert, that is, literally in Latin, "to turn about." Choosing Christ meant not choosing evil. So what Mark and the others just did was a dramatic concrete act of what is always meant by conversion, by faith. They were moving from unbelief to belief. They were making their public choice between Satan and Christ.

Once more we comment that another age (our own modern one) would find it hard to see twenty-six year old Mark and the others standing there in a darkened room, turning from west to east, with outstretched hands and exclaiming their rejection of Satan and acceptance of Christ. This is again because we cannot sense the realities or the drama which they did. Once more, Mark and the others did not consider Satan or evil spirits a mere academic idea. They were real to them. They actually felt the demons encircling them in that dark room, vying for their souls. They felt the invisible power of evil. It was tangible. They felt the tug-of-war. They had no choice but to so confront the devil and his demons. He had been their master so long through sin and a pervasively evil environment. They knew it would not be easy to extricate themselves from the grasp of Satan and to make new contact with Jesus. This whole turning, renunciation scene in the darkness was a powerful, mutually supportive act of faith. Christ, the demons, the Israelites, Pharaoh, the angels— they were all there, all present, all actors in the drama they were undergoing.

Having thus turned from west to east and professed their faith, they were standing there now, with hands at their sides. Mark saw the bishop approach him and the others. He had some oil and anointed Mark on the head. This was the seal, the *sphragis*. Since they declared themselves for Christ, so let them receive his brand. After all, shepherds put their mark on their animals and owners on their slaves. Why should not they be so marked for Christ? Why should they not be strengthened for the struggle against evil and be noted as an "athlete for Christ?" Mark and the others, by this anointing, are blessed with their freedom to live everyday life to the full. They are all now ready to confront the world, live in it, transform it, be a part of it to the fullest for Christ's sake.[7] So the sealing with the oil summarized all this and all that had gone on in the renunciation of Satan and the acceptance of Christ. The anointing completed this part of the ceremony; it was a summary much like the mirror the barber holds up so that the customer can see what *has* been done. So this sealing with oil, this anointing, was an illustration of what had just happened. Moreover, it marked a semicolon in the ceremony. The candidates were now ready for the next step.

The group now moves further in to a kind of pre-chamber to the baptistry. Here they know what they must do. They strip off all their clothing. Mark feels a slight embarrassment standing there stark naked with all the others. On the other hand, this is not something he is completely unaccustomed to. Public nakedness was not a novelty in the warm Mediterranean world used to segragated nude bathing and public baths like the Japanese have today. Besides, Mark is preoccupied with other thoughts. Taking off of his clothes was a very personal symbol of St. Paul's "putting off of the old man" (Colossians 3:9) and getting ready to put on the "wedding garment" of grace that figures in Jesus' parables. The stripping off of the clothes was also a symbol of returning to the primitive innocence of Adam and Eve who went naked and "felt no shame" before sin entered into the world. It also meant the decisive gesture of putting off vanity, frivolous ornaments, luxury, bad habits—in a word, anything that was incompatible with his new life as a Christian. But, as a former pagan, Mark knew other meanings also to this stripping. He and his pagan friends believed that evil spirits clung to one's clothes as they moved about here and there; they could even get into the smallest recesses of one's apparel like fleas. The Christians knew this and took advantage of it. They had the candidates disrobe, for it would be a mockery to wear their clothes, laden with evil spirits, to the brink of the baptismal font. Only in the Christian mind this was no longer associated with magic, but with sincerity. If these former pagans were sincere then they should remove any semblance of evil as they saw it. There was one more symbolism floating in the background. Their clothes were made of wool; wool comes from animals and animals are unclean and a sign of death. Later, after the baptism, the candidates would be clothed with linen robes. Linen comes from vegetation, plants, and therefore is a sign of life.

Mark's musings are interrupted. Deacons approach him and begin anointing him once more with oil, only this time from the top of his head to his toes. This again is a modified old pagan rite. In pagan culture sickness was considered always to be the work of evil spirits. The anointing of the sick was a common medicinal practice. The Christians took that over, figuring that, after all, the candidates were indeed spiritually sick and the anointing with oil would cure them. Oil was a preservative also and this would be a sign of the preservation from sin. Body rubbing with oil was also common among the Greek athletes especially in the body contact sports such as wrestling; and surely these new Christians would have to wrestle with the power of evil. Therefore it was only fitting that they too should be rubbed all over and be made "athletes for Christ." One of his teachers had suggested one more meaning to the oil. After all, it came from the olive tree; and just as the olive branch can be grafted onto a new trunk, so Mark and the others were now "grafted" onto Christ, have a new union with him. It was the vine-branches metaphor of Jesus in action.

After this body anointing, Mark and the other candidates, still naked, were led to the baptistry itself. There he sees the pool, the watery grave of St. Paul's theology where he will be buried with Christ. Like Christ, then, Mark has symbolically just come from the cross and is about to be "buried" prior to his new resurrected life. While he is awaiting his turn, Mark notices how the shape of the pool itself is like a tomb or even a womb, a sign of rebirth in water and the Spirit. He recalls Jesus' words, "Unless a man is born again of water and the Spirit he cannot be saved." Mark is also aware of the great archetypal symbol of water itself. Water–death–life–Spirit. Here was the primitive watery chaos about to recede into order before the breath of the Spirit (ruah). Mark had heard of other baptistries with their octagonal shapes reminiscent of the eight sided Roman baths he knew. Then he noticed the drawings on the wall. There was one of Jesus as the Good Shepherd, another of a deer drinking from a pool. He read some of the inscriptions:

> From this noble spring saving water gushes
> which cleanses all human defilement.
> Do you wish to know the benefits of the sacred water?
> These streams give the faith that regenerates.

Another inscription read:

> Here a people of godly race are born for heaven;
> The Spirit gives them life in the fertile waters. . .
> Here is to be found the source of life,
> which washes the whole universe,
> which gushed from the wound of Christ.
> Sinner, plunge into the sacred fountain to wash
> away your sin.

The water receives the old man, and in his place makes
the new man arise....[8]

While he was reading the inscriptions there was a brief blessing of the pool by the bishop. After all, as his teacher remarked,
"Not all waters have a curative power; only that water has it
which has the grace of Christ.... Water does not heal unless the
Spirit descends and consecrates the water."[9] Now the baptism is
at hand. It is almost midnight, Saturday night. They want to
time the baptism so that it is finished by the first moments of
Easter Sunday. So Mark steps into the water which comes up to
his chest. The bishop kneels by the side of the pool and puts his
hand on Mark's head. He applies a little pressure. Taking his
cue, Mark ducks under the water and comes up. The bishop
asks, "Do you believe in the Father?" Mark answers yes and is
ducked. "Do you believe in the Son.... Do you believe in the
Holy Spirit?" To each of the three questions Mark answers yes
and so the bishop says, "Mark is baptized in the name of the
Father and of the Son and of the Holy Spirit." Mark now comes
out of the pool, is dried off and is then anointed with a special
perfumed oil called myron on his five senses. This anointing is
given with the prayer that Mark receives the Holy Spirit. It is a
fitting prayer for that is what anointing means: to be "Christ-ed"
or to be made a "Christ-ian." That very name Christ is the Greek
word for Anointed One. So Mark in this anointing is reminded
that, in the whole ceremony, he has received the Spirit of Jesus.
Now Mark is clothed in the white linen robe denoting the Risen
Christ, purity of life and the forgiveness of sin. He will wear this
robe a full week until Low Sunday. He is handed a lighted candle and given the kiss of peace. Mark is radiant, not only with the
oil still glistening on his face or the white linen robe or the
lighted candle. But it is Easter Sunday morn now, and like the
Risen Lord Mark is radiant with his new life of faith. Immediately with the others he is led to the awaiting assembly to be
greeted by them and partake, for the first time, in the eucharist.
No longer will he be dismissed after the liturgy of the word, but

can now stay through it all. This completes Mark's initiation into the Christian religion.

We leave our imaginary Mark and return to some comments, not only about him and his initiation, but in general the whole spirit of Christian initiation in the first six centuries. First of all, we see clearly now that initiation is not at all what we call simply the sacrament of baptism. It is a rather elaborate rite which, in our hindsight, includes three sacraments: baptism, confirmation, and eucharist. All were but three steps of the same act in the process of becoming a Christian. They were a unit, all aspects of the same rite. It would be left for a later age not only to separate them but to rearrange their order and even to interject another sacrament (penance).

Secondly, we can now see the origins of many of the customs with which we may be familiar even in the old baptismal rite. We recall the use of oil, the candle, the white cloth (robe), the Creed and Our Father, the triple pouring of the water from the shell on the baby's forehead. We can now sense how truncated these ceremonies are, practically a remnant. With such abbreviated symbols and use it is no wonder that the awe-inspiring rites of Christian initiation were not so awe-inspiring after all in the baptisms we may have witnessed. We can also now see the fate of the end-of-Lent Holy Week and the Easter Vigil. The fate is the worst of all: indifference. When both adults and infants were no longer baptized at the culmination of Lent at the Holy Saturday vigil in the moving ceremonies we have just seen, but rather as soon as possible after birth at *any* time, then Holy Saturday was preempted as a climax. People lost interest and some older Catholics can remember the days when all of the elaborate ceremonies we wrote about in this chapter were truncated and hurriedly and sleepily performed at six o'clock in the morning with no one present. The Holy Week ceremonies in general and Holy Saturday vigil in particular have been restored to their proper nighttime place, but they still have not caught on in the popular mind. People really do not understand what all the water and candle and oil-pouring and breathing and strange movements are all about; moreover, there is seldom anyone initiated at that time anymore, these ceremonies mean even less. Perhaps the only thing that will really revive the Easter Vigil is to "save up" enough candidates so that actual initiation can take place in the ceremonies designed for it.

Thirdly, we can clearly see what great emphasis there was on the community aspect of initiation. The community sponsored the candidate, instructed him, prayed for him, and was assembled to greet him and welcome him after his baptism. The community, in a word, was quite active. It was reaching out and giving the first centuries' equivalent of "welcome!" And it was not only a welcome in the sense that one is now a part of the community, but welcome also in the sense that the community would be there in the ongoing process of becoming a Christian. Baptism was only the beginning. The candidate was now part of a pilgrim people and he would need the support of the community as he made more real the life in Christ he had entered. In the last analysis, then, the ritual of baptism really spoke more to the community and its obligation to continually mediate the faith to the candidate. The candidate's entrance into the church and the community's responsibility of supporting him and creating that Christian climate within which he would grow spiritually were but two sides to the same baptismal coin. With this in mind we may note the necessity of the public aspect of baptism: that it be done before the community, that this increase to the Body of Christ be a mutually acknowledged matter. The Christians of the early centuries would be totally baffled and disturbed at the private baptisms on a Sunday afternoon with no one there—not even the parents—which was common fare before the current revision of the rites.

Fourthly, this is the place to remind ourselves that this whole catechumenate which we have described in this chapter has been restored to the church today. The document on this restoration is called The New Rite of Christian Initiation of Adults, issued in 1972.[10] Understandably this restoration had its roots in the mission territories where the anxiety of properly preparing and introducing converts to the faith has been paramount. But, again, notice that it is a restoration, not a new invention. As the introduction says, "Approved by the ancient practice of the church and adapted to contemporary missionary work throughout the world, this catechumenate was so widely requested that the Second Vatican Council decreed its restoration, revision, and accommodation to local traditions" (no. 2).

We will have some practical pastoral things to say about this restored catechumenate in the closing chapter, but for now we wish to quote some of its exact text so that we may appreciate how closely it follows the process we have described concerning our imaginary convert, Mark. The document on the New Rite of Christian Initiation of Adults explains:

> The initiation of catechumens takes place step by step in the midst of the community of the faithful . . . there are stages or steps by which the catechumen moves forward . . . These stages led to periods of investigation and maturation. . . .
>
> a) The first period consists of inquiry by the candidate and evangelization and the precatechumenate on the part of the church. It ends with entrance into the order of catechumens.
> b) The second period, which begins with this entrance into the order of catechumens and may last for several years, includes catechesis and the rites connected with catechesis. It is completed on the day of election. [This "day of election" is the day that the church or local faith community chooses the candidate because of his or her proven sincerity. Now the candidate's name is inscribed in the book of the elect, "elect" being the technical name for him or her from now on (no. 22).]
> c) The third period, shorter in length, ordinarily occupies the Lenten preparation for the Easter celebration and the sacraments. It is a time of purification and enlightenment or "illumination." [And, at the end of Lent, during Holy Week, the candidate is asked to take off from work, especially on Holy Saturday, and spend the day in prayer and fasting (no. 52).]

d) The final period goes through the whole Easter season and is called the postbaptismal catechesis or "mystagogia" for gaining spiritual fruit, and for entering more closely into the life and unity of the community of the faithful (nos. 4 to 7).

This, then, is the modern catechumenate. We might add, moreover, that the old concept of the sponsor has also been retained. The sponsor accompanies the candidate. Indeed the sponsor is properly designated by the local Christian community. The sponsor is there at the day of "election," the celebration of the actual initiation rite and during the postbaptismal catechesis (nos. 42 and 43).

Finally, we can hardly not be impressed with how seriously the early Christians took baptism or initiation. It was beyond doubt everything foreshadowed in the Old Testament: newness, death, and resurrection, receiving a whole new Spirit to live by. Nor, as we have seen, was it prosaic, academic, or primarily intellectual. The initiation rite was public and gutsy. It involved the whole person, the five senses, and the community. There were all those masterful actions, all of the actors: the renunciations, the turning from west to east, the evil spirts, oil, touch, perfume, nakedness, wool, linen, candle, water, kiss, bread, wine, Christ, Satan, demons, angels, deacons, ministers, bishop. It was, as we have so often suggested, a real *drama.* And it demanded the surrender of the whole self and a total act of faith. "Nothing is further from the spirit of primitive Christianity than any magical ideas of sacramental action. Sincere and whole-hearted conversion is the condition required in order to receive baptism."[11] Certainly, it must have been a most impressive spectacle, spiritually edifying, emotionally satisfying and even physically exhausting. But it was moving and it was meaningful for all: the candidates and the community. For any of us who might remember the routine, private baptisms of our infants in a near empty church building with the community absent and the parents at home preparing the food and drinks, the contrast is indeed profound.

NOTES FOR CHAPTER 4

1. David M. Stanley, S. J., *The Apostolic Church in the New Testament* (The Newman Press, 1967), p. 145.

2. Hugh M. Riley, *Christian Initiation* (Consortium Press, 1974), p. 223. It should be noted that not all were convinced of this interpretation and so chose to live the ascetical life as a sign that they were still separated from the world.

3. What follows is a free composite reconstructed from selected elements in Hugh Riley's book (see above) which gives the catechesis of Cyril, Theodore, Chrysostom, and Ambrose.

4. Actually the words of an early convert named Aetheria, quoted in Edward Yarnold's *The Awe Inspiring Rites of Initiation* (Slough, England: St. Paul Publications, 1971), pp. 8, 9.

5. St. Augustine's words, quoted in Yarnold, *The Awe Inspiring Rites*, p. 13.

6. Cyril's words, quoted in Riley, *Christian Initiation*, p. 62.

7. Hugh Riley writes, "So much is made in this regard of the turning, kneeling, and rising, and the personal confrontation with the adversary precisely because they carried with them implications for membership in the Christian church which were based on an actual confrontation with the problems of the day.... The fathers are not presenting a detached, scholarly investigation into the liturgy, nor a mere esthetic exposition of liturgical ceremonies. They are dead serious, and their catecheses are for concrete candidates wrestling with concrete problems of the Christian life" (*Christian Initiation*, p. 141).

8. Actual inscriptions quoted in Lucien Deiss, *Early Sources of the Liturgy* (The Liturgical Press, 1963), pp. 197 and 198.

9. Ambrose's words, quoted in Yarnold, *The Awe Inspiring Rites*, p. 23.

10. In theory, the catechumenate has always been around, but since 1917 has gone almost totally into canonical limbo. It was the missionary experiences of countries such as France, Africa, and Japan which have revived it for the rest of the world. The numbers in the text following all refer to paragraphs in the new Rite of Christian Initiation of Adults.

11. Jean Danielou, S. J., *The Bible and the Liturgy* (University of Notre Dame Press, 1956), p. 34.

5

Infant Baptism

1

One suspects that it was one of those very human things that the early Christians did. They acted from a very natural instinct first and left it for others to justify their actions later. (This is not an unusual trend: the church acts first and theologizes about what it has done later.) But in the process these early Christians did leave succeeding generations the most sensitive and complicated of problems: the baptizing of infants. We will explore in the next section the reasons that lay behind their actions. For now, we want to take the objective look and see just what scripture has to say about the matter.

The first thing we notice is that there is no direct evidence in the New Testament that infants were baptized. Rather, the record shows that adults were preached to, asked to respond with faith and to freely accept baptism. "... In the age of the apologists (second century) there is no evidence for infant baptism, but there is, on the contrary, some striking evidence to show that only adults were baptized."[1] Yet, by the third century infant baptism is in evidence and in a few centuries more becomes the norm. A man named Hippolytus (whom we shall meet again) was writing in Rome around the year 215. He gives a description of baptism and says, "When they come to the water, let the water be pure and flowing. And they shall put off their clothes. And they shall baptize the little children first. And if they can answer for themselves, let them answer. But if they cannot, let their parents answer or someone from their family."[2] A Church Father named Origen who died in 253 wrote, "By the sacrament of baptism the pollution of our birth is taken away," and elsewhere he remarks that the apostles themselves baptized infants for they knew there were inborn corruptions of sin in all people which must be washed away by water and the Spirit.[3] In fact he quotes Job to this effect, "No one is free from uncleanness" (Job 14:4).

Obviously, therefore, infant baptism began early. Of course for all we know, it might have been a part of the New Testament practice and, negatively, we find no prohibition against it. In fact, there are some hints and suppositions that might support it. For example, we know that the Jews were highly family conscious. If a Jewish father and mother were converted to Christianity and baptized, it would not be too difficult to see that they would want all the family members to be so initiated so as not to have a divided family. Some scholars (Jeremias) see this in the New Testament reference that "whole households" were baptized. After all, the Jews did circumcise their infants as an entrance rite into the community of Israel. Likewise, there is a possible hint of infant baptism in that Timothy was raised in the faith by his mother and grandmother (see 2 Timothy 1:5). In any case, family solidarity, the mentality that thought in terms of the extended family rather than individuals, may have been the subtle cause of infant baptism even though we find no explicit proof in the New Testament. Then, too, there must have been some outside influence of the contemporary pagan cults. They carried with them magical overtones of automatic justification and the right to salvation. This could have crept into Christianity. This is not so far-fetched as it may seem. We know that some pagan notions had in fact inserted themselves and had to be rebuffed. For example, St. Paul mentions that some people were receiving baptism on behalf of the dead in order that the deceased might gain the benefits believed to be attached to the rite (1 Corinthians 15:29). Such a mentality would find it an easy step to baptize infants that they too might receive its blessings.

There also may have been some pressure from the growing idea that the church alone was the instrument for salvation and therefore it was important to enter it quickly. This would be a derivative from the subtle movement from seeing baptism as a total initiation demanding an intense personal faith response to an emphasis on the external rite and its "objective" power.

Whatever its origins, once started, infant baptism caused no outcry, no protests, no crisis that this practice was deviating from what was handed down. Gradually, by the fifth century, infant baptism became the norm—although we read of fourth century bishops who did not baptize their children and that as late as the eighth century adult baptism was customary in Spain. But the trend towards infants was not only started, it received some mighty encouragements. There was the fifth century heresy of Pelagius who said that man, by his own unaided efforts, could be saved. Therefore God's grace was not that important. Infant baptism then became a kind of living refutation which in effect said, "Look, even babies need God's grace—even babies who cannot earn it. That's how necessary it is." Then, too, people began to think more about those famous words of Jesus that "unless one is born of water and the Spirit he cannot enter the kingdom of God." This had its impact. Next, Augustine, who was the chief foe of Pelagius, gave infant baptism its theoretical underpinnings. He emphasized the reality of original sin and therefore the dire necessity of baptism to be free of it. Since even infants were born in this sad state, they should find cleansing and adoption into God's family as soon as possible or else they would be lost. Add to this the high rate of infant mortality and the increase of infant baptism was virtually assured. And even though, as we shall see, the church preferred baptisms at the liturgical times of Easter and Pentecost, parents did not want to wait that long and so had their babies baptized as soon as they could. Even legislation went contrary to official preaching. In England, for example, as early as 693 the king of Wessex commanded that children were to be baptized before they were thirty days old.

There was another factor. A new penitential discipline gradually arose in the church allowing sins to be forgiven (at least one more time) after baptism. (As we shall see later, baptism was the one and only time of forgiveness in the first century.) This meant that people did not have to wait, as some of them did, until their deathbed to have their sins taken away by baptism. Therefore baptism could "safely" be given to infants who would now get another chance if they slipped from their baptismal innocence someday. Finally, the most natural and practical cause of the growth of infant baptism was that eventually there were no more adults (practically speaking) left to baptize. The "whole world" was Christian. It certainly seemed so after the Roman Empire made Christianity the state religion and the mass conversion of the barbarians was underway. The church ran out of material, as it were, so the only available candidates for baptism (outside of the "perverse" Jews and "infidel" Moslems) were those being born—although both earlier and later we find some famous adults with one Christian parent who continued to delay their baptisms: Saints Gregory Nazianzen, Basil, Paulinus of Nola, Jerome, and Augustine.

2

The practice of infant baptism raises basic problems, some theological and others pastoral. First of all, there is no clear, unambiguous foundation for infant baptism in the New Testament as we have just discovered. Secondly, the practical, everyday theology we do find in the New Testament seems to exclude infant baptism. The talk there is constantly about conversion, the forgiveness of sin (note the Nicene Creed: "I believe in one baptism for the forgiveness of sin"), repentance, faith, and the great ethical demands involved in becoming a Christian. An infant does not qualify in any of these categories: he has no sins to be forgiven, he cannot make an act of faith, he cannot accept the demands, he cannot pledge himself to the Christian way of life.

All of those elaborate ceremonies we have examined in the last chapter—the scrutinies, the exorcisms, the prayer and fasting, the probation, the instruction, the threefold response to the Trinitarian plunging into the water—all of these ceremonies (oddly kept intact for infants until modern times) make no sense when applied to infants. And then there is faith. This is always demanded by Jesus, always by the apostles and the whole institution of the catechumenate is based on it. So strong is the faith motif that somehow it was brought to bear even in infant baptism. Even when the emphasis is placed on the objectivity of grace in baptism, an immediate qualification is made by emphasizing the faith of the infant or the sponsors or (for Catholics) the faith of the church supplying for the infant.

Among the various Christian bodies, the Baptists have, at first look, proven to be the most logical and theological about infant baptism. They provide by far the best arguments against it, and they practice what they preach by having only a "believer's" baptism; that is, one given to a faith-responding mature person. The other mainline Protestant communities suffer from inconsistency. They began by holding to the rallying slogan "justification by faith" when they rightly rebelled against the Catholic sacramental system that seemed too much like magic. Yet they continued to give infants who in no way could make an act of "justifying faith" the sacrament of baptism. Does all this mean that Protestants and Catholics have no theological basis for what they do? Obviously not. Once the practical fact was forced on the church, then the church was able to justify what instinct had brought into being—and a rather good justification at that.

Basically the justification for infant baptism rests on the initiative of God himself. (This is the "Godward" thrust as opposed to the "manword" thrust of the Baptists.) It is God who reaches out to man, who forgives sins, who makes holy. God's activity (grace) is a free act. No one can earn it. God is master of his gifts. Man does not deserve them and cannot earn them. Any notion, therefore, that the good deeds or the faith of any human being *must* precede God's action, his grace-filled activity, in order for

God to act, would imply curtailing God's power. He loves us when we do not deserve it. He shows mercy when we have no right to expect it and compassion when we did not think it was possible. Remember compassion and pity are his great names. As he said to Moses, ". . . In your presence I will pronounce my name 'Lord'; I who show favors to whom I will. I who grant mercy to whom I will" (Exodus 33:19). The Jews were often reminded of God's freely given love, "For love of your fathers he chose their descendants and personally led you out of Egypt by his great power, driving out of your way nations greater and mightier than you. . ." (Deuteronomy 4:36). God's grace, then, is so primary, his initiative is so basic, that essentially no response is necessary, at least in order to cause God to act or get him moving. After all, to move into New Testament references, Christ did die first to save men before anyone responded to faith.[4] So, it is on this biblical understanding of a God who is master of his gifts and who "first loved us" that the reaching out in baptism to an infant is justified. It is the emphasis of a Godward approach.

But what about sin? Most modern theologians find any notion of sin in the infant repulsive. But if they dismiss sin as something personal, they do not dismiss it as an overarching reality of life. All mankind needs liberation and salvation and infants are no exception. What Frank Sheed wrote years ago about Mary could be applied to infant baptism and sin: "Notice again that it was not a question primarily of redeeming individuals, but of redeeming the human race to which these individuals belong. . . . The sin of the world was the breach between the human race and God, and it stood between men and the sonship of God. Christ healed it. It is in this widest sense that he is the Savior of mankind. The individual does not have to sin in order to have Christ as his Savior . . . Our Blessed Lady, Christ's mother, who had God's grace in her soul from the first moment of her existence, could still call God her Savior, not only because he saved her from committing sin, but because he had saved the race of Adam whose sinless descendant she was."[5] So, in the same manner, infants just by being a part of the human race need salvation. In this sense, not in any sense of having personal sins, the infant is "forgiven": he is freely touched with the saving actions of Jesus.

Now if we see the justification for infant baptism in God's first initiative towards this child, if we concede that infants, as well as adults, can be the objects of his freely given and gracious grace, then baptism is quite obviously future-orientated. It is the first step, the beginning, the setting onto a path in life. Baptism initiates the infant into the Christian life and into the Christian community. "The loving Father is seeking out his child from his earliest days. That God plans to bring him to joyful acknowledgment of his heavenly Father is empirically clear from the fact that he has sent him in a Christian home. . . . The sacrament of baptism is a sign that God is graciously leading the child to faith and to a life that will exhibit both the fruits of repentance and the fruit of the Spirit in ethical conduct. . . . Of course, infant baptism is not unfailing in its effect; but neither is it unknown for those baptized as adults to fall away. . . ."[6] As Vatican II expresses it: "Baptism itself is only a beginning, a point of departure, for it is wholly directed towards the acquiring of fullness of life in Christ. Baptism is thus orientated toward a complete profession of faith, a complete incorporation into the system of salvation such as Christ himself wills it to be, and finally toward a complete participation in eucharistic communion."[7]

These concepts now help us to see what was perhaps unconsciously in the minds of the first Christians when they baptized their infants and what should be in our minds. These considerations may also help us to answer those adolescents who demand to know by what right their parents had them baptized without their consent. Their parents, they say, have placed a burden on them which they may now not be willing to carry. First of all such adolescents will learn someday that no one exists in a vacuum. "To be" always means "to be in relationship." There is no such thing as a human being unattached to a family or society into which he is born and within which he is shaped for better or worse. His initial and lasting view of reality will come from his first relationships. That is why psychoanalyst Erik Erikson has suggested that the most critical task of the child's first year on the planet is whether he will learn to trust or distrust the world. Only his parents—especially his mother's verbal and emotional dialogue will resolve this question. If this dialogue is warm and generous; if there are the many approaches of fondling, caring, touching; if there are many subtle affirmations of concern and discipline—then the child will learn trust. He will have acquired an optimistic and hopeful attitude. It is this hope, says Erikson, that is the foundation of faith.

What does this have to do with infant baptism? A great deal. For believing parents, the Christian life is profoundly the basic hope and trust in life. In Jesus all will ultimately be well and victorious. Since baptism plunges us into Jesus' death *and* resurrection, moves us into the "last times" and outpours the Holy Spirit—how could believing parents not share that as a life's basic thrust? Believing parents could no more not insert their children into a hope-giving, redemptive community of believers than they could deny them their basic immunization shots without their consent. And here we probably catch the essence of why Christians started baptizing their infants to begin with. It was *out of their common life in faith* that they came to accept the appropriateness of celebrating baptism with infants and children even though the *process* of faith and conversion is essentially an adult experience.

We could express it another way. Think of the alternative. The alternative would be the unusual and curious situation in which deeply committed Christian parents would have their children live among them as non-Christians. This would be an impossible psychological tension. Committed Christian parents can no more raise their children "neutrally" than Chinese parents can raise their children neutrally. From the very first moment that the Chinese baby enters the family in China, with all of its customs, traditions, world outlooks, language, the "Chinese-ing" process begins. There is simply no way, short of giving the child away, for a baby of a genuine, self-conscious Chinese family to be raised non-Chinese. The baby's "Chinese-ness" is a foregone conclusion. So too, it must have been for the first Christian parents who wanted their babies baptized. Infant baptism would be as natural for them as it would be most unnatural for them, as practicing and celebrating Christian parents, to attempt to raise their child in a neutral matter so "he can make up his mind when he grows up." The nature of commitment and belief precludes such psychological nonsense. The only way parents can raise a child in a neutral manner so he can make up his own mind later is for *them* to be neutral. Then, we may have the poignant story of the Harvard sophomore who wrote:

> If I had been brought up in Nazi Germany—supposing I wasn't Jewish—I think I would have had an absolute set of values, that is to say, Nazism, to believe in. In modern American society, particularly in the upper middle class, a very liberal group, where I am given no religious background, where my parents always said to me, "if you want to go to Sunday School, you *can*," or "if you want to take music lessons, you *can*," but "it's up to *you*," where they never did force any arbitrary system of values on me—what I find is that with so much freedom, I am left with *no* value system, and in certain ways I wish I had a value system forced on me, so that I could have something to believe in.[8]

Many of our youths' turning to drugs, sub-movements, the occult, the eastern mysticism sects and astrology may be strong indications of what happens when values are not transmitted early. All this does not mean, of course, that the child cannot reject his parents' nutritional habits, care, patience, love, and faith, and perhaps should do so. This is his or her business. All that the argument says is that the parents are compelled by their very role as parents to share the "good news" (gospel) as they saw it. They are not committing their child in spite of himself, and he does have his future to use to make up his own mind. Parents are merely and profoundly giving the child a value system that includes enormous love and salvation in Jesus Christ. He is free to alter or reject this initial thrust. He really has no grounds to dispute their faith-desire and fondest spiritual hopes anymore than he can get angry because they started a trust fund at his birth for his college education.

So, getting back to the notion of baptism as future orientated, we say that now this infant has been publicly started; he is now related to the kingdom, and placed into the "last times" awaiting their fulfillment. He has been chosen, marked, set on his way and that is quite important to the child, his parents and to the Christian community to know this. Even some of the Baptists see merit in this. As one of them says, "There is everything to be said in favor in the church's providing for children a solemn rite of entry into its midst. . . . Baptists are aware that there are needs that infant baptism seeks to meet and that ought to be met by some means or other."[9] Again we cannot help but feel that this sentiment was what started infant baptism to begin with. Another Baptist theologian says, "Infant baptism may be affirmed on the ground of the eschatological nature of the sacrament. It may be claimed that it has an inescapable proleptic [future-orientated] element . . . that it is 'unto faith.' This is a powerful defense. It may be that upon it, at the end of the day, the case will stand—and stand firm."[10]

It may be that some Baptists are cautiously willing to say such words because, as admirable as their insights may be, they have problems of their own. They will acknowledge that, with the pressure of parental and community expectations, oftentimes their "believer's baptism" is psychologically and sociologically more like a deferred infant baptism. It has also happened that a Baptist will be admitted to his profession of faith without having been baptized at all, and at times communion is given before baptism and totally apart from it. The so-called believer's baptism has backfired in some areas where the Baptists form the political and cultural power. Then, again, there is much pressure to get baptized from convention rather than from exalted free choice. Finally, as one critic points out:

> The location of baptism exclusively within adulthood fails to interpret and support the place of the child in the church. I

hope it is more than a debater's point to suggest that we have it on good authority that there is something normative in the life of the kingdom about a child. The adult is the odd one who must change and become like a child in order to enter. A system which seems to say, "Except you become as a grown-up, you shall in no wise enter. . . ." at least does not have all the arguments in its favor. Does God reach us only through conscious, rational processes? Are there not pre-conscious materials basic to the reasoned-out formulations which bind together Christian with Christian and elders with children in the life of Christ? . . . Baptist parents do not treat their children as exiles from Christ and from grace until they come to adult faith. But godly parental impulse needs to be supported, interpreted, and directed by theology, a theology of the child in the church which, in Baptist circles, appears quite faint.[11]

It seems that no one Christian body has all the answers and all have special problems—although it may be some consolation to know that the early Fathers were divided on the problem: Irenaeus (180 A.D.) says, "In effect, Jesus comes to save all men by himself: all those, I say, who are reborn in God by him—babies, young children, adolescents, adults, and the elderly. Thus he himself lived through all these ages, and became a baby for the babies in order to sanctify the babies. . . ."[12] Cyprian (251 A.D.) writes, "Concerning infants, you said that they should not be baptized the second or third day, but that we should model ourselves upon the ancient law of circumcision, and thus not baptize and sanctify the newly-born before the eighth day. Our assembly thinks differently on the matter."[13] Tertullian, however, in 200 A.D. writes, ". . . Taking into account the condition, the disposition, and even the age of each one, it is preferable to delay baptism, but especially when it is a matter of young infants. . . . Certainly the Lord said, 'Let the children come to me.' Yes, let them come, but let them come when they are older. . . . Let them at least be capable of requesting salvation, so that we may see that it is given only to those who seek it."[14] Perhaps then the Christian world will have to live with—and maybe should live with—the tensions of both infant and adult baptisms. The tensions can serve as a corrective to each other. Anyway, the practice of infant baptism as such is not our problem as Catholics, and in these pages we feel that we can justify the practice. Our problem is pastoral. Infant baptism is built on the solid presumption of an organic society, of a society which is both explicitly and implicitly Christian. But are those assumptions valid anymore? If they are not, then we have the vast task of coming to terms with what can only be called unchristian baptisms.

NOTES FOR CHAPTER 5

1. Robert M. Grant, "Development of the Christian Catechumenate," in *Made Not Born* (University of Notre Dame Press, 1976), p. 35.

2. E. C. Whitaker, *Documents of the Baptismal Liturgy* (London: Alcuin Club, SPCK, 1970), p. 5.

3. Commentary on Thomas, 5:9.

4. Oscar Cullman's remark.

5. Frank Sheed, *Theology and Sanity* (Sheed and Ward, 1946), p. 200.

6. Geoffrey Wainwright, *Christian Initiation* (John Knox Press, 1969), p. 54.

7. Decree on Ecumenism, no. 22.

8. Steven Kelman, "These Are Three of the Alienated," *New York Times Magazine* (October 22, 1967), p. 39.

9. Quoted in "What Can Catholics Learn from the Infant Baptism Controversy?" by Michael Hurley, S. J., *Concilium* 24 (1967), p. 18.

10. Quoted in *Baptism, A Pastoral Perspective,* by Eugene L. Brand (Augsburg Publishing House, 1975), p. 38.

11. Daniel B. Stevick, "Christian Initiation: Post-Reformation to the Present Era," in *Made Not Born* (University of Notre Dame Press, 1976), p. 106.

12. *Contra Haereses,* 11, 22, 4.

13. Letter to Fidus, 64.

14. *On Baptism,* 18.

6

Unchristian Baptisms

1

In the last chapter we made the point that the baptism of infants is justified on the ground that it is future orientated. Infants are initiated immediately into the Christian community even though we all know, as we said, that the *process* of becoming a full Christian will have to wait until adulthood, to the time of conscious moral decision. Since this is so, however, it raises for us today some very sensitive and serious problems on the pastoral level. The problems all boil down to this one: if baptism is future orientated, then should we celebrate it where that future is highly in doubt? This doubt is not without foundation these days and has two sources: one is the family and the other is today's society. Let us look first at the family. The following scenario will do. Mr. and Mrs. Smith just had a baby boy, Edward. When Edward was a few months old, they brought him to St. Barnabas Roman Catholic church to have him baptized. After his baptism Edward was raised by his parents who never went to church except on the social holidays (Christmas and Easter). When Edward was seven they sent him to CCD classes to prepare for his First Communion. He came back a few years later to get ready for confirmation and, after that, he felt religion was over and he dropped out altogether. His involvement with the Christian community in any form was reduced to a minimum although, for lack of an alternate identity, he considered himself a Catholic. Besides, he had other things to occupy him: cars, girls, college. At college he flirted for a time with one of the eastern mystic cults that were so popular and took up with transcendental meditation for a while. After college and a job he met a girl and married her in the Catholic church. The pastor did not see them again until they called to have their baby baptized. Four weeks later the baptism was performed privately on a Sunday afternoon. The church now had a new member and the cycle was completed. Or was the cycle just beginning all over again?

In this account we have the first problem that bedevils all of the mainline Christian religions: If we continue to baptize infants and justify it on the grounds of God's gracious touch to that child with the decided inner thrust to the future, what if there is no future in the faith that we can see? In other words, what do we do about the nominal Catholic? How do we break the cycle? Should we break it? How do we get rid of or reduce the scandal of indiscriminate baptism? Shall we continue to produce millions of baptized pagans? Or is it time, as many have suggested, to allow the name of Christian to quietly die out where the realities of living faith, worship, and hope have already in fact dried up? The Anglican community took a poll some years ago and its survey estimated that out of every hundred babies born in England sixty-seven are baptized Anglicans, but of these only nine "remain faithful to the extent of making their communion once a year at Easter."[1] Yet, in spite of such an amazing disparity, the Church of England could not overcome its materialistic approach to the sacraments for it concluded: "Refusal of baptism must in the last resort be the decision of the parents and not the responsibility of the parish priest, for we find it difficult to believe that any individual could make a child's right of Christian membership dependent upon his own assessment of the suitability of the child's parents or guardians." (Oddly, they make all kinds of external judgments about the suitability of their candidates for the priesthood, and surely it is more odd to expect parents to openly declare themselves unsuitable while requesting baptism for their offspring.) A modern Lutheran theologian remarks:

> Would it not be better to say that infants are baptized *into* faith, i.e., we risk baptizing them because we trust that given the environment of a Christian home and the fellowship of the church, faith will grow and mature? And would that not, in turn, imply a selective practice of infant baptism? . . . Should not one speak only of baptizing infants born into viable Christian families?

This distinction is worth making. In its polemics against Abrahamic guarantees, the New Testament makes it clear that one is not a member of the fellowship by natural birth, but only by water and the Spirit. It is, therefore, unnatural to keep the children even partially outside the larger Christian family in which the parents share. They should be sealed by the same Spirit and thus marked for the kingdom as were their parents. To do this wholesale, however, without any assurance of the growth of faith in response to exposure to the word in its myriad forms, is just as suspect as to herd adults together and baptize them indiscriminately with a fire hose. It reflects a mechanistic concept of grace which is unacceptable.[2]

Catholics and others could come up with similar statistics. We know that one of the latest surveys has shown that Catholic Sunday Mass attendance—long a staple of Catholic practice and identity—has declined some 22 percent.[3] The cultural rather than the committed Catholic is one aspect of the problem.

The other aspect is a dechristianized society. If some families are so indifferent and so nominal as to very likely produce indifferent and nominal Catholics, then society is of no help either. Rather society reinforces the disintegration of the faith. We no longer live in a Christian society whose symbols and atmosphere reflect a Christian way of life. Religion has been reduced to a very private affair of private individuals, one contender among many other interests for the average citizen in a secular society. A recent survey[4] among the youth makes these revelations: in two comparison years:

"Premarital sex is wrong."
    a) noncollege youth in 1969 ....57% agreed
    b) noncollege youth in 1973 ....34% agreed
    c) college youth in 1969 ....34% agreed
    d) college youth in 1973 ....22% agreed
"Living a clean moral life is a very important value"
    a) noncollege youth in 1969 ....77% agreed
    b) noncollege youth in 1973 ....57% agreed
    c) college youth in 1969 ....45% agreed
    d) college youth in 1973 ....34% agreed
"Religion is a very important value"
    a) noncollege youth in 1969 ....64% agreed
    b) noncollege youth in 1973 ....42% agreed
    c) college youth in 1969 ....38% agreed
    d) college youth in 1973 ....28% agreed

This survey only points up the truism that today's moral atmosphere is increasingly hostile to practical belief in God. One writer has observed, "I think it possible to suggest that the decline of the belief in personal immortality has been the most important *political* fact of the last hundred years—nothing else has so profoundly affected the way in which the masses of people experience their own worldly condition."[5] And another has observed, "By the twenty-first century, religious believers are likely to be found only in small sects, huddled together to resist a world-wide secular culture."[6] Again, another says, ". . . Being Catholic in America will mean belonging to a church that will have lost a large number of its institutions and a large part of its membership to the post-Christian secular society. It will mean maintaining a faith in the transcendent and eternal in a culture increasingly unable to appreciate it. It will mean being sharply at odds with prevailing moral standards. It will mean continuing conflict with other groups in the population as the drive is pressed to remove from the law the moral values built into it during the Christian centuries."[7] The point of all of these quotations is to demonstrate that society at large is no longer supportative to the faith. In fact, it is hostile to it. If, therefore, the family reneges religiously, there is no backstop society to take over as surrogate. It is hard enough for true believers to maintain the faith in such a society, but if such parents are neglectful and send children ill-formed in the faith into a pagan society, then the policy of baptizing such children becomes more acutely questionable. There must be a better answer.

2

In search of a better answer several proposals are circulating among Catholics and other Christian communities. One such is to ban infant baptisms altogether—at least until a reasonable amount of spiritual pruning is completed. These proponents declare that we should wait until the children can speak for themselves. Let us wait until they can make their own commitments, if they ever choose to do so. It's a thought, but basically we cannot agree with this. It is the "believer's baptism" all over again and, as we have indicated in the last chapter, it leaves no room for God's gracious grace and the natural instincts of good parents. Others would then counter and say that we *should* baptize infants but *only* those infants of practicing Catholics. We could certainly presume that such good Catholic parents will indeed pass on the faith. They would most likely be familiar with the newly revised rite of baptism which places such heavy emphasis on the duties of parents and the desirability of having the child baptized before the believing community at Mass. In this context we would have not so much a case of infant baptism as the baptism of an infant born into the Christian congregation.[8] What about the merely nominal or cultural Catholic? Do not baptize their children at all and let the conversion chips fall where they may when they grow up. This suggestion is not to be dismissed altogether out of hand, although it does carry with it the danger of using baptism as a weapon and a punishment against nonpracticing parents.

There are other more creative approaches. One is not to baptize any baby at all but rather enroll them all in the catechumenate (remembering again that the catechumenate is an honorable status). This means that shortly after birth infants would be enrolled in a public ceremony before the congregation as catechumens and their names so recorded. When they grow up, then give them the full rite of initiation once more in its original unity of baptism, confirmation, and eucharist. This is an excellent suggestion although it might put a strain on those truly practicing parents who instinctively would want baptism for their newly born child and so have a total and naturally Christian household. However, in the interest of putting some dent into the scandal of indiscriminate baptism even these parents might be urged to go along with the general catechumenate for all. Such a step, if ever taken, would obviously need a great deal of catechesis and the practical implementation of the long term steps of the catechumenate as found in the new adult rite of initiation.

There would be a second benefit to the catechumenate for infants first and initiation later. It would restore, as we have indicated, the wholeness of the initiation rite. It would effectively replace the multistaged rituals we now have. It would pull back into focus the conversion and commitment that are now scattered and emotionally displaced over the years. One writer describes the fuzziness in these words:

> When baptism is only a first stage which admits one to only a qualified participation in church life, it is a diminished sacrament. As long as something essential remains to be granted by some later stage of this progressive initiation, we seem to be saying that by baptism we are only partially related to God. If baptism requires something later as its "completion," we imply that it is incomplete. . . . Gifts of the Spirit, priesthood, anointing, sealing, spiritual combat, commitment to the world, and many others—*are all baptismal meanings.* If they are associated in any exclusive way with confirmation, baptism is deprived of them. If they are shared by the two rites, they duplicate one

another. The unity and decisiveness of baptism becomes qualified. As a sacramental rite confirmation makes sense only in close association with the baptismal action. It cannot gather independent meanings around itself; it has no independent meanings. As regards first communion, it should be noted that the church makes a person a member of Christ and the church by baptism, but immediately suspends him from the normal sacramental practice of Christian life. When the church later lifts the suspension and admits that person to the eucharist, it allows the occasion to take on a festal air of doubtful appropriateness.[9]

A final suggestion fits in between the others. It says that we should baptize the infants of practicing Catholics, and deny baptism to infants of nonpracticing parents. However the twist is this: restore the catechumenate, not for the infants, *but for the parents*. Enroll them, even though baptized but nonpracticing adults, into the postbaptismal catechumenate such as the early Fathers had. Give them an opportunity to reclaim their faith, a time of spiritual development and probation. After all, the new ritual does say, "You are the first teachers." If this is so—and this is endlessly repeated in encyclicals and catechetical documents—then it is fitting that such parents are in fact given a chance to recapture the integrity of their faith and form that believing community which shall nourish their baby spiritually. Upon their decision and proven practice in the community's life of faith, then their child will be baptized.

3

Realistically, it will be a long time before any of these suggestions are publicly and openly tried. And this is so even though the new rite of baptism for infants speaks of "pastoral considerations" to delay baptism while sufficient preparation for the parents and planning the celebration are needed. One paragraph says quite explicitly, "When the parents are not yet prepared to profess the faith or to undertake the duty of bringing up their children as Christians, it is for the parish priest, keeping in mind whatever regulations may have been laid down by the Conference of Bishops, to determine the time for the baptism of infants."[10] Not many will take this to heart, at least without exceedingly strong leadership from the bishops. There are probably three reasons for this. One is the traditional inability to refuse baptisms at all, to "take it out on the child," as the emotional phrase goes. We have developed no criteria for the measurement of faith since "the kingdom of God is within you." Still, the church is hardly a total spiritual reality; it is a Mystical Body but a body for all that. It is an external, structured, visible assembly of people with concrete laws, ritual, creeds, and leaders. Initiation is quite external. Therefore, it is not out of order to demand external criteria without prejudicing the interior qualities of parents which in fact may be of the highest degree of sanctity. All outward, external organizations such as the church are humbly confined to outside measurements. It is not unnatural for the church to seek external criteria along with the fervent hope (it can be no more than that) that the interior dispositions come close to the exterior initiation act. But we have been intimidated by inevitable uncertainties. We are too sensitive to people's interior lives, too democratic to question their spiritual sentiments and too unsure to know even what questions to ask:

The first is evident in the present inability of the church to say no to any who present themselves for sacramental incorporation into the church. It is not surprising that it cannot say no. It does not even know what questions it should put to those who so present themselves. It does not dare to ask whether they can pray, whether they live as disciples and servants of other members of the local church, whether they know how to make their occupations and professions a ministry for justice in the world, or whether they can give a real account of the hope that is in them. The church does not even dare ask such questions of those who approach the Lord's table on a Sunday morning, because its worship operates in the fashion of the established church with an independent cult, not as expression of ecclesial life. And it does not dare ask such questions because it does not have the means to provide concrete answers.[11]

With such uncertainty, many feel it is better to go ahead and baptize in the hope that someday, like a delayed innoculation, "it might take."

The second reason why many would hesitate to defer baptisms is the long-held fear of original sin and what would happen to any baby so unfortunate to die in it. Who would want the burden on his conscience of preventing a baby from getting to heaven? Yet, we must remember that long before St. Augustine, who is the architect of the theory of original sin we hold, babies were being baptized but with no urgency of panic to get them out of original sin. It was, as we indicated, the natural desire for unity in the family, the natural tendency to share the good news with one's offspring. But, as so often happens, Augustine knew of this fact first; namely, that babies were indeed being baptized, and so came up with the theory to support the practice. The theory was that therefore there must be some innate sin which would and could affect even a child. A child is apparently born in a state of estrangement from God, an estrangement or state of sin inherited from Adam and Eve. He needs to be freed of that. Else, Augustine taught, he would go to hell if not freed by baptism.[12] The church fortunately rejected Augustine's teaching that unbaptized babies go to hell as it did his teaching that some people were predestined to that place. Instead, the sensitivity of the collective church reacted sufficiently against any helpless unbaptized baby being in an eternal hell that it invented a place called limbo—the perfect compromise between the demands of God's salvific will (1 Timothy 2:4) and Augustine's powerful influence as a theologian.

People would have to learn a better understanding of original sin. They must see it as a collective term for the unmistakable fact that sin has indeed preceded every human being born into this world and has always done so as far as we can determine. The result is that we are all born into a spiritually deprived atmosphere, created by long traditions of sinning men, going back to the first—whether Adam or Eve or several human originators—forming our moral and religious attitudes in such a way that threatens our response to God's constant call. Original sin, then, is not so much a personal fault as it is the cumulative weight of evil that burdens every man because of his solidarity with a mankind prior to his own sins. His own sins merely ratify and prolong the tradition of sin which he has inherited.

It is in this sense that there is a "sin of the world" to be reckoned with—and one not confined to infants. We have put so much stress on them that we think that original sin is a baby problem and once the child is innoculated by baptism the problem is over. Rather, original sin is present for all. All are sinners and all human beings need saving (1 Corinthians 15:3). Therefore it is not a question of getting three-week-old babies out of original sin as soon as possible by some kind of sacramental corrective surgery called baptism. Rather baptism is designed for all, whether infant or adult, to bring them into the saving embrace of the Father, to incorporate them into the Spirit-filled community of his Son. Baptism takes the infant and the adult from the solidarity of sin and places them in the solidarity of being in grace with Christ. But the struggle goes on. Baptized adults are not immune from it; they are still in this world and original sin is an atmosphere in which they too move, live, and breathe. But now, through their baptism of long ago, they are "in Christ," united with him, a part of his body, the church.

For those not so baptized and therefore not placed in solidarity in Christ, there are other ways. We have mentioned before that God is not confined to his sacraments and no one has a monopoly on grace. If, as scripture says, "God wills all men to be saved and come to know the truth" (1 Timothy 2:4), then there is no need to despair over the millions of Chinese or African or Moslem or Jewish or Hotentot babies who might never be baptized at all. Nor, therefore, is there need to despair (though we surely should regret, and prayerfully so) that little Suzie of non-practicing Catholic parents, practically guaranteed no immediate faith nourishment whatever, will be lost. But if she dies, where will she go? The answer is simply, no one knows, although the presumption based on God's Self Disclosure as a loving Father greatly favors the answer to be heaven. And limbo? As we indicated, this was prompted by the instinctive rebellion from Augustine's harsh doctrine that unbaptized babies go to hell. As a theory, limbo was first put forward by St. Anselm in the eleventh century and was elaborated in the thirteenth. Interestingly, although widely held, it has never been defined and definitively held by the church. In any case, there is still too much trouble even with this more benign answer. The trouble, basically, is that limbo compromises God's omnipotence and love. God can and does reach out to others in ways we do not know. Limbo does not have to be the only alternative for unbaptized babies and to insist it is, is to leave little room for God's inventive grace. Limbo, although a solution offered by human compassion, simply fails to give due respect to divine compassion. That's its sharpest criticism.

Besides, there *are* other reputable theories to deal with unbaptized children who die. One sound one says that such infants are saved by the faith of their parents; that is, the basic desire of the parents to will their children good, which obviously includes their faith—this is sufficient to save the child. Their deep wish for such a good, in other words, is a form of baptism of desire. A famous cardinal of the sixteenth century, Cardinal Cajetan, argued this. He compared unborn children to the catechumens in the early church who were often martyred before receiving baptism of water. So he says, "It would not be unreasonable to say that in case of necessity baptism in the desire of the parents would seem sufficient for the salvation of little ones, especially with some outward sign." The Council of Trent saw merit in Cajetan's views and modern scripture scholars (Jeremias, Cullman) support this view. They quote St. Paul who says, "The unbelieving husband is consecrated through his wife, and the unbelieving wife is consecrated through her husband. *Otherwise, your children would be unclean, but as it is they are holy"* (1 Corinthians 7:14). This means that a saving grace has in fact been communicated to the child by the faith of the believing parent. Should that child die, he shall be saved by that faith.[13]

The third and final reason why some hesitate to refuse or defer baptism is the fear of creating an elite church. This is probably the most difficult to come to terms with, and perhaps we will always live in a certain tension regarding elitism. The problem is having a church that is so external and institutionalized, so unquestioning, so undemanding, so broad that anyone and everyone can enter and remain. The result is mere formalism, nowhere more devastatingly portrayed than in the famous *Godfather* baptismal scene where the words and gestures of the baby's baptism were rapidly intercut with that same baby's familial "faith-community" simultaneously performing a series of sadistic murders. On the other hand, high demands and penalties for failure conjure up the old bible-toting fathers, so dear to movie directors, who in the name of the Lord are totally paranoid and beat their kids to an inch of their life for some minor moral infraction. This caricature of the elitist church can be paralleled in Prosper Merimee's classic short story *Matteo Falcone,* which tells of a father who fulfills the code of honor of his people by taking out his small son who has stolen a watch and shooting him while the boy's mother stays terrified at home. Or else, without resorting to such extreme caricatures, the image of an elitist church is seen as a small clique of judgmental people addicted to all the evils of that pharisaism that Jesus so castigated. And we all want to avoid the Salem witch trials. And, at the very least, there is the sensible realization that the church is not an assembly of saints awaiting with joy and confidence the Second Coming. It is a mixed bag of saints and sinners, of motley pilgrims.

Yet, there must be a middle ground. The church cannot be so loose that it cannot deny membership to those unready or unwilling nor can it be so strict that it has no room for compassion, no room to call itself a church of sinners as well as saints. Jesus, after all, had certain demands. He could not work miracles in Capernaum because of their lack of faith. He did not plead with those who walked away muttering after his discourse on the eucharist, but merely asked his disciples, "Will you also go away?" Moreover, as we shall see in another chapter, in document and theory all of the revised rites for the sacraments are highly insistent on sincerity and honesty and have a quite pervasive "conversionist" tone. Radical demands are made upon the candidates, yet we lack the open church policy of what to do and how to handle the clearly and doubtfully indifferent; and often the threat of elitism pulls us all back into line.

Since nothing is without risk and since so often things occur in cycles, it may be the time in history to lean more to the elitist side; and if we do have latent fears, we must in our era, go back and consider the alternative which we have been living with too long: millions of baptized pagans. At the very least we ought to work hard to give that old catechumenate some standing and legitimization once more, both pre- and postinitiation. Since it originally arose from the very practical pastoral need to confront a pagan world, perhaps its time has come again, for there are very few who will deny that our world of the twentieth century is richly entitled to that same adjective.

NOTES FOR CHAPTER 6

1. Quoted in "What Can Catholics Learn from the Infant Baptism Controversy?" by Michael Hurley, S. J., *Concilium* 24 (1967), p. 19.

2. Eugene L. Brand, *Worship* 50, no. 1 (January 1976), p. 34. See also the in-depth study by the noted Lutheran theologian Edmund Schlink, *The Doctrine of Baptism* (Concordia, 1969). See also Bernard Häring's remarks in *The Sacraments and Your Everyday Life* (Liguori Publications, 1976), pp. 81 ff.

3. See the survey made by the National Opinion Research Center in Chicago, reported in the *New York Times,* December 29, 1974.

4. Survey by Daniel Yanovich, *New York Times,* May 22, 1974, p. 37.

5. Irving Kristol, in *Commentary* LIV, 5 (1972), p. 42.

6. Peter Berger, in the *New York Times,* February 25, 1968.

7. Francis Canavan, "Problem of Belief in America," *Communio* (Winter 1975).

8. Eugene Brand's suggestion. See Brand, *Baptism, A Pastoral Perspective* (Augsburg Publishing House, 1975), p. 40.

9. Daniel B. Stevick, "Christian Initiation: Post-Reformation to the Present Era," in *Made Not Born* (University of Notre Dame Press, 1976), p. 115.

10. The Rite of Infant Baptism, no. 8, sec. 4.

11. Ralph A. Keifer, "Christian Initiation: The State of the Question," in *Made Not Born* (University of Notre Dame Press, 1976), p. 147. Bernard Häring in the work cited above gives his opinion of the whole question: "Except in cases of imminent danger of death, there should be firm refusal to baptize infants who are not in any way really inserted into the community of faith. Official church legislation forbids one to be baptized if there is no hope of a postbaptismal catechumenate" (*The Sacraments and Your Everyday Life,* p. 84).

12. Augustine said that infants are born in sin and cannot enter heaven in such sin. But baptism "obliterates original sin in infants," said Augustine (*Pecc. orig.* 19:21) and so is obligatory. When the Council of Carthage did in fact condemn Pelagius in 418 it more or less made Augustine's views official. However, in justice to Augustine, he also wrote: "When the question of the punishment of children is raised, it troubles me sorely, I assure you, and I am at a loss what to answer."

13. This insight comes from Father Joseph T. Nolan in "I Just Want to Get My Kid Baptized," *U.S. Catholic* (May 1976), pp. 10 and 11.

7

Confirmation:
In Search of a Theology

1

Among the scholars, confirmation is often called the sacrament in search of a theology. There is much truth in this for perhaps no other sacrament has so many controversies on so many levels. After twenty centuries, one of our more respectable theological encyclopedias can still say, "... It is undeniable that the theology of confirmation presents very different characteristics between one epoch and the other.... The early Scholastics seem to be at a loss when they find themselves confronted with confirmation as a separate sacrament.... We may conclude that the magisterium leaves plenty of latitude to the theologians as regards the theoretical interpretation of the essence of the sacrament."[1] Some of these "theoretical interpretations" we shall attempt in the next chapter, but for now we want to trace the origin of the confusion from two sources: tradition and scripture. Then we will examine some popular expressions about confirmation which, while they do capture something of the truth, fall far short as whole and satisfying explanations.

First, tradition. Recall that when we were examining baptism we saw that at first there seems to be a very simple routine: preaching or proclamation, conversion, and water-baptism. Everything seems to be summed up and completed there: the remission of sins and the imparting of the Spirit. The New Testament and indeed the first documents immediately after apostolic times are silent about anything more than water. St. Paul, for instance, knows nothing of a separate rite to convey the Spirit. He says quite openly, "You were washed, you were sanctified, you were justified in the name of the Lord Jesus Christ and in the Spirit of our God" (1 Corinthians 6:11). Again, "It is God who establishes us. . . . He has put his seal upon us and given us his Spirit in our hearts as a guarantee" (1 Corinthians 1:21), a passage which refers to baptism only according to the scholars.

There is nothing in the first Fathers of the church up to the time of Irenaeus to show that Christian initiation meant anything more than water-baptism. A man named Hermas (whom we shall meet again in connection with the "second baptism," penace) speaks only of the "seal of water" in the middle of the second century. He doesn't mention anything about a postbaptismal imposition of hands or an anointing. Yet, in a short time, when we come to the writings of people like Tertullian (around the year 200) and Hippolytus (who wrote his work around 215) we find evidence that the simple water-baptism has acquired striking additions. Of particular interest is the anointing with oil of those baptized by the priests, and later the bishop's anointing, laying his hand on or over the candidate and praying for the blessing of the Holy Spirit. There is also a specific renunciation of Satan and a later addition of the long-term catechumenate.

But the practical question that causes so much trouble is this: does this complex rite as presented in these writings represent the way it originally was, or are the elements mentioned additions? If these elements, particularly the postbaptismal anointing by the bishop, are only an addition, then it is clear that they represent merely a beautiful but accidental elaboration of the basic water-baptismal rite. But if the anointing with oil by the bishop and the imposition of his hands (which we have come to call confirmation) were indeed there from the very beginning, then they may well represent an essential part of Christian initiation and are necessary to confer the Holy Spirit. In other words, if we hold to the first approach, there really is no such thing as a sacrament of confirmation and what we call confirmation is essentially a baptismal ceremony and explication. But if we hold to the second approach, then confirmation is needed to confer the Holy Spirit and is an independent sacrament. There are scholars on both sides and even the ancient Fathers appeared to be as divided as modern theologians. Therefore, some would hold (for example, Gregory Dix) that the water-baptism is really a preliminary rite and that the anointing and imposition of the bishop's hands—confirmation—is the decisive sacrament of initiation, so much so that a merely baptized but unconfirmed person is not a Christian. Others (for example, G.W.H. Lampe) would hold that water-baptism says it all, does it all, and the postbaptismal anointing and/or hand-laying (confirmation) is merely an elaboration, a baptismal spin-off. There's the problem and if left alone, it might have remained only an academic squabble among scholars. But history was about to intervene and the way history turned out brought the squabble into public domain, and various approaches, theories, solutions have been active ever since.

Practical problems were determining. For one thing, Christianity was spreading and many converts were entering the church, especially after the fourth-century peace of Constantine. The bishops, of course, presided over Christian initiation, but now there were difficulties. They could not handle all the converts personally. Then, too, Christianity was moving to the rural areas and the bishops tended to stay in the large cities. Now, there were not only numbers but distance. Something had to be done to handle the pressure of all those candidates for baptism. Then there were always emergencies. What about a sick adult or child in the rural areas or one who lay dying? How could they get to the bishop for initiation? Add to these one more eventual factor: St. Augustine's teaching on original sin and the consequent necessity (as people understood it at the time) of having infants baptized as soon as possible. No decent parent was going to delay baptism, especially one who lived in the countryside and didn't get to the city very often. So the pressure was mounting and, curiously, the church in the East and West reacted differently.

The East decided to do what it had done in regard to the celebration of the eucharist. Since the bishop could not be there personally to preside over every eucharist he delegated the presbyters to do this. They became the priests. So, too, in the initiation rite. The Eastern bishops decided to keep it intact and delegated the priests to carry out the whole ceremony. However, they did keep their hands in the affair symbolically: the oil used at the initiation rite had to be blessed by the bishop. So the East chose to maintain the unity of the initiation rite at the expense of the bishop's presidency. But the West did the reverse. It decided to keep the bishop's presidency intact and at the expense of ritual unity. And this is what caused the problems.

We are not certain why the West made this decision, but some good guesses are in order. We know that the Roman Empire in the West collapsed in the fifth and sixth centuries, leaving the barbarians to overrun and devastate all of Europe. The Roman emperor had already moved the capital of the empire to the East at Constantinople where he and the East were untouched by the havoc. But in the West it was different. The civil administrators fled before the onslaught, creating chaos and a political vacuum which the Western bishops, already natural leaders of the people, holding some measure of civil authority given them by Constantine, filled. They and their clerics and the monks almost single-handedly pulled Europe and civilization back from the brink of extinction. Under their guidance, especially under the genius of the bishop of Rome, the pope, the barbarian was eventually christianized and some semblance of order restored. The point is that in the West the bishops, under the circumstances, became even more a kind of center of civil, social, and religious gravity. It was needful and desirable to keep their image and position intact. Therefore, when the dilemma arose over working out the initiation rites for large numbers of people, it was natural that somehow the bishops' presidency would be determining. The question was, how would it work out? What would they do? Their answer was to break up the initiation rite. Some parts would be done by the priests, others by the bishops. Nor was there any difficulty in figuring out who would do what. Already, under the pressure of Augustine's teaching, the priests were doing the water-baptisms, especially in emergencies (which were frequent enough in those days of war and infant mortality). Therefore the postbaptismal anointing with oil and the imposition of hands with its accompanying prayer to the Holy Spirit would be reserved to the bishops.

From this point on the West presents a notoriously uneven development in what would emerge as the sacrament of confirmation. Local rites would be somewhat similar in structure but filled with all kinds of differing details and a wide variety of ceremony, all of which would ebb and flow, change, relocate, and reappear until a consensus coalesced. What happened was that a time lapse occured between the water-baptism and the episcopal anointing. For example, the custom grew of having the imposition of the bishop's hands a week later on the Octave of Easter. But this intervention of one week gradually spread itself into many months and even years leaving a "floating" anointing or hand-laying with nothing to attach itself to. Clearly an anchor was needed to stabilize this rite. With this need were born the theories to underpin, explain, and locate what in fact was already occurring: an episcopal anointing or hand-laying separated in years from its original initiation unity with baptism.

We can trace somewhat the development of the different theories. The justification was emerging in the suggestion, then opinion, and later "teaching" that the episcopal anointing and hand-laying after baptism conferred the Holy Spirit. People like St. Cyprian (d. 258) and St. Irenaeus (d. 200) began to talk like this. Such cautious talk escalates to a "need" for water-baptism to come to completion through the bishops' activity. There are more references to the Spirit descending after baptism (St. Hilary) and the two operations of the Spirit (St. Ambrose). The trend is to see the Spirit as giving other graces besides that of baptismal rebirth. As usual St. Augustine's influence is important. He holds that the Spirit does indeed give rebirth at baptism but that the Spirit is also needed to strengthen, fortify, and bring love to completion. As far as Augustine was concerned, there was a difference between receiving a sacrament and having it activated and made fruitful. It was therefore the Spirit who made baptism fruitful. He even referred to the holy chrism as "the oil that supplies the fire, the sacrament of the Holy Spirit."[2] In fact Augustine was misread enough to supply a vocabulary for a separation of rites. The foundation for the entrenchment for the sacrament of confirmation was being laid and the bishop's role was likewise getting entrenched even in the official Western church documents. Here is a rule from the Council of Elvira held in 305: "It was agreed that when a deacon who has charge of faithful people baptizes some of them in the absence of a bishop or presbyter, it shall be the duty of the bishop to confirm them; but if any depart this life before confirmation, he will be justified by virtue of the faith in which he has believed."[3] Be it noted here the beginning of a long and firm tradition which has never held that confirmation, like baptism, was necessary for salvation. Let us add an excerpt from a famous letter of Pope Innocent I written in 416 to the bishop of Gubbio:

> Concerning the consignation of infants, it is clear that this should not be done by any but the bishop. . . . The right of bishops alone to seal and to deliver the Spirit of the Paraclete is proved not only by custom of the church but also by that reading in Acts of the Apostles. . . . It is permissible for presbyters, either in the absence of a bishop, or when they baptize in his presence, to anoint the baptized with chrism but only with such as has been consecrated by the bishop: and even then they are not to sign the brow with that oil, for this is reserved to bishops alone when they deliver the Spirit the Paraclete.[4]

We have now an explicit statement that confirmation deals with giving of the Holy Spirit and it is the bishop's prerogative to bring this about. Actually, this position will need much retelling in future ages because, in practice, the average Christian citizen was not impressed. As we indicated, the people were often far from the bishop's cathedral and there were many disruptions such as banditry and war to discourage them making the trip. Therefore many people never did get to town to see the bishop for the postbaptismal anointing (confirmation) or else their babies were adolescents by the time they did so. Then, too, they were confused by the theology and could not see just what the bishop "added" to baptism. Their priests had baptized their infants who had therefore already received the Holy Spirit (they were baptized in the name of the Father and the Son *and* the Holy Spirit). No one had ever said that the bishop's anointing or hand-laying was necessary for salvation while no one ever denied that baptism was. So why bother? The result was that many children remained unconfirmed for the rest of their lives, unless by accident they happened to stumble on a traveling bishop who then and there dismounted and confirmed them. This confirmation, divorced now as it was from baptism, had lost its impact and was devalued in the eyes of the people. Many sermons, some of them famous and influential, would be preached to rouse an indifferent public to receive confirmation. More theologizing would be done to give it status. We shall see some of the themes invoked later.

We should again note that all of this development was taking place quite unevenly throughout the West for centuries. This alone is a good indication that what was going on was an effort to meet changing times rather than a clear-cut theory or doctrine at work. There was no uniformity of practice until very near modern times. France, for example, had no custom of the imposition of hands but did have an anointing; but this was conferred by the priest, not the bishop. Ireland, England, and Spain followed the same custom. However, matters became somewhat more standardized when in the eighth and ninth centuries the Emperor Charlemagne launched his reforms. He wanted to unify his far-flung Frankish empire and, in a Christian era, this desire necessarily included the drive to standardize church policy and liturgical reform as well. So Charlemagne went to Rome, returned with its liturgical books, and sent out word that in his kingdom things were to be done thus and so. Among the "thus and so" was the insistence that baptisms be celebrated only at Easter and Pentecost (as in ancient times) and that confirmation be celebrated by the bishops only.

He had little luck in holding baptisms to those traditional seasonal times, but he was more successful in establishing more widely the bishop's sole prerogative in confirming. In this he received considerable help from a famous forged document of the time known as *False Decretals*. This was a document, supposedly written in the fourth century (actually in the ninth) to a certain Pope Melchides (nonexistent) whereby Constantine granted him and his successors full spiritual and political power in the empire. The document was designed to enhance the power of the pope and the bishops. In this vein it would be expected that the document specifically mentions the right of bishops to confirm. The result of all this, plus all of the centuries' sermons, theorizing, and practice came in the twelfth century when we begin to find a rite of confirmation written out separately from that of baptism. The split, already long existent in some parts of the empire, was now official. Confirmation had arrived as something unrelated to baptism and justified on its own terms.

We haven't mentioned too much about the East's tradition except to say that it kept the initiation rite intact. Here, however, we might add that it too had acquired early a prebaptismal anointing in some parts. At Antioch, for example, a great missionary center of the church, there is record of a baptismal rite which shows an anointing on the head of the candidate before the water-baptism and the laying on of the bishop's hands and a sharing in the eucharist. The prebaptismal anointing gets several interpretations, such as a seal or brand; and it is interesting that the recently revised rite of confirmation used the term seal: "Receive the seal, the Holy Spirit," says the bishop now. It was really only later that the East, influenced by the West, developed a postbaptismal anointing (there were exceptions such as the Syrian church) which was said to confer the Holy Spirit. " . . . The earliest attestations of a post baptismal anointing are to be found in the *Apostolic Constitutions* (c.a.d. 375) and the *Catechesis* of Cyril of Jerusalem, and these most probably represent an importation from the churches of the West. By degrees this anointing after baptism was adopted throughout the churches of the East where it is now accepted as a sacrament. . . ."[5] This is why we acknowledge that Catholics in the Eastern tradition are baptized and confirmed in the same ceremony.

And Eastern versus Western mentalities had a lot to do with the different approaches too. The Easterners tended to think more in overall patterns. They simply saw Christian initiation as one circular rite which had many facets, including the postbaptismal anointing. One item did not follow consecutively after another in their minds. The whole rite was one circular rhythm with no determined beginning, middle, or end; it was a whole motion. But the Western mind was different. Under Roman legal influence, it thought in "straight line" patterns, with one step logically following upon another. Therefore it was quite easy for the Westerners to see what the Easterners could not: the postbaptismal anointing as a separate movement which could easily be detached from the whole rite. It of course "belonged" to initiation, but, not being seen as circular and involved, it could also find another time and place with perfect (Western) logic. The East, however, could not psychologically dismantle what they saw as a whole. That is why, as we have just seen, even when they, under Western influence, did get around to calling that post baptismal anointing "confirmation" and accepted it as such, they still could not bring themselves to separate it from the overall rite. Their temperaments forced them to keep it "attached" to baptism anyway.

But, getting back to the West: in the later Middle Ages the scholars simply took over quite uncritically the arrangement of a split ceremony bequeathed to them by their predecessors. They had no historical documents accessible to tell them differently. In the twelfth century, Peter Lombard wrote a standard theology textbook which narrowed the term sacrament, listed seven of them, and included the new distinct confirmation in the list. He categorized it as the giving of the Holy Spirit. The Fourth

Lateran Council of 1215 further defined the seven sacraments. By the early twelfth century, Hugh of St. Victor is speaking of confirmation as a sacrament and in 1439 it was declared so by the Council of Florence. The great St. Thomas Aquinas added his thoughts. Unfortunately, he was probably familiar only with the twelfth century Roman pontifical and based most of his theology of confirmation on Melchides, that fictional pope of the *False Decretals*. So he called confirmation the sacrament of "spiritual growth . . . perfection of spiritual strength." The matter and form for confirmation were determined to be the words of the bishop and the anointing with holy oil combined with the laying on of hands. The edge, however, was given to the anointing with oil as the real "essence" of the sacrament even though, as we shall see, the initial action and the one attested to in scripture is the laying on of his hands.

We have here an instance where the church did change the material of the sacrament. In the eighteenth century Pope Benedict XIV restored the laying on of hands and the church's Canon Law of 1917 incorporated it into its text. Still, the hand-laying was not considered essential to the sacrament for the Holy See said that if by chance the hand-laying were omitted, the sacrament of confirmation was still valid if the anointing had been given. And, of course, the bishop as the sole administrator of confirmation, outside of emergencies, was now firmly entrenched. The newly revised rite of confirmation of 1973, acknowledging all of this untidy history, more cautiously calls the bishop the "original" minister of the sacrament, not the only or ordinary minister.

2

We have seen how the tradition concerning the sacrament of confirmation developed. In that tradition there was the need to justify it by scripture as well. Unfortunately, scripture is ambiguous at best and, as a result, inconclusive. For example, in the favorite New Testament source, the Acts of the Apostles (from which it has been said one can prove anything), there are several references to the Holy Spirit and the laying on of hands. Yet, the fact is, that out of the nine apostolic hand-laying references, only two refer to the gift of the Spirit. Furthermore, in the Acts there is no discernable pattern, and there is no mention of the anointing with oil which would become the necessary material in a later age.

There are two favorite texts which supposedly support the institution of confirmation. In one text we have an account of Sts. Peter and John laying their hands upon the Samaritans who had been baptized by the deacon Philip. "The pair upon arriving imposed hands on them and they received the Holy Spirit" (Acts 8:17). Modern scholars tend to see this incident as highly unusual and one designed to remove some imperfect dispositions that hindered the baptism of the Samaritans. The Spirit was already given in their baptisms, but their improper dispositions hindered his effect in their lives. "Whatever the interpretations of this passage, we must at least agree ... that the Samaritan situation is not considered normal by Luke, and it certainly does not provide a justification for promoting or even expecting a baptism which does not confer the Spirit."[6] A few chapters later, there is another incident claimed as a foundation for confirmation. Here St. Paul meets certain disciples at Ephesus after they had been baptized. He asks them, "Did you receive the Holy Spirit when you became believers?" They answered, "We have not so much as heard that there is a Holy Spirit." Paul found out that they had been baptized in the style of John the Baptizer, so he himself baptized them "in the name of the Lord Jesus. As Paul laid his hands on them, the Holy Spirit came down on them ..." (Acts 19:6). But there is nothing to prove that this is a confirmation ceremony. Instead scholars see this incident as the handing on of some kind of charismatic office to be exercised in the church.[7] It seems that G.H. Lampe's remark is more on target that "the laying on of hands in Acts is a confirmation of baptism rather than a confirmation of the baptized."[8]

Outside of the Acts we do have other references. In Paul's epistles to Timothy we encounter hand-layings, but these are obviously associated with conferring a ministry or a mission (1 Timothy 4:14; 5:22 and 2 Timothy 1:16). In the epistle to the Hebrews there is a verse which reads, "Let us ... advance in maturity ... : repentance from dead works, faith in God, instruction about baptism and laying-on of hands ..." (Hebrews 6: 1–4). This need not imply a hand-laying confirmation for hand-laying was also used for other reasons, such as the forgiveness of sins. Karl Rahner, in reviewing the evidence, says this: "Hence a mere charismatic interpretation of the apostolic imposition of hands might be suggested as the right explanation of many passages."[9]

There are other uncertainties. There is no pattern to the conferral or receiving of the Holy Spirit and therefore this would indicate no special sacrament of confirmation. The Holy Spirit is given to the Gentile household of Cornelius *before* the water-baptism (Acts 10:44). St. Paul himself also receives the Holy Spirit before his baptism by Ananias (Acts 9:17). Incidentally, it is worth noting that Ananias, although not an apostle, lays hands on Paul. This would seem to refute those who hold that the hand-laying is strictly an apostolic (episcopal) affair. On the other hand, we have instances of the reverse order. St. Luke describes Jesus' own baptism in water first and then the Spirit comes upon him (3:21). There is no pattern. We have the conferral of the Spirit first and baptism later and, in other places, baptism first and then the conferral of the Holy Spirit. We have two mentions of hand-laying with baptism and eight mentions of baptism without the hand-laying. It seems, therefore, that we can detect no indisputable proof about confirmation being attested to in scripture.

3

If later scholarship cannot find definitive foundations for confirmation in tradition or scripture, this did not prevent those in another age, for whom records and documents were scarce, to justify it. Once the initiation rite did in fact break apart and the anointing spun off as a preserve of the bishop, then there were many attempts to underpin this sacrament of confirmation. In time some of this theologizing about confirmation was done without its original reference to baptism and we have, until lately, inherited such theories. Let us look at three of them and see that, although all the theories contain some element of truth, they suffer severe limitations by being organically disconnected from baptism.

1. *Confirmation confers the Holy Spirit.* We recall that as far back as the fourth century in Rome there is that prayer at the end of the initiation rite reflecting the conferral of the Holy Spirit. This prayer and the anointing that preceded it has been used, as we saw, as an indication that here was a true separate rite and one, moreover, which conferred the Holy Spirit. It was genuinely different from the water-baptism. But, again, we saw the reality. This prayer refers to what went on in the entire rite. The already present Spirit (active in the water and the font) is being invoked in reference to the entire rite of initiation. There was no room in those early documents (or early mentalities for that matter) for any kind of breakdown into an item by item process. The whole thing was an initiation rite into Christianity. There is no warrant to mean that the anointing and prayer to the Holy Spirit somehow sets it off from baptism. After all, the Spirit *must* be given in baptism. Who else could be the cause of regeneration and the forgiveness of sin which are its prime achievements? As one writer expressed it almost eighty-five years ago, "It is hard to see how the recipient of baptism as such could be a child of God, yet destitute of that 'assurance of son-ship' which comes from the Spirit of adoption; could be 'in' the church and yet not 'in the Holy Spirit'; could be incorporated into the body mystical, yet not really be 'inhabited' by the 'Giver of life' who is the very informing and vitalizing principle of that body."[10] As Lampe says, "There is no intermediary state between the state of sin and the state of being in Christ and his Spirit ... The Spirit is not merely complementary to the Christ.

He is the bearer of Christ to the church ... in whatever sense, degree or measure the Spirit does not dwell in us, in the same degree or measure the Christ also does not dwell in us, nor we in him."[11]

Some have resorted to the writings of the fourth century bishop, Cyril, whom we met in our chapter on initiation, for they profess to find in him a clear delineation of the sacrament of confirmation. A scholarly assessment might therefore be in order:

> Because of Cyril's almost ingenuous use of traditional materials associated with the communication of the Holy Spirit, one is tempted to say this anointing is "confirmation." But this would be an unjustifiable application of later thought categories to more undifferentiated beliefs of earlier times, and can only result finally in an indiscriminate polemic or theological deadend. That Cyril uses the ceremony of the anointing as an apt vehicle for a mystagogical interpretation of the fact that the Holy Spirit is communicated in Christian initiation is clear, and his motive is clear: greater emphasis on the role of the Holy Spirit, and its meaning in Christian initiation. . . . However, one cannot say this anointing which Cyril the mystagogue treats so effectively is the "sacramental sign" of "confirmation." The careful analysis of the texts of Cyril . . . lead more and more to the conclusion that Cyril was not writing with such later theological thought patterns in mind, and that he was not really treating the question in a way in which later theology puts it. Therefore, one must not come to Cyril's mystagogy to find an answer to the question of where was the *locus*, the "sacramental sign" of "confirmation." The communication of the Holy Spirit takes place in Christian initiation. . . . When Cyril says that the neophyte received the Holy Spirit in the anointing after baptism, he is thinking "inclusively" and not "exclusively," for in the Eastern Fathers, the communication of the Holy Spirit is seen in the totality of Christian initiation.[12]

What all this is saying is that *baptism* does and must confer the Holy Spirit. To state boldly that confirmation does implies that baptism does not and therefore we have to wait till we're older to receive him.[13] It's like becoming a member of the church at baptism, but not quite. No, it is in baptism that we receive the Holy Spirit and many of the prayers of the baptismal ritual remind us of this fact. ("We pray for these children; set them free from original sin, make them temples of your glory, and send your Holy Spirit to dwell with them.") If this anointing we call confirmation is kept intact with the initiation rite of baptism, then there is no problem; but if the rite called confirmation is separated (as it is) by many years from baptism and is declared to confer the Holy Spirit, then the impression is unmistakable: the Spirit is given ten or twelve years after a supposedly Spirit-less regeneration of baptism. This is the kind of implication which the medieval Christians rejected and which led them to ignore confirmation. If therefore we are going to continue to speak of confirmation as conferring the Holy Spirit, we are going to have to qualify what we mean and present the statement under a different aspect.

2. *Confirmation makes one a soldier of Christ: it is the sacrament of strengthening.* This is the theme most Catholics have inherited. There are resonances of this theme way back when in some places the anointing of the baptismal candidate was thought of in terms of sealing one for Christ and thereby making him strong to resist the wily devil. This theme was brought into public domain when a certain Abbot Faustus in the year 460 preached a sermon on confirmation. It was he who said outright that confirmation prepared one for life's battles, for soldiering for Christ. True, he said, the Spirit is conferred at baptism, but now there exists a separate rite to assist the faithful in their daily Christian struggle. We should remember that his sermon was intended to motivate people who were already at this early time neglecting the separated rite of anointing by the bishop. In the ninth century another phrase caught hold. A man named Rabanus Maurus (d. 856), copying from Charlemagne's mentor, Alcuin, came up with the words, "witnessing to the faith." This said that confirmation was the sacrament that readied one for

the active apostolate. This whole soldiering-witnessing motif is seen in the curious evolution of the kiss of peace the bishop used to give the candidates after their baptismal initiation. This kiss descended into a caress which, under the new emphasis, deteriorated into a slap on the cheek to remind one how much he must suffer and endure for the cause of Christ. (The new rite of confirmation has restored the slap to its original sign of peace.) As a whole picture, this strengthening aspect of confirmation is not so firm. It is hard to see why the other sacraments could not and should not inherently strengthen a person. How, for example, in this regard is confirmation different from the eucharist, the preeminent sacrament of spiritual vigor and strength?

3. *Confirmation is the sacrament of maturity and commitment.* Yes and no. Some people have tried to make confirmation a kind of Christian bar-mitzvah, a coming of age, of physical maturity. This is probably due to the mixed-up history of the sacrament. Originally, as we have seen, the initiation rite was all of one piece even when conferred on infants. When the separation came, the ages varied widely, but the net result was that baptism was thought to be appropriate for infants and confirmation for the later years. Various church councils over the centuries decreed the ages of one or two years old for confirmation; then, later, the "age of discretion" which ranged anywhere from seven to sixteen. The Council of Trent laid down the rule that children were not to receive confirmation before seven and no later than twelve. We notice the shift that what was formerly given to infants is now forbidden to them. Another development came in to urge a later age: the introduction of religious instruction as a prerequisite to seeking confirmation. Strictly speaking, to demand instruction before confirmation is as illogical as demanding instruction before baptism; yet there was a lot of pastoral good sense to this demand. In any case, there is no theological or historical basis for making confirmation a Christian coming of age. It is not a sacrament of maturity in that sense. It is not designed to help beginning adolescents cope. "Confirmation is not ordered by its purpose as a sacrament to the personal and

spiritual struggle of adolescence: the sacraments for this are the eucharist and penance."[14]

Furthermore, we cannot make confirmation carry the sole burden of Christian commitment. Baptism is the place for commitment (or the whole initiation rite) and, as we have already indicated, we must be exceedingly anxious to restore baptism to its primary status as *the* place for conversion and commitment. To so insist on confirmation as the "real" sacrament of commitment is to reduce baptism. It is to make one think that he is *merely* baptized while he awaits the fuller commitment of confirmation at adolescence. No, full commitment *is* baptism and the church should make it totally clear that the burden falls on this sacrament. The church, in its pastoral and liturgical practices, should not give the popular impression that confirmation has replaced baptism as the moment of commitment. On the contrary, it must always be insisted that "confirmation is a confirmation of the baptismal gift; Holy Communion continually renews and sustains it; but it needs no second act or stage."[15] If anything, confirmation is a ratification of baptism, not a replacement. That is why Vatican II said, "The rite of confirmation is to be revised and the intimate connection which this sacrament has with the whole Christian initiation is to be more lucidly set forth; for this reason, it will be fitting for candidates to renew their baptismal promises just before they are confirmed...."[16] We must note, therefore, the next time we share in a confirmation celebration and the candidates renew their baptismal vows, that this is not implying that now at last they are speaking for themselves independently of their previous life in the church. Rather it is to show the ancient unity of what they are doing now with what in fact occurred at their baptism. This is why some liturgists have suggested that we really ought to rejoin the whole initiation rite again—baptism, confirmation, and eucharist—and then invent some paraliturgical service that, at meaningful moments of people's lives, restates the commitment already made at baptism.

Sometimes people say that confirmation "completes" baptism. This is true if we mean that it is a further organic step in the initiation process. It is less than true if we mean that baptism left something unfinished, something dangling, which a later supplementary rite must supply. If this was literally true then we would not confirm an adult *immediately* after his baptism as the new rite commands us to do. Rather it seems obvious that the confirmation given to an adult candidate immediately is not "completing" his baptism, but rather is there as an *integral part of the rite*. As liturgist Aidan Kavanaugh puts it, "According to the ancient practice maintained in the Roman liturgy, an adult is not to be baptized unless he receives confirmation immediately afterward provided no serious obstacles exist. This connection signifies the unity of the paschal mystery, the close relationship between the mission of the Son and the pouring out of the Holy Spirit, and the joint celebration of the sacraments by which the Son and the Spirit come with the Father upon all those who are baptized."[17] The "completing" notion is ambiguous. Its use breaks the mental rhythm we should feel about the Christian initiation.

So these are three common misunderstandings or misemphases about confirmation. It would seem, therefore, that if we are ever to get at confirmation's meaning we must do what we have suggested so frequently in this chapter: we must establish the primacy of the sacrament of baptism and the integrity of the whole rite of Christian initiation. We must raise questions about baptism, promote a strong catechesis surrounding it and, as suggested before, perhaps restore the catechumenate to prepare for it; for baptizing indiscriminately is as harmful to confirmation as it is to baptism itself. As one writer expresses it: "The church has always recognized that the sacraments of baptism and confirmation can do little for a child if the environment in which it is brought up is not favorable to the growth of faith. For this reason the indiscriminate baptism of children of non-Christian parents has never been allowed. If the society in which we now live is inimical to the growth of infant faith, we must surely question the expediency of infant baptism rather than try to twist the sacrament of confirmation into a second sacrament of commitment."[18] Once we can strengthen and promote a good baptismal (initiation) catechesis and official church policies, then we can better position confirmation and try to give it a perspective and an approach that will avoid the pitfalls we have just seen and yet at the same time make it truly meaningful.

NOTES FOR CHAPTER 7

1. *Sacramentum Mundi* (Herder and Herder, 1968), pp. 407, 409.

2. P. Weller, trans., *Selected Easter Sermons of St. Augustine* (B. Herder, 1959), Sermon 227, PL 38, 1099.

3. *Documents of the Baptismal Liturgy,* comp. E. C. Whitaker (SPCK, 1970), p. 222.

4. Ibid., p. 229.

5. E. C. Whitaker, "Confirmation," in *A Dictionary of Liturgy and Worship,* ed. J. G. Davies (Macmillan, 1972), p. 146.

6. George Montague, "Baptism in the Spirit and Speaking in Tongues: A Biblical Appraisal, " *Theology Digest* 21, no. 4 (Winter 1973), p. 345.

7. *The Jerome Biblical Commentary* comments that apparently the hand-laying was part of the baptismal rite and the rest of the verse may imply that the imposition of hands had another function, namely, that of a charismatic office to be exercised in the church (*The Jerome Biblical Commentary* [Prentice Hall, 1968], p. 202).

8. G. W. H. Lampe, *The Seal of the Spirit,* 2nd ed. (London: Alcuin Club, SPCK, 1967), p. xxi.

9. Karl Rahner, *Confirmation Today* (Dimension Books, 1975), p. 14.

10. J.D.C.G. Fisher, "History and Theology," in *Confirmation Crisis* (Seabury Press, 1968), p. 28.

11. Lampe, *The Seal of the Spirit,* p. xxiv.

12. Hugh M. Riley, *Christian Initiation* (Consortium Press, 1974), pp. 398 and 399.

13. We say "him," although in the East the Holy Spirit is feminine.

14. Charles Davis, *The Sacraments of Initiation* (Sheed and Ward, 1948), p. 135.

15. Lampe, *The Seal of the Spirit,* p. xxix.

16. Constitution on the Sacred Liturgy, no. 71.

17. The Rite of Christian Initiation of Adults, no. 34.

18. Austin P. Milner, O.P., *The Theology of Confirmation* (Fides, 1971), p. 105.

8

The Spirit of Confirmation

1

We will let theologian Karl Rahner summarize the difficulties we explored in the last chapter:

> The difficulty is . . . it is not easy to distinguish between baptism and confirmation. Baptism is not merely a sacrament for the forgiveness of sins and for the acceptance of the individual into the church. It is also the sacrament of rebirth, of the grace-filled inner-justification of man, the sacrament of the communication of the Spirit, without which the forgiveness of guilt, rebirth, and sanctification cannot even be conceived. And even if one stresses that in confirmation the Spirit is communicated to the recipient for particular tasks and special challenges, for a spiritual strengthening of the person to help him confess his faith before the world, it must be admitted that the Spirit received in baptism also confers on the individual the disposition and strength for undertaking special tasks.[1]

It would seem that this eminent theologian (and our previous chapter) leave no further room for discussion, and confirmation still ends up as a disguised baptism. All the same, there are certain perspectives we will explore in this chapter which may help us to give some focus to this disputed sacrament.

Recall our association of wind, breath, Spirit. Remember how they were coalesced into an understanding of the work of God's Spirit. That Spirit was designed by God to be poured out on all

111

mankind, but, first, that revelation unfolded slowly. The preliminary work, as it were, the initial indication was to come
through the Jewish prophets who were to be living hints of what
God had in mind for all. So Moses and the elders, for example,
received some of the Spirit of God: "Moses ... gathered the
seventy elders of the people and brought them around the Tent.
Yahweh came down in the Cloud. He spoke with them, but took
some of the spirit that was on him and put it on the seventy
elders. When the spirit came upon them they prophesied, but
not again" (Numbers 11:24). The prophet Isaiah tells how God's
Spirit came and anointed him, "The spirit of the Lord Yahweh
has been given to me, for Yahweh has anointed me. . ." (Isaiah
61). And we have already taken note of the Joel prophecy
(quoted by Peter on Pentecost) about the Spirit being poured
forth at the "last times" (Joel 3). All of these are foreshadowings
that God's gracious Spirit, active now, shall someday become
apparent, complete, public, open to all.

There was a transition to that public completeness and the
New Testament is basically a chronicle of that transition. It tells
openly and specifically that the Spirit of Israel is passed over to
Jesus for the benefit of all mankind. John is the link of the
transition. He is the last of the Old Testament Spirit-filled
prophets. As such he deliberately recedes into the background,
departs into prison and death so that he can give way to Jesus in
whom the Spirit would reach his fullness and whom, in turn,
Jesus would leave to his church. Now the church would be the
new "repository" of the Spirit. It would be the new Israel, filled
with the Spirit of Jesus and doing "wonderful works" in his
name (Acts 2:11).

The New Testament chronicle wastes no time. Jesus is con-
ceived by the power of the Spirit. The Spirit leads him into the
desert to undergo all of ancient Israel's trials. Later, as we have
seen before, Jesus is filled with the Spirit at his baptism and
announces to the synagogue assembly that the ancient prophecy
of Isaiah concerning the Spirit being upon him is now fulfilled.
Still later Jesus promises that this same Spirit which is his full measure, shall be given to his followers. "On the last day of the

festival Jesus stood there and cried out, 'If any man is thirsty, let him come to me! Let the man come and drink who believes in me!' As scripture says: From his breast shall flow fountains of living water. He was speaking of the Spirit which those who believed in him were to receive. . ." (John 7:37). (Notice the water-Spirit symbolism.) Again, "If I fail to go, the Paraclete will never come to you, whereas if I go, I will send him to you" (John 16:7). So Jesus suffers, dies, and is raised up. Now, at Pentecost, that Spirit, long active in a cautious way among the Israelites, is poured forth in abundance upon the New People of God.

The Acts of the Apostles tell us just what that meant. The Spirit is active in mutual charity, prayer, worship, power, and miracles. The people of God, the church, are indeed living according to Jesus, living by a different tempo. They are guided by a different set of values as personified in Jesus. Theirs was to be forgiveness where most people might urge revenge; theirs was to be mercy where most would demand justice; theirs was to be a sharing where most would promote avarice; theirs was to be a community of open love where most would opt for isolation and alienation; theirs was to be the experience of the grain of wheat—the dying to self—where others thought that they saved life by hugging it to themselves. They were indeed a Spirit-filled people with new capacities, insights, and a wide-ranging love. And all because the breath of life, the "*ruah,*" the pristine Spirit had breathed on them.

But notice. This Spirit sent by Jesus, held to the old tradition: he was given in the water-sign. That is to say, the water-baptism brought the Spirit into the lives of people. Now it is important to realize what we are saying. The rite of baptism is not the reality itself. It is a *sacramental sign.* And of what is it the sign? The Spirit. As always, everything starts with and ends with the Spirit which Jesus came to unleash in this, the last times. It is the Spirit who is active, who summons, calls, motivates, and sanctifies. It is only by his power that anyone can cry, Abba, Father! Baptism is but the ancient, externalized, water-Spirit sign of what is going on. This is why the rites of baptism have so many references to the Spirit. For example, in the newly revised rite there are petitions that the newly baptized may become more perfectly like God's Son, more fully like Jesus and that they may be witnesses and proclaim the faith and the Good News—items we usually associate only with confirmation. Some of the baptismal prayers go like this:

> We pray for these children,
> set them free from original sin,
> make them temples of your glory
> and send your Holy Spirit to dwell with them.

Again:

> God the Father of our Lord Jesus Christ,
> has freed you from sin,
> given you a new birth by water and the Holy Spirit,
> and welcomed you into his holy people.
> He now anoints you with the chrism of salvation...

One of the general intercessions reads:

> Once they are born again of water and the Holy Spirit,
> may they always live in that Spirit,
> and make their new life known to their fellow men.

Over the font is said:

> In the waters of the Jordan
> your Son was baptized by John
> and anointed with the Spirit.

All of these quotations from the revised baptismal rite are meant to tell us that it is in the water-baptism that the Spirit is given. Baptism is the externalized acknowledgement of the Spirit's initiating and primary activity (grace). Through baptism the candidate is pulled into the whole history of creation and re-creation, into all that the Spirit has done since the beginning of time and brought to completion in Jesus: "The baptized person is drawn into a new story of creation, which has begun with Christ, who is the divine act of creation. This is the basic idea which can be traced through the descriptions of the gospels. But the principle which gives shape to this cosmic history is the

Spirit, who now takes possession of the believer himself. Thus there is a deep significance in the later administration of baptism in the name of the Father and the Son and the Spirit."[2] These words add one more emphasis to what we have been saying all along: it is in the water-baptism that the Spirit is given. "None of the New Testament texts, even in Acts, supports the thesis of a genuine Christian initiation deprived of the Spirit. There is, then, only one baptism, not to be separated even chronologically from the water-rite as an integral part of Christian initiation. Man is born again of *water and the Spirit*."[3]

2

It seems that we have arrived right back at the old dilemma: what to do with confirmation? What role does it play? If we hold that originally there was only the simple water-baptism and *it* conveyed the Spirit, then where did confirmation come from to begin with? We saw the answer to this in the last chapter: it was the choice of the West to honor the primacy of the bishop at the expense of the initiation rite by reserving the initiation anointing to him. But as the bishops became more remote and took with them this prerogative, then the anointing got delayed and separated from the water-baptism. This we saw. Here, however, we might suggest three subconscious reasons for the rise of a separate rite called confirmation. The three are only speculations but they might be worth considering as an aid in positioning this sacrament in our own day.

The first speculation is this. Man is a ritual being. He is prompted by his own psychology to spell out in symbol his beliefs and the truths he lives by. The water-baptism, as we have seen, is one of those ancient symbols which spoke to the people of the water-wind-Spirit of God being poured forth. But, as time went on, human nature dictated that this water symbolism be expanded. The ritual was extended to show "more" of its meaning. So, as we have seen, candles, white robes, exorcisms, and so

forth were eventually added to the initiation rite. Mostly, however, a very early addition was the anointing with oil. It was a
particularly good symbol that said much to the Jews and Christians. There was a whole history of being "chosen" by being
anointed with oil. Priests, prophets, and kings were so proclaimed. Jesus himself, as *the* priest, prophet, and king was
anointed by God and indeed, his "last name," Christ, is but a
Greek translation of "Anointed One." Therefore, in baptism, in
the initiation rite, it would be an easy and short step to mate-
rialize the anointing by the Spirit by actually using physical oil
and adding a prayer to the Spirit. The anointing would be a
metaphor materialized. It would say in a physical way what was
happening in a spiritual way at baptism: "I have been anointed
by the Spirit of God in this initiation rite." If the water-baptism
collected one into a community, the external anointing showed
that this was a Spirit-filled community.

All of this stayed stable for a long time even as other additions
were made. But then we may estimate that two things happened.
One was overload. As more prayers, scrutinies, anointings, exorcisms, candles, robes, etc., were added, the initiation rite became
overloaded. Scholars remind us that good symbols can stand so
much overlay before they collapse. So with the initiation rite. It
could not carry all of the meanings attached to it any longer. It
was a case of too many plugs in the metaphorical socket. Something had to give. What gave was the anointing. As an anointing
signifying the Spirit, transferred from the water part of baptism,
it was ripe to take on something of its own independent tone if
only in an incipient way. When, as we saw, the rite did eventually
split apart in the West, it was a "natural" that the anointing
ceremony spun free. More than any other additions or "explanations" of the water-baptism this had more "substance," more
tradition. In time it came to be called confirmation. It still retained its Spirit-orientated meaning and its baptismal connection, even if later this was forgotten.

A second speculation is that somewhere along the line there
was a feeling (still unconscious) of a sense of loss concerning the
experience of the Holy Spirit. After all, he was an experience, not

an abstract proposition. Marvelous events and special charisma had accompanied the activity of the Spirit as we read in the Acts of the Apostles. But then such charisma declined. Certain heresies made the church suspicious of any "too spiritual" events it could not control. Then, there was the rise of infant baptism. This certainly limited any experience or proclamation of the Spirit. The Holy Spirit was in danger of being reduced to an idea, a doctrinal statement. So, in the West, the church wanted to revive that experience for people who were capable. This meant people with some use of reason and intelligence who could take part in what was going on and so, to that degree anyway, experience the Spirit and openly proclaim him. So the church capitalized on the already separated anointing, eventually called it confirmation and stressed it as a sacrament. (Even the East, under Western influence, later followed suit although it still retained the unity of the initiation rite.) This sacrament took on (at least theoretically) the experiential aspect of the Spirit so stressed in the New Testament. Unfortunately, the action of such stress had the reaction of divorcing it from the baptismal initiation process. However, because such a connection has been restored by modern theology and the revised rites of baptism and confirmation, we can now understand better the comments of theologians such as the following: The first is by Christopher Kiesling:

> Thus confirmation does not celebrate a reality substantially different from that which baptism celebrates—the gift of life in the Holy Spirit. But confirmation perfects or completes baptism by celebrating more explicitly and emphatically the Spirit's role in that life and the consequent richness and possibilities of it.
>
> In the new confirmation rite, all the prayers and all of the petitions asking various gifts of the Holy Spirit have their equivalent in the baptismal rite.... So confirmation celebrates the same mystery as baptism does, namely, life in the Spirit, but explicitly and emphatically celebrates a facet of that mystery which baptism leaves in the shadow, namely, the Holy Spirit's fullness in us.

In the process of developing the liturgy around baptism in water, the Christian community became conscious of confirmation as one of the important elements in the church's sacramental nature, that is, its being the visible manifestation of God's invisible grace among men, the mystery of Christ in us. The community developed the baptismal liturgy to make its members more explicitly aware of the many facets of the mystery celebrated in the simple rite of washing a believer in water in the name of Jesus or the Trinity. So it is not surprising that confirmation celebrates basically the same reality as baptism does, but stresses an aspect of it which baptism does not.

The community has a public act in which it calls its baptized members' attention to the Spirit's fullness in them and to the holy, prayerful, loving, apostolic life which is theirs through his help and guidance. This public act is the sacrament of confirmation.[4]

The second is by Marian Bohen:

The effects of this pouring forth of the Spirit vary. But nowhere are they seen as arming for combat. Rather, the effects of the postbaptismal gift of the Spirit all refer to the perfection of the neophyte as neophyte, as one recently re-born and enlightened, and this communication of the Holy Spirit, crowning the initiation rites, enables the neophyte to partake of the peace, prayer, and Bread of the Christian community. According to the evidence of these early documents, then confirmation emerges as the simple completion of baptism. It is less a strengthening (making firm) than a perfecting seal placed on the baptismal gifts.[5]

It is the concept of experiencing and proclaiming the Spirit, at least in principle, that justifies confirmation according to our theory of subconscious needs. In this vein we may continue to keep and use those themes of commitment, maturity, and strengthening *provided* we remember that we are basically celebrating an extension of an initiation rite; provided that we realize that we are "completing" baptism, deliberately placing the "perfecting seal on the baptismal gifts." Confirmation says that because we have been initiated into the church of Christ and regenerated by his love, we have a whole new way of looking at life. We are not only filled with the Spirit of Jesus, but we live *out* of that Spirit. Let us develop this further.

We often speak of the "spirit" of a class or a group or a parish. We sense a spirit of aliveness, a sense of comradeship, a spark which makes the members of the group of one heart. They see reality differently from others. They have, we say, a certain spirit. So, too, we speak of the "Christmas spirit" or an "anniversary or birthday spirit." These are atmospheric overtones that grab people and cause them to experience a new way of appreciating, savoring, and seeing reality. So with the Holy Spirit. He is not just a spirit with a small *s*, but a Person, a very Power of God, sent by the Father and Son who enters into the deepest recesses of our beings and "makes all things new." In this sense, we cannot really speak *about* him as someone we know. We can only speak *out* of such a Spirit which reveals, not himself, but the living Lord. The prophets—Jesus, the apostles—all spoke from the Spirit, with the Spirit, in the Spirit, not about him.

When we speak of the Holy Spirit, then, we are speaking about "a God-given horizon or context for vision, experience, and action. The Holy Spirit is the context out of which we can experience and then confess that Jesus is indeed alive and the Lord, our Lord. . . . The Holy Spirit is an experience, an experience which gives us a particular vision whose center is Jesus and whose object is God. . . . The Holy Spirit is not some neutral object but is a revealing, claiming, liberating, challenging experience to which some response, positive, negative or indifferent is unavoidable."[6] *So confirmation celebrates the baptismal experience, or at least the public, conscious proclamation of the Spirit.* Therein it openly tells the world that the candidate has a certain definite vision of life and from that vision (Spirit) he hopes to speak, act, live, witness, and die. This is the vision, the Spirit out of which we live, that is the basis for Catholic Action or the apostolate and community of good works so emphasized in the textbooks. This is the experience of the Spirit that grasped Isaiah, John, and Jesus at his own baptism. It was this Spirit who was poured forth at Pentecost and who is given to us in the baptism-confirmation experience. Confirmation therefore becomes a "datable event, verifiable in time and space, and an objective reference point by reason of which I know that the Spirit is present and active in my life."[7] Confirmation becomes a more evident act of witnessing the indwelling of God's holy love given in baptism. Confirmation continues the "baptismal catechesis which emphasized entrance into a community committed to conscious cooperation in the work of God's love in the world."[8]

The third and final speculation is this. From the very beginning there has always been some catechesis associated with baptism. There was the simple but powerful proclamation of Peter and there were the long term information and formation of the catechumenate in which catechesis was included on many levels. However, when infant baptism became the norm, then the catechesis was excluded. At least it could not be given before baptism to the pagan child. Therefore it had to be developed *after baptism* for the Christian child. Eventually this took the form of the invention of the catechism in the sixteenth century and subconsciously may have contributed to the rise of confirmation and its later age of conferral. In other words, confirmation provided another step for the child to get "baptized" all over again, but this time with the catechesis intact beforehand. It would seem that the custom of the past centuries of learning one's catechism and even being publicly questioned by the bishop is an exact copy of the old scrutinies before baptism. Confirmation may have its unconscious roots in the collective attempt to come to terms with a catechumenate that had to be delayed because of baptism in infancy and now reclaimed for a later time. (In this sense, too, the parochial school and religious instruction classes—CCD—are related to initiation because they are in effect a postbaptismal catechumenate.) This is why the Reformed churches have always seen confirmation primarily in catechetical terms and why all the mainline Protestant and Roman Catholic churches make a strong point of learning the catechism before confirmation.

3

Speculations aside, given the established relationship to baptism, or more properly, to the whole initiation rite, then, not surprisingly, there are two schools of thought on the subject. One, which we favor, is to restore the unity of the rite. Either celebrate the entire baptism-confirmation-eucharist complex at infancy or enroll all infants in a catechumenate (remember, this is not a shameful downgrading: the catechumenate is a genuine, valid position in the church's tradition) and celebrate the rite later on in adolescence or adulthood. But keep the rite intact. In fact, many argue that, given the new rite for the baptism of adults (which does keep all three sacraments united), this is *normative* and separation of the elements is exceptional. It is not likely, however, that this will happen right away. Meanwhile? Meanwhile we would suggest an approach based on our three speculations, that makes the best of a less than happy situation. We will take a look at the other side.

The other side would argue that perhaps, after all, we should let the rite be chronologically separated (although not theologically). They say that in a society which is clearly no longer supportatively Christian perhaps the Western split-off might have a point. It does have the merit of offering a personal articulate side of the initiation process, now clustered around confirmation. Of course, we would have to be careful to keep the baptismal connection because, as it has turned out in practice, confirmation gets all the preparation, instruction and the bishop's personal presence—which is quite an overshadowing of baptism. We would have to catechize differently and teach the confirmation candidates that the Word which is Christ has already been spoken to them in baptism but is now spoken more distinctly and more urgently in confirmation, wherein "our freedom, as to whether we choose our well-being or our disaster, is awakened and is gently invited to choose life."[9] Moreover the emphasis on the bishop's presence must be that he is there not as glorifying confirmation at the expense of baptism but as reminding the candidates that he was there symbolically in baptism already (in the chrism blessed by him) and now this is his personal baptismal visit where he will witness their experience of the Spirit. His presence reminds them more forcefully that he, as representative of the universal church, is deputizing them for that same universal church.

What we are saying is that, given the present insistence on infant baptism, the initiation triad of baptism, confirmation, and eucharist is not necessarily normative for all times. In fact, we saw that at the very first there was just the water-baptism. The additions and expansions were due, not to any great theory or doctrine, but precisely to meet the pastoral needs of the centuries. Our pastoral needs today (again, if we maintain the practice of baptizing infants) might be to continue the split-off chronologically but keep the unity theologically. As one writer says, "It is not a choice between a unified rite and a fragmented rite. It is a choice between two kinds of unity. One brings inner, personal experience into connection with a portion of the early ritual. The other is ritually complete, but it has lost the unity with teaching, discipline, and faith which the church's early rite had."[10]

So, for all of the problems it has caused, the Western breakdown of the rite into two and three sacraments at least comes to terms with the reality of infant baptism and affords later on a public, open opportunity to experience the Spirit who is always at the heart of initiation anyway. This is why one popular textbook widely used for young people preparing for confirmation says, "So, although you had no part in the decision to be baptized or Christ-ened, you are now being given the opportunity to decide personally and personally to accept the consequences of your baptism. *That is the real purpose of this special preparation for confirmation.*"[11]

This view, then, tries to be realistic. It probably would also opt for the integrated rite as of old, but knows it is not forthcoming immediately. *Therefore,* supporters would say, in the interim, make the best of it by presenting confirmation as that articulate opportunity to experience the Spirit, to dramatize the radical baptismal conversion.

Moreover, let us go one step further and argue that this articulation would be intimately tied into the concept of ministry. Since the Spirit is so often associated with peacemaking and reconciliation in the writings of Saints John and Paul, this ministry might seek to develop these themes. This would give confirmation its distinct and unique aspect of the baptismal grace. Young people (and adults as well) would be summoned, through this sacrament, to commit themselves to the work of reconciliation. So it would come about that "confirmation marks the stage where, through his reconciling actions, the Christian gives witness to the Spirit's presence in the Christian community. . . . Testifying to this power of the Holy Spirit by actions of peacemaking and reconciliation is the obligation that confirmation lays upon the Christian of mature and committed faith."[12]

This leads into the question of age, if we hold this view. There has always been a debate on what age is best for confirmation. From what we have said, the theoretical answer is that any age that makes possible the experiencing of the Spirit is correct. In practice, the church has fluctuated over the centuries. The church used to confirm infants, then seven years old and up. The Council of Trent recommended not before seven and no later than twelve—although we know that in 1553 Queen Elizabeth of England at three days old was baptized and confirmed at the same time. Today we have what we call the psychological school versus the theological school. The one opts for an emotionally mature age while the other argues for the same age as baptism whenever that is conferred. Pope Paul did not settle matters, and the United States Bishops Conference has adopted Trent's guidelines but with the understanding that in practice there will be a wide variety in practice. However, whatever age, the rite must be attractive enough to be desired, and the message of initiation must be clear.

Finally, we cannot close this chapter without a word about the phrase "baptism in the Spirit" which is a catch-phrase among the charismatic groups. Basically, it refers to a deep (and sometimes sudden) awareness of the presence and activity of the Spirit, urging one to conversion, surrender, and active love. Sometimes this "baptism of the Spirit" is an exceptional occurrence in which those so touched believe they are possessed by the gifts of the Spirit, and sometimes this includes the gift of tongues, the speaking in unintelligible words that basically are rhythmic praises to God. For some, this experience of being seized by the Spirit has been quiet as it has been definitive; and sometimes it resembles very much the variety of religious experiences undergone by many people throughout history that are described by psychologists. For others, the being taken up to God's especial presence and gifts is dramatic, emotional, and exceptional. In any case, there is a radical transformation in the lives of those so involved, and they experience a striking and liberating presence of grace (the Spirit's activity).

Ideally, the institutionalized sacrament of confirmation and this highly personal experience of the Spirit in the "baptism of the Spirit" should coincide. Every person getting confirmed should experience the Spirit as we have seen. Yet, in practice this is not so and need not be so. We must make a distinction between a "fundamental and sacramental promise of the Spirit making himself felt in terms of grace . . . and the living, powerful efficacy of this Spirit and of this grace announcing themselves in the daily chores of everyday activity."[13] In other words, receiving the Spirit does not necessarily demand the extraordinary events we associate with charismatics. We must remember that St. Paul lists some rather common and prosaic aspects among the gifts or charisma of the Spirit. The Spirit is not to be identified with miraculous and ecstatic matters only but rather as simply being operative wherever quiet but determined faith, hope, and love are given and received.

The great boon of the charismatic groups may be to remind us all of what the Spirit demands and can do. The phenomenon of tongue speaking, for example (to be found also among the unconfirmed) should not divert us from the basic fact of ongoing conversion and dedication that should be the posture of every baptized-confirmed Christian. The institutional sacrament of confirmation can look to the charismatic experience as the yet unfulfilled potential of everyone so called to celebrate this sacrament.

NOTES FOR CHAPTER 8

1. Karl Rahner, *Confirmation Today* (Dimension Books, 1975), p. 10.

2. Ethelbert Stauffer, "Baptism in Primitive Christianity," in *Twentieth Century Theology in the Making,* ed., Jaroslav Pelikan (Harper and Row, 1969), p. 303.

3. George Montague, "Baptism in the Spirit and Speaking in Tongues: A Biblical Appraisal," *Theology Digest* 21, no. 4 (Winter 1973), p. 347.

4. Christopher Kiesling, O.P., *Confirmation and Full Life in the Spirit* (St. Anthony Messenger Press, 1973), pp. 74–109.

5. Marian Bohen, O.S.U., *The Mystery of Confirmation* (Herder and Herder, 1963), p. 28.

6. Joseph M. Powers, "Confirmation: The Problem of Meaning," *Worship* 46, no. 1 (January 1972), pp. 26 and 27.

7. Joseph C. Cunningham, *Confirmation: Pastoral Concerns* (The Liturgical Press, 1973), p. 63.

8. Mary Perkins Ryan, "Sacraments in Context" (St. Mary's College Press, 1974), p. 5.

9. Rahner, *Confirmation Today,* p. 27.

10. Daniel B. Stevick, "Confirmation for Today: Reflections on the Rite Proposed for the Episcopal Church," *Worship* 44, no. 9 (November 1970), p. 556.

11. Sister James Margaret, S.S.J., *Live in the Spirit* (Sadlier Sacramental Program, 1975), p. 8. Cf. Robert Ludwig, "Updating Confirmation," *Today's Parish* (April 1976).

12. Robert Barry, O.P., "Confirmation in a Modern Perspective," *The Priest* (October 1976), p. 18.

13. Rahner, *Confirmation Today,* p. 12.

9

From Supper to Sacrifice

1

The eucharist is the last of the three sacraments of initiation. Like confirmation it too eventually broke off from the original rite—although as with the other two sacraments, the newly revised rituals have attempted to return it to context. Today the baptism of adults and infants, for example, is encouraged to take place within the Mass so that baptism, confirmation, and eucharist can be seen once more as one. So, too, with confirmation. The renewal of the baptismal promises at a confirmation celebrated within the Mass is designed to meet the same end. But, as we said, this is an attempt at restoration, for the eucharist did break off. In the West this breaking off was starting here and there, but it finally became a reality around the eleventh to thirteenth centuries.

Up to this time, all the evidence is clear: communion was always given with baptism, even the baptism of infants.[1] There was a rather consistent reasoning behind this. If no one, including infants, could get to heaven without baptism, then neither could they get to heaven without communion. The two sacraments were considered together as necessary for salvation. Therefore infant communion was quite normal. What began its disuse was some controversies about the eucharist. The reaction to the controversies was a great overprotectiveness, a great reverence and a shift of emphasis to the sacred species as such. This reverence and emphasis on the materiality of the species led to the withdrawal of the chalice from the laity. For a while, as a nod to the old tradition that communion was also necessary for salvation, infants were permitted to lick a little of the Precious Blood from the priest's finger. But even this ceased. Finally, the Fourth Lateran Council in 1215 decreed that those who have reached the age of reason must receive communion once a year. This was, of course, an implicit approval of delaying communion until the age of seven or twelve. It put the official blessing on the separation of this final element of the original triad. Still, so strong was the tradition of infant communion that the sixteenth-century Council of Trent felt it necessary to state very explicitly that infant communion was not necessary for salvation—although, it hastened to add, infant communion was not without merit. Later, the Roman Ritual of Pope Paul expressly forbad communion to infants.

All of this produced the interesting contradiction that the child was virtually instantly excommunicated upon his reception into the church. Although now a full Christian, he was forbidden to participate fully. He had to wait till he was seven or later for the "excommunication" to be lifted and he was allowed to participate in the eucharist; and then, the preparation, emotional satisfaction, and ceremonies easily overshadowed baptism. A child's First Communion, in practice, became far more important than his entrance into the Christian community, his baptism. Once more, as in the case of confirmation, the religious hoopla tended to downgrade baptism, reducing it to a kind of public registration while leaving the "real" commitment and the "real" spiritual development and the "real" highpoint of the Christian life to confirmation and first communion. The early Christians—not to mention St. Paul—would not know what to make of this.

As in the other sacraments, there is a movement afoot today which seeks the return of communion even to infants to complete the initiation rite. The reasoning is that if we instinctively baptize infants so that they can be brought quickly into the believing community, by what logic do we deny them full membership? The return to infant communion is not based on some kind of sacramental theology. It is based more on the whole notion of community, of what it means to belong to the church and, as we mentioned above, of the sensible desire not to be excommunicated upon entrance. One writer expresses the case thus:

> People who still regard their communion as a private matter between themselves and God will continue to see the privilege on the altar as an "adult privilege." For them the sacrament tends to be related to understanding, or faith or contrition. But where people have caught the vision of the eucharist as a corporate meal, the question must eventually arise, Why can't the children participate?
>
> It is, of course, inappropriate to divorce the sacraments from the church. . . . The question of the participation of children in the eucharist must be answered not in terms of the theology of the sacraments (narrowly conceived), but of the theology of the church.[2]

It would seem, therefore, that in the coming years we may see some modified return to full initiation which indeed does include the eucharist for infants as well as for adults.

So much for the final sacrament in the initiation rite. However, this whole question of the eucharist, and therefore of the Mass, invites us to explore further, in this chapter, something of its whole origin and history. To round out our consideration of this sacrament of the eucharist we should know how we ever arrived at our present attitudes and, perhaps more personally, how we ever arrived at the eucharistic celebration we have today.

But first an illustration. In a famous story of Edgar Allen Poe a hidden letter was not found precisely because it was right there in front of everyone. So it is with the liturgy of the Mass. Let me explain. I am visiting the home of a very wonderful but very conservative Catholic. He is bemoaning the changes, especially those in the Mass. It should have stayed the same; the old Latin Mass with the priest standing at the altar and the people in front of the altar rail with heads bowed and with obvious reverence

and piety. Well, we could concede that perhaps something has
been lost and that if the old Mass had too much of a Godward
focus, the new one might have too much of a manward focus.
Doing our liturgical thing might have replaced doing *his* thing.
Anyway, the point is that this man is telling me all this while he is
sitting underneath one of the most copied pictures of art in all
the world: da Vinci's Last Supper. My friend has never made the
connection nor observed large discrepancies. In this picture of
the artist's conception of the first Mass, there is no altar, no altar
rail, no white hosts, no altar boys, no Latin, and no vestments.
Rather the "congregation" is gathered around Christ, right up
there with him sharing his physical and eucharistic presence in
common bread and wine in their native Aramaic. And what's
more, singing hymns. "After singing hymns of praise, they
walked out to the Mount of Olives" (Mark 14:26).

It is beneath this picture that, in describing the old Latin Mass
he was raised on, he is telling me, "But that's the way it always
was!" Someday he is going to study that famous painting and
suddenly realize that between it and his experience there is a
wide gap. Someday he'll realize that the new Mass of the 1970's
should more properly be called the "latest" Mass. Let us look.

Our first consideration must be the obvious but often over-
looked one that we cannot understand the Mass unless we
understand the Last Supper. We cannot understand the Last
Supper unless we understand the Jewish Passover meal. We
cannot understand the Passover meal unless we understand
what it celebrated; namely, the Exodus deliverance of the Israelites from the slavery of Egypt. Therefore, any discussion of the
Mass must respect the unalterable fact that what Jesus and his
disciples were doing at the Last Supper was celebrating a ritual
meal. What were they ritualizing in this Passover meal? Liberation. Freedom. God stepped into Israel's history and by his
mighty power delivered the Israelites when they did not expect
it. He showed them mercy and compassion when they knew they
did not deserve it. Out of love he did this. Out of love he formed
a covenant with them. The Exodus became for them the
paradigm of all kinds of deliverance and freedom. The Passover

meal celebrated what God had done, could do, would do. He would lead his people everlastingly into freedom.

So what Jesus was doing at the Last Supper, what he was doing in celebrating this liberation-memorial meal had something to do with freedom. Somehow what he did, the change he made and the emphasis he put on this already highly established, symbolic ritual meal, would bring the theme of freedom to its fulfillment. Somehow his death the next day ("... my body broken for you ... my blood given for you ...") would give genuine release to all. So he did not invent the themes and motions of the Passover meal. No, he took a meal already there, heavy with liberation themes, and gave it a new dimension. And that new dimension—*that* was to be uniquely Christian. *That* was to be done in memory of him. His taking the bread and wine and doing something different with them in the old ritual meal somehow expressed the meaning of his impending death; that just as the bread was the product of wheat ground and the wine the result of grapes crushed, so Jesus' death, ritually shown in these Last Supper symbols, would effect reconciliation between God and man.

In other words, the Last Supper was an acted out parable. Through it Jesus was announcing his approaching sacrificial death. "The bread that he breaks and passes around to be eaten, the wine—blood of the grape—that he hands to his disciples in the chalice, in his own chalice, is his body given up for all, his blood shed for all. And this takes place within the setting of a meal characterized by the synoptics [the first three gospels] as a paschal meal at which all thoughts center upon liberation from the condition of slavery, a liberation in time past and a still greater liberation to come. Through this analogy Jesus indicates the redemptive suffering and death he is about to take upon himself."[3] Through the Mass, then, the sacrifice of the cross is made present and is continued through the centuries and the event of redemption is made present. Every time we celebrate the eucharist we are entering into Jesus' experience of death and of its meaning for him and for us.

So, in the eucharistic ritual we do not celebrate merely some special presence of Jesus in the appearance of the meal's food of bread and wine. True, he is there in some way, but his being there only makes sense in the larger context of what he is there *for*. He is not there (as later it would develop) to be a presence or passive object to be looked at and admired. He is there as celebrating the ritual meal (eucharist) of deliverance from sin and death, to deliver God to us and to reaffirm and extend the revelation of the Father in his life and in ours. The eucharistic food is the sharing of a meal by which we enter, as a people, into the mystery of Christ's sacrifice on the cross which reveals the Father's liberating love.

You see, what mattered to the early Christians was not that Jesus was truly present in the sacred species (he was) or how he was so there, but rather what he was doing in them and what demands he was making in that ritual meal. Jesus to them was not there as passive, but active. He had something to say and they would be the spokesmen in their lives of what in fact he did say and of the liberation he did effect. The eucharist is a ritual mystery, but it is a mystery which is not to be solved, but one which must be confronted and celebrated by the entire community at Mass. It memorialized Jesus as the true Paschal Lamb, laying down his life that we might live. We *are* at a ritual sacrificial meal when we "go to Mass." The food is still there: bread and wine. There is a sharing and an eating and drinking. There is song and prayer. Most of all, the themes behind them are still active: the themes, ever old and ever new: deliverance from sin and death and the offer of everlasting freedom in Christ. So the Mass started out and remains a ritual sacrificial meal, originating in God's deliverance of the Israelites and culminating in Jesus' deliverance of all mankind on the cross.

2

There is some debate whether Jesus and his disciples were celebrating the once-a-year Passover meal or even the weekly

Friday evening thanksgiving meal (called the *chaburah*). The debate is not that important because the Last Supper was certainly grounded in the Passover meal and had Passover connotations and ceremonies. It had a Paschal character and was understood as such. That is why St. Paul says, "Christ our Passover has been sacrificed" (1 Corinthians 5:7) and St. John sees the crucified Jesus as the Paschal Lamb whose bones remain unbroken (John 19:36). In general the outline of such a Passover or ceremonial meal went like this: (1) There was a benediction which meant basically a summons to praise God; (2) a remembrance of God's wonders as a motive for praise; and (3) a return to another benediction which took the form of a formal ending or doxology (such as our "Glory be to the Father. . ."). This basic outline formed the style of the Passover meal and the Christian Mass canon. It is interesting to note further similarities as seen, for example, in the blessing of the bread and the cup of wine. The leader or host of the Jewish ceremonial meal would take some bread, break it and say, "Blessed are you, Lord our God, eternal king, for bringing forth bread from the earth." Then he gave a piece to everyone at table. Each one present would then bless his own cup of wine during the meal saying, "Blessed are you, Lord our God, eternal king, for making the fruit of the vine." On more solemn occasions, after the meal there was a long prayer of thanksgiving. We can quickly sense the similarity of these prayers with the one we say in our own Mass canons today: "Blessed are you, Lord God of all creation, through your goodness we have this bread to offer, which earth has given and work of human hands. It will become for us the body of Christ. . . . Blessed are you, Lord God of all creation, through your goodness we have this wine to offer, fruit of the vine and work of human hands. It will become for us our spiritual drink."

Again, as we have just seen, the Mass has its origins in a ritual meal and one that has a certain format, derived from the Jewish service, and never lost in Christian development. At the very first, the Christians met in private homes or larger halls to celebrate the Christian ritual meal. The occasion was one of community. They understood that the Risen Lord Jesus was alive and was with them and that they were doing this action in his memory. The Lord's Supper, as it was called at this time, was the time and place when Christians, already united to one another in baptism, deepened their union with each other and with Jesus so that they could more effectively proclaim the reconciling and liberating death of Jesus. The Lord's Supper was an occasion of community, a mutual cohesiveness by which the participants knew that they were more than the sum total of their individual selves. They were in fact the very Body of Christ. They were church, and "though there be many of us, we form a single body" (1 Corinthians 10:17).

At the beginning there were two distinct services. The liturgy of the word (scripture readings and homily) was held on Saturday mornings. This was separate from the eucharist which at this time had two phases: a common table-fellowship meal and the celebration of the eucharist itself. Quickly this meal element was separated from the eucharist. As a result of removing this attached meal, only one table was kept and the dining hall changed its character and became a room for a religious assembly. This separation of the meal from the eucharist came about mostly because of a change in understanding and emphasis. As the notion of thanksgiving became more prominent, the notion of a meal, solely as a meal, receded. Moreover, this thanksgiving was not for its own sake, but was tied in with the notion of sacrifice. We were thankful because of our redemption celebrated in this eucharist. The mystical offering of Jesus on calvary in reparation for our sins and effecting our reconciliation to the Father was the basic reason for the thanksgiving.

In other words, the eucharist was a sacrifice, a true offering of Jesus, seen in the breaking of the bread. This shift of emphasis was duly noted in time with the repositioning of the priest. He used to face the people. Now he began to come around and stand on the same side with them. The idea was that since it was a sacrifice that was being offered in the Mass, then both priest and people were standing together making this gift to God. We may also note that from this time on—the first century—no longer was the term Lord's Supper or meal or banquet ever used of the Mass in any liturgy. These terms were only revived in the sixteenth century by the Protestant reformers and in our own day by some who wished to stress the meal aspect of the Mass (and at times at the expense of seeing the Mass as a ritual meal which was sacrificial). By the second century, around the year 150, as we learn from an account of Justin Martyr, the eucharist, now separated from the fellowship table meal, was joined to the liturgy of the word and the whole package was transferred to Sunday. This has been the structure of the Mass ever since.

The oldest term for the Mass was, as we have noted, the Lord's Supper or the breaking of the bread and then, later on, the Greek term eucharist, a word meaning praise and thanksgiving. But the word Mass has been predominant since the fourth century. Actually, it means "dismissal." We should recall that the catechumens were dismissed in a quite solemn way by the bishop after the liturgy of the word. This first dismissal must have impressed the pagans when they saw all the people exiting together from their meeting. From this association came the word Mass ever since. Pope Innocent III wrote, "Missa comes from 'dismissal,' because the catechumens are sent away at the moment when the priest begins to consecrate the eucharist."[4]

Once more, we must take into account the deep sense of community which we saw in speaking of the other sacraments of initiation. And to have a strong sense of community there is needed a leader whose gifts and talents can be a force of cohesion. Therefore, what emerges very quickly in the eucharist is the preeminence of the bishop. He is the leader of the community, and he either presides over or celebrates the eucharist. Pope Clement of Rome, St. Ignatius of Antioch, and Polycarp of Smyrna—all of the second century and widely apart—see in the eucharist presided over by or before the bishop the preeminent sign of Christian unity and cohesiveness. So strong was the community aspect that, when more Christians demanded more groupings, they met with the bishop's surrogate, the priest.

A few more developments. The people, as all ancients were accustomed to do, brought their own contributions to the Jewish Friday night meal. They continued to do this at the Christian eucharist. This custom is at the bottom of our offertory procession. At first, the prayers recited at the eucharist were freely improvised by the bishop, although they followed the general pattern of the "Jewish canons" of praise and thanksgiving. Gifted bishops could do this, but when those less gifted came on the scene it became a growing custom to use texts composed by others. This would lead, in later centuries, especially in the West, to considerable standardization under such original popes as St. Leo, Gelesius, and Gregory the Great. Naturally, all this was going on in the predominant Greek tongue. In the year 384, Pope Damasus, seeing that the people had largely forgotten the Greek and were in fact speaking Latin, changed the worship into that language so that the people would not be prevented from participating or understanding. It is worth noting that the *next* time the church changed the official language for worship was in 1963. Only Easter was celebrated in the early church with its fifty days extension (derived from Judaism) and every Sunday was considered a little Easter. Later, other festivals were added, plus the feasts of the martyrs. By the sixth century there was completed the essentials of a liturgical year. An interesting footnote: there were two favorite Christian acclamations which died out in the year 100. They were, "Maranatha!" (Come, Lord, come) and "May the grace of Christ come and may this world pass away." Such acclamations were based on the expectation of the imminent return of Christ. As this return was delayed, these acclamations dropped out of use.

We mentioned that we have an early document from Justin Martyr from the year 150 which gives an outline of the Mass. It mentions the scripture readings, the kiss of peace, and the long canon or preface or eucharistic prayer. Around the year 220 we have another explanation of the Mass from Hippolytus who, we must remember, is describing the rite of Christian initiation which included the celebration of the eucharist. His was widely used, although, as we said, bishops were free to make up their own. That is why Hippolytus said afterward, "Let the bishop give thanks as we said above. In giving thanks to God he does not have to use the same words we gave before as if he were studying them by heart, but let each pray according to his own ability."[5] An outline of what Hippolytus wrote would be as follows:

1. The people come and offer their gifts from which the deacons select the bread and wine to be used and bring them to the bishop.
2. The bishop then begins the eucharistic prayer with the very same beginning we have today. He says, "The Lord be with you.... Lift up your hearts.... Let us give thanks to the Lord our God." This is followed by a long institution narrative recalling what Jesus did at the Last Supper, a reference to the memorial of his death and resurrection (anamnesis) and a calling down of the Holy Spirit upon the bread and wine (epiclesis) with a concluding doxology to which the people respond with the great Amen.
3. There is no Sanctus (Holy, holy, holy) which later on (fourth century) would be inserted to break up the flow of the eucharistic prayer. There are no remembrances of the living, the dead, or the saints.
4. All of the early Mass prayers were addressed to the Father *through* the Son. (It was only later, in reaction to Arianism, that prayers began to be addressed to Christ himself.)

These, then are beginnings and shifts of emphasis. As the title of this chapter indicates the movement has been from the Last Supper as mere meal to the Last Supper as the redemptive sacrifice of Jesus. The tone and outlines are still Jewish, but the matter and heart are Christian. The church is doing what Jesus commanded in his memory: assembling to give thanks and praise by the very means of offering the redemptive death of Jesus once more to the Father. Not a new death, but the same once-and-for-all death (Hebrews 9:11) now made present for the benefit of all.

NOTES FOR CHAPTER 9

1. All this is documented in J.C.D. Fischer's book, *Christian Initiation: Baptism in the Medieval West* (London: SPCK, 1965).

2. Eugene L. Brand, "Baptism and Communion of Infants: A Lutheran View," *Worship* 50, no. 1 (January 1976), p. 30. Sometimes people quote Paul in 1 Corinthians 11:28 where he says we must be able to "discern" the Body of the Lord. If this "discernment" means intellectual understanding, then children are excluded. But if it means an instinctive sense of belongingness, then they can well be included.

3. Josef A. Jungmann, S.J., *The Mass* (Liturgical Press, 1975), p. 101.

4. *DeSacro Mysterio*, PL 217, col. 912.

5. Quoted in John Barry Ryan, *The Eucharistic Prayer* (Paulist Press, 1974), p. 16.

10

From Sacrifice to Silence

1

The old Roman Canon described at the end of the last chapter, with some later additions, was probably fixed in outline and development by the fourth century—certainly by the time of Pope Gregory the Great. This Roman Canon was and remained the *only* Mass canon for fifteen hundred years. It is only since Vatican II that several more official canons in the West were introduced. Since we mentioned Pope Gregory the Great we should further remark that he represents the beginning of a new era in the Mass. He inaugurated the first reforms. The Roman liturgy was made more solemn and additional prayers, chants, gestures were joined to the old structure. The people still stood close to the bishop and the Mass was still clearly a community affair. But here we find the beginning of the most single important influence on the Mass in the West. What the popes did at Rome became in time the pattern of all Masses in the West. The papal Mass will evolve into the ideal Mass and everything since (in the West) will be measured against it.

To this papal Mass came all of the bishops, priests, and dignitaries of Rome and the outlying districts—a true external sign of the universal church. Later on, as congregations grew and the clergy had to remain with their people, the practice arose by which the pope took a piece of the sacred bread and sent it to the parish priests of Rome. The priest at his Mass would drop this fragment into the chalice. The action was to underscore the unity of the church. That custom died out in the seventh century, but the underlying notion has persisted to this day, for Vatican II says that the local "pope" or bishop "is to be considered the high priest of his flock. In a certain sense it is from him that the faithful who are under his care derive and maintain their life in Christ. Therefore all should hold in very high esteem the liturgical life of the diocese which centers around the bishop, especially in his cathedral church. Let them be persuaded that the church reveals herself most clearly when a full complement of God's holy people, united in prayer and in a common liturgical service, (especially the eucharist) exercise a thorough and active participation at the very altar where the bishop presides in the company of his priests and other ministers."[1] And the object of all this "is not to give a ceremony more outward splendor, but to shed more light on the sign of the church's mystery, which is the sacrament of unity."[2]

In practice, as we have had occasion to remark before, Mass with or before the bishop is not held in high esteem, and the sign of unity is mostly academic for people whose only contact with a real live bishop is a confirmation visit. Again, liturgy will not work until dioceses and parishes are made smaller.

The time from Pope Gregory the Great (sixth century) to the time of Pope Gregory VII (eleventh century) sees many changes, not only in the Mass, but in the general political and liturgical context of the times. These changes were very uneven, but they were real. Jewish influence, of course remains as is seen in the following list: the liturgy of the word, the Jewish scripture, the structure of the canon, the seven day week, the weekly day of worship, the festivals of Easter, Pentecost, the cult of the martyrs, the reckoning of the liturgical day from sundown to sundown (hence the basis for our newly given Saturday evening Masses "counting" for Sunday), the notion of the doxologies, and acclamations such as Amen, alleluia, hosanna, and the custom of the laying on of hands. But, as we have seen, Greek influence was working its way in and many would endure to this day: the exorcisms, anointings, night-time baptism, turning to the East for prayer, and some of today's technical terms, such as the word liturgy itself, eucharist, mystery, advent, acclamation, and hymn.

An interesting sideline was developing in the style of the bishops who celebrated these liturgies. We must recall that Christianity was illegal for four centuries. The Emperor Constantine gave it legal status and used the bishops of this new religion to obtain some measure of civil and religious unity in his far-flung empire. The bishops, then, became kind of quasi civil servants as well as clergymen. Since Constantine gave them some measure of civil power he had to give them insignia in keeping with the imperial protocol. So it is here that we find the beginning of clerical special insignia: the pallium, the special footwear, headgear, the ring, and the throne. In a special way the bishop of Rome was honored with insignia and in time he soon came to have almost equal status with the emperor. Some bishops had their doubts about all this civil transfer but most went along with it until the dress and insignia became standard enough. After the fall of the Roman Empire, however, most of these civil trappings and insignia lost their original meanings in the minds of the people and even in the minds of the bishops themselves. Their special dress simply became a sign of their spiritual office. Still, the touch of the court ceremonial was there and would have its effect in medieval Christendom. More than that, it would have its interplay with a strange theological shift that was about to happen.

2

The cause of the shift was heresy. There were several famous ones in the early church and the church councils were invented precisely to deal with such emergencies. These councils gave us the great formulas which enshrined the truths of revelation. Now one of the most devastating and widespread heresies was the one called Arianism, the heresy which St. Jerome remarked was so pervasive that the world woke up one morning and was amazed to find itself Arian. This heresy was proposed by a certain bishop Arius who basically denied the divinity of Christ saying that he was but man. This was a stubborn heresy which claimed even the Emperor Constantine on his deathbed and spread to the barbarian tribes. But the point we wish to make here is that the church reacted—as indeed it had to—but the reaction has been with us ever since.

So strongly was the church determined to eradicate this heresy and so deeply did it react against Jesus being only a mere man, that ever since it has stressed his divinity. Jesus was true God and true man declared a church council, but the emphasis came down hard on the God aspect. Moreover, the emphasis began its own distortion by tending to pull Jesus out of the realm of the human altogether. Jesus more and more became enshrined in the absolute and abstract Trinity. He was divinity, a very God, a power, and—in the natural imagery of the day—emperor-like. In a word, Jesus was slowly removed from earth, so to speak, and made a fearsome imperial divinity in clouds of mystery. The mosaic above the main altar in the National Shrine in Washington, D. C., shows us exactly what happened: there we see a Byzantine, powerful, royal Christ with lightning flashing out of his head. This is a far cry from an early picture in one of the old baptistries portraying Jesus as the good shepherd.

This change was duly noted in the Mass liturgy. The Nicene Creed was added to the Mass as were prayers to the Trinity. The point of the shift was clearly that of distance. If formerly the Mass was a gathering of the baptized around the altar surrounding the bishop (as in da Vinci's painting) now it became an occasion of separation. People were suddenly overawed and unworthy. Hence the introduction of many confessions before Mass. An altar rail was gradually introduced to emphasize the distance. There was a preoccupation with reverence, cleanliness, remoteness. The absolutions and washings were introduced. Communion in the hand, a tradition from the beginning, was stopped lest dirty hands soil the sacred bread. The bread itself became a small, white, pure, antiseptic host. People were no longer worthy—and said so three times—to receive the eucharist. The church was forced to order this reception at least once a year in the thirteenth century. Naturally the bishop's role and the priest's role changed. No longer was either the one who orchestrated the liturgy, bringing into harmony the various people and parts. In due time, each would take over all the parts, become a caste apart and eventually even wear special clothes, not just when celebrating the liturgy but all the time. The momentum had been started.

In the period before the sixteenth-century Council of Trent matters moved steadily ahead to change the focus of the Mass. The Roman influence passes into the Franco-German world by way of Pippin and his son Charlemagne. Under their influence the Roman liturgy became common—though it is an amalgam of old Roman, Gallican versions. Liturgical books become the norm and standardization sets in. One such codification was done under Pope Gelesius in the year 500 (the Gelesian Sacramentary) and another a hundred years later under Gregory the Great (Gregorian Sacramentary). However we should remember that "neither Gregory the Great nor his immediate successors foresaw or required that their liturgical books should alone and everywhere be regarded as authoritative. In Rome people were generous enough to permit the titular churches to keep their books and their liturgy which deviated somewhat from the normal practice. During the whole of the sixth and seventh centuries, in fact, it is impossible to speak of an absolute unity as regards the liturgy of the city of Rome; for the bishop used the Gregorian Sacramentary, and the presbyters kept to their own book."[3]

From the eleventh century on, as we have indicated, the popes continued to dominate the liturgy. They demanded that all of the episcopal sees in the Western church follow exclusively the usages and the customs of the Roman See. The only ones to really resist this centralizing thrust were the liturgies of Milan and Spain. An interesting footnote in liturgical history is the role of the newly established order of Franciscans. It was they who in their wanderings, preaching, and influence carried with them the convenient liturgical books from Rome. Therefore they had a large hand in spreading Roman uniformity all over the West. But there also came at this time another major influence which has persisted to modern times and which is a first cousin to the reaction against Arianism: the introduction of the private Mass.

Private Masses (Mass with no congregation) started in the monasteries. At first this was not even thought of for the very practical reason that all the monks were not priests. They simply had one or two priests come in to celebrate the Mass liturgy with them. However, when Gregory the Great began to draw the monks out of their monasteries to go into missionary work, then things changed radically. Missionary work could not be carried out without the priests to baptize, confirm, and celebrate Mass. Therefore the most practical solution was to ordain the lay monks. The net result was that the number of monks in a monastery who were also priests grew considerably.

This was one factor in promoting the multiplication of private Masses. The other was the invention of the so called "votive" Mass; that is, a Mass offered for a special intention: for the sick, for fortune, for health, for the deceased, etc. This concept of celebrating Mass for some intention is not entirely foreign to the nature of the Mass, but it became terribly disproportionate and made a noticeable shift in the meaning of the Mass. Mass came to be seen in relation to a particular case of need or for specific groups rather than as the worship of the entire church with God in mind, rather than man. Little guilds and confraternities were having "personal" Masses all over the place. Intentions multiplied, especially for the deceased. All this necessitated the multiplication of Masses and did violence to any communal concept of worship. Another result was that at this time grace was being seen in almost mechanical terms. A need was felt to obtain it frequently and as often as possible. The Mass, of course, was considered one of the most efficacious ways of "getting grace" and so insuring one's salvation or the salvation of others (deceased). These factors fused to promote not only the rise of many Masses but also the rapid rise of the private Mass.

The result of all this was that all communal aspects rapidly disappeared. The priest had to do the readings (no one else, except possibly an illiterate altar server, was present). He had to do all the singing since no choir was present. Since he had no congregation and the space for his little side altar was limited, he had no room to leave the area to do the readings; so he compensated for this by simply moving the book from one side of the altar to the other. Since, however, in theory the lessons were really meant to be read to the people he turned the book at a slight angle on the altar as a sop to this reality. Naturally any offertory procession ceased. Finally, with the situation we have described, there was no longer any need for the various liturgical books. Rather all the parts were soon collected under one cover called the Missal and after the thirteenth century this was the common single book used at Mass. Finally, the Mass became completely silent since there were other priests "saying" Mass simultaneously and no one wanted to disturb the other. The priest no longer vested at the altar and all of the preparatory prayers were pulled into the beginning (the prayers, in the old days, at the foot of the altar) and the entrance hymn was read as the first opening prayer (introit). By the end of the Middle Ages, the conviction was so well entrenched that it was the solemn duty of every priest who was sincere to celebrate Mass every day privately.

Now the split was widened. Formerly, as we saw, the people were quite active. The Mass prayers and the canon were said aloud. The people gave their responses and at the end of the canon they shouted out their "Amen" to show that they had heard, approved, and concurred. Now, the canon was reduced to a whisper and so became the exclusive concern of the priest. The notion seemed to be that a great reverence had arisen about the eucharist and that to say the words of the canon or the consecration out loud was somehow irreverent. By the year 1000 it became a matter of obligation to recite the canon in a whisper.

The people were delegated to watching. To this alienation was added another factor: the removal of the free-standing table altar to its fixation to a wall. This placing of the altar against a decorated wall started in the sixth century in the West—the East seems to have done this from the beginning—and by the year 1000 it became the standard practice. Candles were added about a hundred years later and a cross atop the altar around the thirteenth century. Of itself there was no special problem in this new altar location. On the contrary, the position of both priest and people on the same side of the altar was a real demonstration of their collective posture of worship to the Father. It was rather all of the other elements added to this that conspired to give physical and emotional distance and passivity to the laity.

Besides the introduction of the altar rail which we have already mentioned, the chalice was eventually withdrawn from the laity. This only served to confirm the impression that here was no sacred sacrificial meal in which all shared and took part, but rather a holy drama which anyone, if present, watched. Devotion to the Passion arose and replaced the focus of the Mass. Actually, this Passion motif was not hostile to the Mass's meaning since, as we saw, it did represent the redemptive passion, death, and resurrection of Jesus. Yet matters started to become too literal. There was no action of the Mass that was not considered a piece of Passion play drama. A man named Amalarius of Metz (d. 850) tried to show that every Mass action was symbolic of something in Jesus' last days. The entrance rite, for example, was the crowd coming into the garden of Gethsemani; the washing of the hands was Pilate proclaiming his innocence; the cord around the priest's waist was the cord that bound Jesus, and so on. This sort of theater was condemned, but it strongly persisted through the centuries. Then, too, the Mass was further devalued because of the sudden outbreak of all kinds of private, favorite devotions of the religious orders and the various confraternities. "For the liturgy, which was once and always should be the communal act of priest and people, became now exclusively a priestly duty."[4]

The move from the Mass as a shared sacrificial meal to an object of passive devotion had other practical ramifications. One would be the reservation of the Blessed Sacrament. In antiquity part of the sacred bread was kept back after every Mass and people even took it home in their hands. They used it for protection and carried it around with them. Some was reserved for viaticum. There also arose the custom of reserving a piece of the sacred bread from a previous Mass to drop into the chalice at the next one in order to signify that, though time separated them, the Masses were indeed one act of worship. This reserved piece of the sacred bread was kept in the sacristy or in a cupboard near the altar or in a suspended container in the form of a dove. A mere bow to this container at the next Mass was all that religious etiquette required.

In the eleventh century, however, there was a controversy over the real presence. Once again a reaction set in. Genuflection to the reserved species was now in order. In the twelfth century it became the custom to place a lighted candle before the container (called the Everlasting Light). A hundred years later the priest began to elevate the bread after the consecration. This was as much a practical demand since the people could not see the bread and wine with the priest's back in the way. There was also a touch of magic for people were at the stage where they thought they would gain some benefit just by gazing on the sacred species. The celebrant genuflected both before and after the elevation. Then, out of respect for the eucharist, communion dropped off and became rare. Then came the feasts. The Corpus Christi feast was first introduced in the city of Liege in 1246 and for the rest of the Christian world in 1264. Later a procession attached itself to it so that people could steal a look at the eucharist. From this custom arose another one: exposition of the Blessed Sacrament. Often this occurred even at Mass itself and indeed became more important. From this came Benediction. Moreover, since the reformers of the sixteenth century attacked this custom, devotion to the Blessed Sacrament then became a talisman of Catholic devotion. Perpetual adoration societies grew up in order to make reparation against such indifference. Finally, in the early seventeenth century the tabernacle was prescribed by Rome for all churches and this tabernacle reached its zenith in the baroque style of architecture developed under the aegis of the Jesuits. A whole ceremonial developed in order to approach Jesus holding court in the Blessed Sacrament. There were couriers and guards (the Knights of Columbus, Fourth Degree), canopies and arches over the altar. The whole impression was a throne room within the church building from which Jesus reigned in the Blessed Sacrament.

All that we have described were but understandable approaches of a people who became convinced that their job in reference to the eucharist was to be passive and watch. In other words, we have moved from the original *action* of a redemptive ritual meal to a Presence. To put it another way, when Christians lost sight of the Mass as a community meal, as doing something in memory of Jesus, then the focus began to shift. No longer was the sacrificial *action* the thing, but rather the elements of bread and wine themselves. Once more we see the tendency to reduce everything to its "essential" elements, which always means that we can use and maneuver them. We have made the eucharist an object, argued over the Real Presence, enthroned the species and immobilized the movement. To return to the eucharist as an action rather than as a presence is the point of the latest renewal of Vatican II.

We might add that the Council of Trent did make an effort at reform concerning some emphases and some real abuses concerning the eucharist. The price of reaction to the reformers, however, was rigidity. By that we mean that formerly each bishop had a great deal of leeway concerning the liturgy. Gradually all this was taken from them and the Council of Trent gave all of their prerogatives over to the Roman congregations set up for the very purpose of universal regulation. All the new books would now carry the adjective "Roman." It was an accurate adjective, for from now on all would have to conform to the centralizing rulings of Rome. This is why the time from Trent on is known as the "Age of Rubrics"—the age of rules and directives and minute prescriptions. Trent did tidy up the Mass and issued much-needed reforms. Unfortunately, it once more did not have the necessary documents and perspectives at hand, and so it failed completely to take into account the community aspect of the Mass. It did what it could, and by its rubrics and printed missals froze everything into position. It was only with more scientific scholarship and the impetus that Pius X gave that the iceberg of rubrics began to thaw. It was up to Vatican II to complete the thaw and refocus the Mass. It is up to our own age and the future to make that focus meaningful.

3

Basically what we have reviewed in this chapter is the historical truism that the church has reflected on the eucharist under various aspects in direct proportion as it was preoccupied with various questions concerning it throughout the centuries. This historical truism provides the key for seeing the eucharist one time as Real Presence, another as the sacrifice of the Mass and still another as the eucharistic meal. One writer sums it up well when he remarks

I think it can be said without great risk of serious historical error that when the attention of the theologians was fixed on efforts to explain how Christ might be really present in the eucharist, there were distinctive behavior patterns in the Christian community that corresponded to this theological accent.

Again, without risk of historical distortion, I think it can be said that when the theological accent fell on the eucharist as sacrifice, there was a corresponding behavior pattern in the community.

Similarly, with the contemporary theological accent on the eucharist as meal, there is a distinct behavior pattern in the community that differs significantly from earlier behavior that corresponded to different doctrinal accents.[5]

The point is well taken as we remember that a fresh "theological accent" does not necessarily negate previous views. It is a matter of emphasis not cancelation.

What about today then? What is our peculiar behavior pattern that makes us consider the eucharist more in terms of a meal? Our pattern is clearly the urgent need for community—a constant theme in all of our investigations concerning the sacraments. It is the assembly of believers, the gathered community that is of such great interest today. Just what does it mean to be church? And if these are our concerns then we are not going to focus especially on the Real Presence with its passive devotions and isolated piety; nor are we going to focus on the notion of sacrifice that might cater to individual worship which is satisfied just by "being there" and gathering the "fruits" of the Mass to oneself or for the deceased. Not that we ignore or dismiss these concepts. Rather, our needs are different, and we are returning to the old and traditional notion of the eucharistic meal. After all, we are "the lonely crowd," living private, isolated lives. We need and we crave a sense of belongingness, of community. It should be expected that we seek them around the altar, in the unity of the eucharist itself.

So we of the 1970s turn our altars around to make them more a community table. It does not matter very much if women approach such a table, even bare-headed and having an active part. A people in search of community could hardly exclude them. We use more substantial bread and pass the cup. And we do this, not only because there is fellowship in such signs, but also because there is symbol. Jesus was broken and passed around; so, too, must we be if community is to be created. We also redesign our church buildings to represent less of a theater and more of a banquet hall, often in the round, so that recognition, familiarity, and closeness can be created. After all, how can one have the eucharist among strangers? How can vast and impersonal territorial parishes be proper settings for its celebration? "Eucharistic liturgy should be a magnet to draw people out of their private hiding places, to help them break down the barriers of egotism and petty self-interest, to overcome the artificial and often destructive divisions of social and economic class, race, and even of age."[6]

This building of community, this creating and celebrating of community by way of the shared eucharist is not meant merely for the local area. It has deep and abiding reference to the world at large, especially those great portions of the world which suffer the basic hungers of food, justice, and truth. The needs of the poor, the starving, the enslaved are the object of every true eucharistic community. "In the eucharist we have an answer to despair about the future of the world: we can still live and bid others live because we are drawn into a covenant with God and all mankind within which to give one's life for others is ultimately to save one's life."[7]

This is the behavior pattern of the twentieth century. It could not be otherwise that, while holding the notions of Real Presence and sacrifice in tension, we look at our eucharist from the perspective of a meal.

NOTES FOR CHAPTER 10

1. Decree on the Apostolate of the Laity, no. 41.

2. *Instituio generalis Missalis Romani,* no. 59.

3. Theodore Klauser, *A Short History of the Western Liturgy* (London: Oxford University Press, 1969), p. 58. This book is the source for most of the outline of this chapter.

4. Ibid., p. 97.

5. William J. Byron, "Eucharist and Society," *America* (August 7, 1976), p. 43ff.

6. Ibid.

7. Monika K. Hellwig, *The Eucharist and the Hunger of the World* (Paulist Press, Deus Book, 1976), p. 88. See also Lucien Deiss, *It's the Lord Supper* (Paulist Press, 1976).

11

The Sacraments
of Penance

1

In this chapter we want to examine the sacrament of penance and trace its origin and uneven development throughout the ages. Unlike confirmation it has no essential part in the initiation rites even though, by accident, it got wedged in between baptism and the eucharist and wound up before confirmation. But like confirmation, the sacrament of penance has its blackout moments. The first sources are not frequent, and what is there is often difficult to interpret. Even with the many excellent researches into the history of this sacrament there is still much that is unsure. So we will try to piece together what we can with as much fact and reasonable speculation that the data warrants.

Whatever doubts about the origin and development of this sacrament of penance, there is no doubt about its subject matter: sin. From his very beginnings man has always known that estrangement and that alienation we call sin. At every time and place he has yearned to be made whole again, to be restored, renewed, reconciled. Therefore, since sin and its attendant evils have been such a deep part of the human experience it was impossible that Jesus would not deal with it. In fact, he made it the theme of his ministry. His very name Jesus is a translation of the word Savior, for, as the angel told Joseph, "he shall save his people from their sins" (Matthew 1:21). Jesus himself described his mission not as calling the just, but sinners. His first words were, "Repent and believe in the Good News" (Mark 1:15). He told stories such as that of the Merciful Father (Prodigal Son) and left as his dying legacy that blood "which shall be shed for many for the remission of sins." After his resurrection his apostles would heed his words and themselves continue the Good News: "In his name, penance for the remission of sins is to be preached to all the nations" (Luke 24:47). On Pentecost day when the people asked Peter what they should do he naturally replied that they should be baptized for the forgiveness of sins (Act 2:38).

Now this last sentence provides us with two important facts. The first is that the church has always been conscious that it indeed, by the power of Jesus' Spirit, could forgive sins. As we shall see, the church for a while may have entertained some doubts as to the extent of this power, but no doubt as to the power itself, "Receive the Holy Spirit, whose sins you shall forgive, they are forgiven" (John 20:19). The second fact is that the church has traditionally always provided a variety of ways and several sacraments in which this could be done. This startles us at first because we have been so accustomed to think that only the sacrament of penance forgives sins. But this is not true. Let us look.

The first way and the first sacrament for the forgiveness of sins is that primal and definitive conversion which we have described in previous chapters as baptism. This above all was the place for radical conversion. Recall that it is in baptism that one is plunged into the passion, death, and resurrection of Jesus. It is baptism therefore which regenerates and forgives sins and was proclaimed as such. It is this same baptism, we again remind ourselves, which we announce in our Creed as the "one baptism for the forgiveness of sins." When the apostles preached forgiveness they meant baptism as we just saw in the example of Peter. And when he did tell the people that they must repent and be baptized for the forgiveness of sins, this is exactly what he had in mind. He was not thinking of a repeated confession of sins, but rather of a one-time, lasting baptismal conversion forever to God. When St. Paul was in the process of being converted, the disciple Ananias said to him, "Rise and be baptized and wash away your sins, calling on his name" (Acts 22:16).

Moreover, the conviction was strong that so final was the cleansing of baptism, so much did it enter one into the messianic community, a community of high self consciousness of being "in the Lord," that sin was not even considered as a possibility. That is why there are so many texts in the New Testament urging assistance, spiritual aid, mutual concern and help lest a brother or sister of the Lord fall into sin. This is also why (as we shall see shortly) that, if this unthinkable tragedy (sin) ever did occur after the definitive sin removal of baptism, the first church was at a total loss as to how to deal with it. So, for the early Christians, as for us today, baptism retains its initial and powerful place as the first forgiveness of sins. We see this primacy upheld in the new Rite of Penance, issued in 1974. In its second paragraph the decree says:

> This victory [over sin] is first brought to light in baptism where our fallen nature is crucified with Christ so that the body of sin may be destroyed. . . . For this reason the church proclaims its faith in "the one baptism for the forgiveness of sins."
>
> Furthermore, our Savior Jesus Christ, when he gave to his apostles and their successors power to forgive sins, instituted in his church the sacrament of penance. Thus the faithful who fall into sin after baptism may be reconciled with God and renewed in grace. The church "possesses both water and tears: the water of baptism, the tears of penance."[1]

After baptism we have what we can only call the premier sacrament of forgiveness, the eucharist, and even such an early theologian as Origen, who died in the third century, stressed the importance of the eucharist as the place for the forgiveness of sins, even mortal sins.[2] So there is an exceedingly long and ancient tradition, quite unbroken, behind this statement. In fact, we may rightly say that the eucharist is the *traditional* sacrament of forgiveness of postbaptismal sins. And this is as it should be. After all, the eucharist celebrates those very acts of Jesus by which we are saved. St. Paul reminds us that "Through his blood, God made him the means of expiation" (Romans 3:25) and later, "When Christ appeared as a priest of the good things that have come . . . he entered once for all into the Holy Place, taking not the blood of goats and calves, but his own blood, thus securing an eternal redemption" (Hebrews 9:11–12). St. John adds, "He is the expiation for our sins, and not only for ours only but also for the sins of the whole world" (1 John 2:2).

This redemption in his blood reached its high point in the fellowship meals which Jesus shared with sinners. It was a bold and even scandalous thing to do before the Jews of his time: to eat at table with publicans and sinners. To do so was a parable in action, telling all that the kingdom of God was a reconciling one, and it was extended to all. Jesus was anticipating that final banquet where all would be harmony and where "many will come from east and west and sit at a table with Abraham, Isaac, and Jacob in the kingdom of heaven" (Matthew 8:11).

Of course, the table-fellowship of the ministry of Jesus was not restricted to the penitent tax collectors and sinners. "These are the extreme examples of the acceptance of the challenge of the forgiveness offered in the proclamation of Jesus. . . . Scribe, tax collector, fisherman, and Zealot came together around the table at which they celebrated the joy of the present experience and anticipated its consummation in the future."[3] It was surely under the impulse of what Jesus did that the words "for the remission of sins" were early added to the Last Supper accounts. They were meant precisely to underscore the primitive insight that the eucharist is a real, expiatory sacrifice of atonement which causes the forgiveness of sins. These words, as a part of such a definite liturgical context, demonstrate the early church's understanding "of the eucharistic sacrifice as the summit and summing-up of the total ministry of Jesus."[4]

Again, it should be obvious that the celebration of the eucharist is a communal activity whereby all share in the one bread and the one cup precisely in order to be reconciled by this ancient sacrifice. As one writer sums it up, "Because of its regular use in the eucharistic celebration, the phrase 'for the remission of sins' must represent the understanding the primitive church had of the eucharistic sacrifice as the summit of the redemptive ministry which Christ continued to exercise in the assembly.... The New Testament offers us no evidence of the ritual of the sacrament of penance. [Furthermore] there is no suggestion that all that we call grave sin excluded from the eucharist and required the use of the sacrament of penance."[5]

This reference to grave sins may surprise us, but the indications are that those in what we call mortal sins approached the eucharist for forgiveness. As we shall see, the official public penance was so severe, extended over so many years and forbidden to clerics that "it is open to doubt whether ecclesiastical penance *in practice* extended much beyond notorious cases of capital sin."[6] This means that other means must have been present to remit sins, mortal but not notorious. In the absence of any reference whatsoever to any private sacrament of penance process, we may conclude that it was at the eucharist that such mortal sins were forgiven, especially as some bishops and church councils began to require that there be more frequent communion.

It seems, therefore, that "the reception of the eucharist is enough to efface all sins where no real malice is apparent" and that "at the eucharistic meal, the church is assured that in the signs of remembrance, by the power of the Holy Spirit alone, the body and blood of reconciliation are truly present to it, not merely so that the church may fittingly praise God but above all so that it may participate once and for all in reconciliation."[7] That this was a rather strong conviction is perhaps evidenced in the fact that it took the church so long—the 1215 Fourth Lateran Council—to prescribe confession of mortal sins before receiving communion.

A final indication that the eucharist forgives sins is found in the Eastern traditions. In the eucharistic prayers of the East there are freely embedded penitential rites for the forgiveness of all sins. The Coptic, Chaldean, Eastern Syriac, Nestorian, and Malabar Christians all have room in their eucharistic prayers for the forgiveness of even mortal sin without private confession.[8]

These Eastern practices do presuppose a high sense of community and a tradition of the public display of one's sinfulness. In other words, they do contain a larger communal context which made it easier and more fitting to have sins forgiven in the eucharist. Nevertheless, this tradition is there and remains so to this day.

In any case, the tradition of the forgiving nature of the eucharist was never entirely suppressed and has found itself vindicated time and time again to this very day. St. Thomas, for example, summed up that long tradition by commenting that the eucharist has the power to remit all sins and derives this power from the passion of Christ which, as he says, is the source and cause of the remission of sins.[9] Trent in the sixteenth century, for all of its canons on the sacrament of penance, could not and would not disturb the tradition which held that sins are forgiven at the eucharist. This council says that, "... the Holy Council teaches that this [Mass] is truly propitiatory and has this effect that if, contrite and penitent, with sincere heart and upright faith, with fear and reverence, we draw nigh to God, 'we obtain mercy and find grace in seasonable aid' (Hebrews 4:16). For, appeased by this sacrifice, the Lord grants the grace and gift of penitence, and pardons *even the gravest crimes and sins.*"[10]

In this our day we have six official Mass canons, some new, others very ancient like the first Roman canon. Yet we can find all through them references to what the Mass is all about: reconciliation. And this theme is presented, not accidentally, but as the whole reason for the Mass' existence. The texts are many: "You were sent to heal the contrite.... Though we are sinners, we trust in your mercy.... In mercy and love unite all your children wherever they may be.... See the victim whose death has reconciled us to yourself...." We have that prayer following the Our Father which says, "Deliver us, Lord, from every evil.... In your mercy keep us free from sin"; and before the rite of peace we pray, "Look not on our sins, but on the faith of your church." The sign of peace itself is a profoundly reconciling sign and the Lamb of God who takes away the sins of the world—repeated three times and then once more as the sacred species are held up—are perfectly clear as to the reconciling nature of the eucharist.

Significantly, even the new rite for the sacrament of penance issued in 1974 speaks in its first opening lines of the reconciliation effected in Jesus' blood: "The Father has shown his mercy by reconciling the world to himself in Christ and by making peace for all things on earth and in heaven by the blood of Christ. . . . Therefore, on the night he was betrayed and began his saving passion, he instituted the sacrifice of the new covenant in his blood for the forgiveness of sins. . . . In the sacrifice of the Mass the passion of Christ is made present; his body given for us and his blood shed for the forgiveness of sins are offered to God again by the church for the salvation of the world. In the eucharist Christ is present and is offered as 'the sacrifice which has made our peace' with God and in order that 'we may be brought together in unity' by his Holy Spirit."[11] Clearly the church is once more affirming the ancient tradition that forgiveness occurs at the eucharist even for grave sins and that the sacrament of penance is to be seen in the perspective of the eucharist.

We might mention here that our ignorance of the eucharist as the normal sacrament for the forgiveness of sin is due to the great emphasis that the sixteenth century Council of Trent put on the sacrament of penance. As we shall see, Trent did not know much of the history of reconciliation; it knew best only its own immediate experience which was the private one-to-one confession to a priest. It was this form that was being attacked by the reformers and therefore it was this form which received all the emphasis. In so defending this one particular (and late) form of reconciliation, Trent did not mean to exclude the other traditional forms, but in practice this is what happened and what we inherited. It will take a great deal of catechesis to refocus the old ways of forgiveness and place them in a fitting context for the modern Christian.

Finally, we may mention another sacrament for the forgiveness of sins and that is the sacrament of the sick. We all recall St. James' famous words which gave us this sacrament and we should recall his notation concerning the sick person that "if he has committed any sins, forgiveness will be his" (James 5:15). We should add to these sacraments the understanding and the ancient tradition that charity does cover a multitude of sins; and therefore good works, almsgiving, fasting, and prayer were used as precisely the means of having one's sins forgiven. So, naturally, with three sacraments plus Christian good works as exact and precise means for the forgiveness of sins—all attested to in unbroken scripture and tradition—then we will want to ask the obvious question: where did we get what we call the sacrament of penance and what does it add to or do in reference to the other means of forgiveness?

2

Before we tackle the origin of the sacrament of penance and trace its development to the form that we know today, some sensible and cautious words from James D. Shaughnessy are in order:

> Even the briefest study of this history produces evidence that there never was a period in the development of penance when the many and varied problems which plague this sacrament were ever solved to the satisfaction of all. It has really been a trial and error effort, without much consistency in the development of liturgical forms and practices.

> To state this is not to suggest the same is true concerning the doctrine of penance. Although there have been differing opinions about frequency, forms of absolution, satisfaction, imposition of hands and disabilities, the one consistent element in the history of penance has been in the area of doctrine. Without deviation and from the beginning the church has consistently exercised the God-given authority to forgive sins and to preside over the reconciliation of penitents, while acknowledging that God's loving forgiveness is open to those

who elicit true sorrow and purpose of conversion, admit their guilt before God and/or the church, and perform adequate satisfaction.[12]

Bearing these words in mind, we may begin our exploration.

Basically we might say that the whole origin of the sacrament of penance (not its institution by Christ, but its use by the church) is rooted in the early Christian sensitivity of community and the all encompassing fervor of a beleagured people. The first Christians were fully aware that they were a minority people. They knew themselves in time as persecuted and hunted both by their fellow Jews and by the Roman Empire. As in all tight-knit, small groups it was necessary to pursue two goals: (1) to keep the initial vision (Christ) intact, and (2) come to terms with those open and public scandals which might undo all that the small community stood for. As for the first—to maintain the vision—we see the constant horror of heresy, the constant hammering away at any deviation. "For even if we, or an angel from heaven, should preach to you a gospel not in accord with the one we delivered to you, let a curse be upon him!" (Galatians 1:8). So exclaimed St. Paul. As for the second, we see the anxiety to keep the community pure and well-advertised as such in the way the first church dealt with public, scandalous sin. All sin, of course, could be forgiven, but some sins were construed to be so scandalous, such bad publicity, that they were considered incompatible with what Christianity was about. The early church seemed to entertain some doubts about its power to forgive such sins, and even if it decided that it could it was unwilling to do so. It would not compromise the high ideals of the faith.

But let us go back and trace this development. The first communities of Christians were so profoundly convinced of the once-and-for-all conversion and forgiveness in baptism that they could not imagine anyone sinning scandalously again after it. One was converted to holiness. Serious public sin after baptism was not envisaged. The early Christians, in this regard, were like our Puritan forefathers who came to America to establish a new paradise, another Eden where there would be no evil. That is why, according to Nathaniel Hawthorne, the Puritans were reluctant to build prisons and cemeteries, for a place of total grace would obviously have no place for either. The names of New Hope, New Haven, Providence, and Salem (short for Jerusalem) were indications of their expectations. So it was to some degree with the first Christians. When the church went out to preach the forgiveness of sins, it had in mind non-Christians, not themselves. In fact, some commentators say that those Easter night words of Jesus, "Receive the Holy Spirit, whose sins you shall forgive. . ." refer to *baptismal* forgiveness. It did not cross the mind of the early church to announce such a message to those already cleansed in baptism. Since this was so, then the church provided no way for the forgiveness of sins after baptism, and indeed nowhere in the New Testament do we find any account of the reconciliation of a sinner with the community.

Still, for all of this high idealism, for all of the expectation that one who was deeply converted in baptism had therefore forsaken all sin for the rest of his life—still, the facts of life set in. Like the first Puritans of America who consciously modeled their towns after the New Testament communities, the first New Testament communities were to feel shock as they discovered sin. Baptized Christians actually committed open, public, scandalous sins. Some went back to their old pagan ways, some during persecution time denied the faith. Of these, some repented and wanted to return to the church, but now the church was at a loss as to how to deal with these public sins. One fleeting possibility was argued over and then dismissed forever: rebaptism. There was a special reasoning behind this. Baptism was an incorporation into a believing community which took a person into its midst and promised to give all the support needed to grow in the life of Christ. The community therefore felt that in so pledging itself it was reflecting the fidelity of God himself—and how could God's fidelity, by its very definition, ever falter?

This is why the Christian community could not bring itself to rebaptize. God's fidelity would stand, no matter what. Man could be unfaithful to God, but God was constitutionally incapable of being unfaithful to man. A sinner after baptism would have to do something—the early church was not sure just what—but the church, reflecting God's fidelity, could not rebaptize him. It could not indicate in the slightest that God had slacked his love and was now restoring it. So, since the church would not and could not rebaptize and was not sure that it had the power to forgive the more open, public sins, it hit on the last resort which was to last almost a hundred years: throw the public sinner out of the church!

This was the answer for the time being. If public sinners could not live up to the total conversion made at their baptisms, when their past sins were forgiven, then they could not stay in the church. They were, in the strong words of St. Paul, "handed over to Satan" (1 Corinthians 5:1-15); that is, they were excommunicated. Paul was unrelenting. To Titus he wrote, "As for a man who is factious, after admonishing him once or twice, have nothing to do with him, knowing that such a person is perverted and sinful; he is self-condemned" (Titus 3:10). To Timothy he wrote, "By rejecting conscience, certain persons have made shipwreck of their faith . . . whom I delivered to Satan that they may learn not to blaspheme." (1 Timothy 19). To the Corinthians he wrote, "Though absent in body, I am present in spirit and as if present I have already pronounced judgment in the name of the Lord Jesus on the man who has done such a thing. When you are assembled and my spirit is present with the power of the Lord Jesus, you are to deliver this man to Satan for the destruction of the flesh that his spirit might be saved in the day of the Lord Jesus" (1 Corinthians 5: 1-5). These "deliverances to Satan" were standard terms for excommunication. The idea is that once the protection of the church is withdrawn from the sinner, he will find himself exposed without defense to Satan, the author of all evil and hurt.

In deference to Paul, we should note that he is not inventing a totally new idea. The same notion is found in the gospels, although these words, according to some commentators, may well reflect the primitive Jewish Christian community. Read Matthew 18 and you will find these words, "If your brother should commit some wrong against you, go and point out his fault, but keep it between the two of you. If he listens to you, you have won your brother over. If he does not listen, summon another, so that every case may stand on the word of two or three witnesses. If he ignores them, refer it to the church. If he ignores even the church, then treat him as you would a Gentile or a tax collector" (Matthew 18:15). We know that Gentiles and tax collectors were the outcasts of the time. They were not even spoken to, and they were separated from the faithful. We may detect this same notion of segregation in the famous Easter night scene where Jesus not only says that the church can forgive sins, but also retain them. This may be a sign that the church can retain or cast out serious sinners, can excommunicate them.

It seems, therefore, that from the New Testament evidence the first Christians arrived at the solution to deal with serious and scandalous sins committed after baptism: and that solution was excommunication. They could not overcome the deep conviction that baptism was total commitment and holiness. In their minds, there was nothing to do for such public sinners but cast them out and commend them "to the mercy of God," in the phrase of the day. And all of those prayers for sinners we find in the early liturgies are not for non-Christians. They are precisely for such former Christians for whom there is no hope now, except in fact that mercy for which they are praying. Perhaps to help us moderns to appreciate this mentality better, we might recall the religious case that was brought to civil court in 1975. It seems that among the Reformed Mennonite church in Pennsylvania, a very strict group with mentalities much like the first Christians, a certain Robert Bear was excommunicated in 1972 for questioning the authority and infallibility of the church's hierarchy. Therefore, since this was a public and scandalous outburst, members were commanded to shun him (shunning is the technical term for excommunication). This included his wife who, as a believer refused to sleep with him or eat with him. She, like her church, was relying on Paul again and quoted him. Paul said, "What I really write about was your not associating with anyone who bears the title 'brother,' if he is covetous, an idolater, an abusive person, a drunkard, or a thief. It is clear that you must not eat with such a man" (1 Corinthians 5:11). Then, to bolster his own stricture, Paul quoted from the Old Testament where it says, "Expel the wicked man from your midst" (Deuteronomy 13:6). Sins, light and serious, could be forgiven in the normal ways of eucharist and good works. But there was as yet no sacrament of penance to deal with open scandalous ones that brought the community into disrepute. In relationship to such scandalous sins it was an either-or situation: baptismal holiness or excommunication.[13]

NOTES FOR CHAPTER 11

1. The Rite of Penance, no. 2. The "water and tears" phrase comes from St. Ambrose.

2. 9 De Oratione, 28, PG, 11, cols. 528–9.

3. Norman Perrin, Rediscovering the Teaching of Jesus (Harper and Row, 1967), p. 107.

4. Jerome Murphy-O'Connor, O.P., "Sin and Community in the New Testament," in The Mystery of Sin and Forgiveness (Alba House, 1970), p. 56.

5. John J. Quinn, "The Lord's Supper and Forgiveness of Sin," Worship 42, no. 5.

6. Karl Rahner, quoted in Jose Ramos-Regidor, "Reconciliation in the Primitive Church and Its Lessons for Theology Today and Pastoral Practice Today," Concilium 61 (Herder and Herder, 1971), p. 79.

7. Jean-Marie Tillard, O.P., "The Bread and the Cup of Reconciliation," Concilium 61 (Herder and Herder, 1971), p. 41 and 52.

8. Ibid., p. 70.

9. Summa Theologica, Tertia pars, 79Q, 3rd article.

10. The Council of Trent, 22nd session. Denz. 940.

11. The Rite of Penance, nos. 1 and 2.

12. James D. Shaughnessy, in Celebration Supplement (May 1976).

13. We must recall that in these chapters on penance we are describing what we know, not what we don't. There indeed may have been some exercise of the sacrament of penance beyond the baptism and the eucharist, but the records of such are nonexistent in the period treated in this chapter, and scholars like C. Vogel hold the opinion that during the patristic period in the West there is no evidence of private sacramental penance (outside of the deathbed conversion). However, we should recall that there may be valid reasons for this. Only adults were baptized, and they were frequently baptized near the end of their lives and even on their deathbeds or only after a long and strenuous catechumenate impressed on them the finality and irreversibility of genuine conversion to Christ. Under such circumstances any sacrament of penance would be minimal and in little use. Old age, death, or solid, mature conversion would make such a sacrament virtually "useless." At the very least there would be little cause to write about it.

12

The Sacrament of Penance

1

No solution was forthcoming for the either-or problem we discussed in the last chapter until around the year 150. Obviously
the problem was on the church's collective mind and in that year
there was a document written by a man called Hermas who was
perhaps the brother of Pope Pius I. This is a rather romantic,
allegorical work treating ethical and moral questions. Among
the questions the document tries to come to terms with is the
knotty problem of remitting public, serious sins committed after
baptism. One of the visions goes like this:

> ... I have heard sir, said I, from some teachers, that there is
> no second repentance beyond the one given when we went
> down into the water (into baptism) and received remission of
> our former sins. He said to me, "You have heard correctly, for
> that is so. For he who has received remission of sin ought
> never to sin again, but to live in purity. [The standard thrust
> from Paul on.] But since you ask accurately concerning all
> things, I will explain this also to you, without giving an excuse
> to those who in the future shall believe. [Now, the departure
> from the standard teaching.]... The Lord knows the heart,
> and knowing all things beforehand, he knew the weakness of
> man and the sublety of the devil.... The Lord, therefore,
> being merciful, had mercy on his creation, and established this
> repentance: and to me was the control of this repentance giv-
> en. But I tell you that after that great and holy calling, if a
> man be tempted by the devil and sin, he has one repentance;

but if he sin repeatedly, it is unprofitable for such a man, for scarcely shall he live...."[1]

This is the first indication we have of some modification of the former once-and-for-all rigoristic baptismal forgiveness. It is a cautious teaching which says that postbaptismal sins may be forgiven, but once only. The early writer, Tertullian, confirms this unique second chance for public sin. "[The devil's] poisons are foreseen by God, and although the gate of repentance has already been closed and barred by baptism, he permits it to stand open a little. In the vestibule he has stationed a second repentance which he makes available to those who knock—but only once, because further were in vain."[2] Tertullian also speaks of the "one plank" left to the "drowning sinner." So we have here the first signs of another way besides baptism to have public, scandalous sins forgiven and this is very significant. This thought alone will be the foundation of the canonical penance system that will soon emerge. The second-century Christian could not only confess one baptism for the remission of sins, but also one other way as well. If this way was used up, then once more the sinner was simply and helplessly handed over "to the mercy of God."

We might mention that there was still some debate as to what constituted serious, public, scandalous sins but there were three sins which were definitely excluded from this second chance: the famous triad of murder, adultery, and apostasy. They were considered so destructive of community and so scandalous that in practice they were not felt to be forgivable at any time. However, in time even these three infamous sins could be forgiven—but still only once. However, note in all this the relation of penance to baptism. It was sometimes called a second baptism. Remember what we saw: baptism is the sacrament of conversion. If one for some reason failed that deep a conversion, penance was introduced to regain it. Penance is designed here towards the reinvigoration of baptism and therefore has an intimate connection with it.

Now something else began to develop which the Shepherd of

Hermas and Tertullian prepared the way for. A long period of preparation before this second repentance was introduced. In other words, just as we have seen that the early church elaborated a long catechumenate for the "first" forgiveness in baptism, so now a similar kind of catechumenate was begun for this "second" baptism of forgiveness. A penitential system was evolved, a long series of stages, lasting for years and even lifetimes before one was admitted to the eucharist again. (When this admission did occur, there were no formal "words of absolution"; just an invitation by the community or the bishop to rejoin them at the eucharist.) Moreover, just as one needed a sponsor for baptism, so sinners needed a sponsor in the members of the community who would work with them in a program of penance. In this sense, the first "confessors" were those who witnessed the sinners' sincere repentance and who worked with, fasted with, and prayed with them. In a word, it was the baptismal catechumenate all over again in penitential dress and the minimum time was a period of seven years. We might note that the old hesitancy remained about the triad because apostasy would not be given a second chance for forgiveness until the deathbed. We must add one more point. Because the penances were so terribly long (maybe a lifetime) and so severe, this system could really only include the more public sins, those sins which caused a man or woman to forego all family and economic life in his or her pursuit of penance (their spouses kept from the marriage bed and the community supported him or her with alms during this time). Further, this system *had* to include only very open and scandalous sins, not what we would call mortal sins in later centuries. It would not be practical to include them in the system of one-time public penance. Besides there was certainly no desire on the part of the community to have public penance a common occurrence and so admit to the existence of a large number of bad Christians. In fact, the existence, much less the use, of such a public system was considered an embarrassment, a misfortune. And that is why it was limited to a one-time use, why it was rare. The dignity and integrity of the church demanded that it be so.

What we are talking about here is the system known as canonical penance. It went in four stages. On the part of the sinner there was (1) an interior admission of sinfulness; (2) recourse to a community authority such as the bishop and perhaps even privately telling him one's sins. The result of this encounter was to be enrolled in a kind of "order of penitents." The bishop would lay his hands on the penitent. Then the penitent might dress in sackcloth or by some similar public gesture show that he was now a member of that group of public penitents; (3) there would be a long period of doing penance, and then (4) finally reconciliation by the bishop usually on Holy Thursday at the eucharist by the imposition of hands.

It is also interesting to observe that this canonical penance system was not something imposed from above. It seems to have arisen from the natural instincts of the people themselves who wanted a concrete and palpable experience of being contrite and converted. Now, this canonical form of penance, public and severe, was the only one available. There was no private form that is officially recognized—although it in fact may have been occurring. We know that St. John Chrysostom of the fourth century was having something like private penance, and he was roundly condemned for it, as were Pope Calixtus I who was lenient in declaring certain sexual sins as forgivable and Pope Cornelius who extended the range even more.

We might mention that such "leniency" as readmitting those who had denied the faith under persecution and admitting to canonical penance Christians guilty of grave and scandalous faults caused severe schisms in the third century in Africa and Rome. The schismatics professed to be scandalized at such softness. Tertullian, whom we have mentioned frequently, joined the rigorist Montanist sect and bitterly condemned the practice of pardoning the alleged sexual sins of a highly placed bishop. The Novatian schism was also rigorist, breaking over the readmission of apostates. Again it wasn't that they said these sins were unforgivable, but they denied that the church had the power to do so or disputed the "soft" policy that it *should* do so.

In any case, we note once more in this public canonical penance, the stress on doing penance and the emphatic role of the community. St. Jerome tells us of an aristocratic lady named Fabiola who went through this public canonical penance system. He says:

> On the day before the Pasch, when the whole city was looking on, Fabiola took her place in the ranks of the penitents, with disheveled hair, a ghastly countenance, soiled hands and sordid neck. She prostrated herself before the bishop, the presbyters, and all the people, as they wept along with her. . . . She laid bare to all her wound, and a Rome in tears beheld a livid scar on her flesh. The sides of her garment were unfastened, her head was bared, her lips tightly drawn. She did not enter the church of the Lord, but like Miriam, the sister of Moses, she sat apart, outside the camp, in order that the priest who had cast her forth might personally call her back again.[3]

This lady certainly worked out her penance in public before the community. And the community did support her in the process. It was common enough for bishops to urge their congregations to share the penances of these people and give them every encouragement lest they give up along the way. Prayers inside the church were offered for Fabiola and others, and the congregation and the clergy did themselves undergo some mortifications to obtain the graces needed for those outside the doors, in sackcloth and ashes, to hold fast. In fact, the community often appealed to the bishop to receive a public penitent back prematurely because of the obvious sincerity of his or her sorrow and penances.

Such was the public canonical penance. It obviously depended on a high community spirit and motivation. When these characteristics waned, so did this system.

2

Because of the long term penitential exercises and the severity of the penances and the one-time chance at it, two things happened in the history of canonical penance. One was that very few people would ever use it for fear of never having another opportunity for forgiveness. We know, for example, that the Emperor Constantine did not have himself baptized until his death so as to avoid the public penance system. St. Monica did not have Augustine baptized even though sick, and several Fathers of the church were not baptized until their twenties. Ambrose was unbaptized when at thirty-four he was chosen bishop of Milan. People did not want to use up baptism and, for the same reason, did not want to use up a one-shot public penance. Some councils of the church as well as pastoral bishops such as Ambrose urged adolescents not to receive this penance until their youthful sins had run their course.

The second thing that happened flows from the first. Public penance became a deathbed affair. The deathbed, always an emergency situation, was more attractive as the place to ask for this second repentance. It at least preempted the long severe penances, not to mention any more opportunities for further sinning. In any case, this was obviously not a satisfactory state of affairs. A better answer had to be devised because in fact the public canonical system was withering away from nonuse.

The answer would come from the islands: England, Scotland, and especially Ireland. There was an old pagan custom in Ireland whereby one had a friend who read his heart, so to speak. He was counselor, advisor—what we might call today, his guru. Now it was natural that this custom would pass over into Christianity, which it perhaps did as early as the fourth and fifth centuries. The transition was easy because Christianity came to Ireland in its monastic form. There was no organizational structure such as there was on the mainland. There abbot, monks, and people formed a rather close, family-like relationship. Moreover the monasteries represented a whole penitential way of life. The monks were more alert to sin and its effects. The penitential spirit which characterized their striving for a fuller spiritual life developed into the form of spiritual direction. Monks would talk things over with the other monks who were not priests. They examined the life of the penitent, as we might call him, discerned patterns, discovered sin, and the advisors gave reassurance that such sins were indeed forgiven by the great mercy of God. Thus assured both penitent and advisor prayed together and praised God together for his great goodness.

These "lay confessions" were enacted in the cases of venial sins and even of those grave sins which in different eras of history were considered as privately forgivable. That is why, later on, St. Thomas Aquinas would refer to such lay confessions as "quasi sacraments." However, in the case of public sins there was that old sense of community and the need to be reconciled with it. So arose the need for a legitimately appointed representative of the church to reconcile one to the church and pronounce God's releasing word in the church's name. Here was born the priest confessor and sacramental absolution. The priestly office provided an "official" ecclesial sign of community reconciliation which the private lay confessions did not.

So the Irish monks, especially noted names like Finian of Clonard and Columbanus, used this system and they make it clear in their writings that it was not confined to the monks. It was available to students who flocked to the monasteries for higher studies and other laity. Moreover, we note that there was no special liturgy, no public act of reconciliation and no recourse to the church's official leader, the bishop. It was Columbanus, by the way, who was chiefly responsible for bringing this type of penance to the continent. People flocked to the monasteries which became centers of spirituality and accepted the Irish penitential procedures.

What we have been describing is the origins of the one-to-one private confession as we know it. It was repeated and repeatable. Now at last we have a second, distinct tradition growing up unofficially beside the official public penance system. Officially, the church recognized only the latter and the bishops used it; but the average person opted for the former and went to the priests, not the bishops, for it. When the Irish monks went to the mainland to evangelize it, they brought this private, auricular system with them and so swiftly did it spread that by the year 813 the public, canonical system was almost gone and frequent confessions, as we may now call it, was urged by no less than the great St. Boniface.

This new private system had pros and cons, some of which we will explore in more detail in the next chapter. Right now we might mention on the positive side that this type of confession was private and repeatable. Now at last the old problem of sins after baptism was solved. We had a sacrament of penance. Secondly, it opened the way to keep the best of the old tradition and lead into a new. By this we mean that it started out in the nature of discernment and praise. There were no declarative words of absolution; there were instead beautiful petitional prayers. The whole event was in the nature of liturgy and praise: praising God for his unspeakable mercy, giving him thanks for his goodness.

On the negative side, we might mention that, realistically, a system of private penance could only grow and flourish where a deep sense of community had been lost and that what worked well in a monastery would have ill effects apart from it. That is, whereas the monks blended the practice and virtue of penance with the sacrament, later ages, outside the monastery, would not keep this pattern and eventually the sacrament would substitute for the virtue. We would have the beginning of a mere "Jesus-and-I" relationship instead of community sensitivity.

Then there developed the penitential books. In themselves they were remarkable. They were the product of those monks who were better at the discernment and confessing process than others. They began to write penitential books for the guidance of other confessors—the first Irish penitential book being written by Theodore, Archbishop of Canterbury, in 680. On one side of the page in these books was the sin, the crime and on the opposite side was the penalty or "tariff" designed to fit the crime (hence the term "tariff system" to describe this era). Here's an example about the sin of gluttony from one of these penitential books: "He who suffers excessive distention of the stomach and the pain of satiety shall do penance for one day. If he suffers to the point of vomiting, though he is not in a state of infirmity, he shall do penance for seven days." The tariffs imposed were scarcely more benign than the old penances of the first Christians. They were harsh, severe, and long-termed.

These penitential books with their tariffs were all right in themselves. Their basic idea went awry, however, when the notion of commutation was introduced. People got someone to substitute for them. This probably started out as a case of emergency—the penitent who was ill or near death who got someone to do his tariff for him—and then became almost the standard. Likewise other penalties substituted for the original ones, and soon the arithmetic and casuistry took over. Here are two examples of what substitution and commutation could do:

One year of fasting can be commuted to 3,000 lashes
But ten psalms can be recited while inflicting 1,000 lashes
Therefore 30 psalms can be recited while inflicting 3,000 lashes
Therefore one year of fasting = 30 psalms
Therefore five years of fasting = 15,000 lashes = one recitation of the Psalter.

This one is from a tenth-century Anglo-Saxon book showing how a seven year penance could be carried out in three days:

The penitent will pay twelve men to fast three days for him on bread, water, and vegetables.
Then he will get 7×120 men to fast three days.
The total of $(12 \times 3) + (120 \times 7 \times 3) = 2,556$ days = 7 years.

It takes little imagination to see that such a commutation system favors the rich who could afford substitutes. The penitential pilgrimage, so popular during the late Middle Ages often caused more scandal than piety. Still, for all of this, the private, repeatable confessions gained steady ground while the official church shunned it. The first reference we have to the private penance is from the Council of Toledo in 589 which condemns it and gives off a peculiarly modern criticism: "We have discovered that in certain Spanish churches people are using a form of penance contrary to the canonical institution [public canonical system]. In a disgusting manner, any time they take it into their heads to sin, off they go to a priest to get absolution." Nevertheless, for all of the official fulmination, this form of private confession was so successful that by the Fourth Lateran Council in 1215 it was decreed that every Christian who reached the age of discernment must receive *private*—not public communal—confession once a year.

We are also at the point to see why, with the other sacraments plus good works being able to forgive sin, we have inherited one tradition in preference to these others. The answer is that in the twelfth century Peter Lombard, as we have noted before, defined (narrowly) the sacraments as seven. He listed as number four the sacrament of penance—which is to say, the private, repeatable sacrament that he knew. The result is that his seven-fold division stuck and the emphasis endured that this fourth sacrament was *the* place for forgiveness.

It is no surprise therefore that the old formula "ego te absolvo. . ." is found for the first time in the twelfth century and will be defended in the next century by St. Thomas Aquinas as the one valid one. The whole weight of the sacrament shifted to the absolution, an emphasis which did not exist for a thousand years where the emphasis was on the acts of penance and the reconciliation at the eucharist by the bishop. What the bishop or any other church minister did was not defined and had no special theology to it beyond any other element. The great scholastic teacher Duns Scotus who, like other scholastics, was looking for some matter and form to this "new" sacrament added his influence with his insistence on the words of absolution as the form and therefore necessary for validity. So true was this, it was held, that a penitent could approach the priest with even "imperfect" contrition, and this coupled with the priest's absolution would effect the forgiveness of even his mortal sins. That's how power-

ful those words came to be. The absolution, in the popular mind,
became the "essence" of the sacrament. This is the theology
which Trent inherited.

3

In the sixteenth century the Council of Trent further consecrated the sevenfold sacramental system and decreed this sacrament of penance as the sacrament of forgiveness of sins. It
went even further. In reaction to the reformers' attacks, it
specified certain demands concerning this sacrament. First, it
said that there must be what is called an integral confession; that
is, people must confess all mortal sins as to number, kind, and
determining circumstance. Moreover, Trent said that this is
what God revealed; it is of divine law. While there is a certain
logic to the integral confession, Trent perhaps said too much.
For one thing the integral confession was not at all a part of
Christian tradition up until then and is not so today in the East.
People always had to be sorry at the time they confessed their
sins: sometimes specifically, sometimes in general. That "divine
law" demanded on each and every occasion number, kind, and
circumstance was saying too much—and in fact, Trent did not
demand that this apply to each and every confession although
it did not specify exactly when it did apply.
    Secondly, Trent made it necessary to have a form of absolu-
tion and one that was declarative, representing the judicial nature of the sacrament. But, again, this was not accurate. In the
past the forms were words of praise, liturgical expressions of
petition and thankfulness for God's mercy. In fact, as we have
seen, there were no words of absolution in former centuries.
Merely a return to the eucharist. And, moreover, the sacrament
of penance was not basically a judicial judgement; it was an
ongoing process of conversion, a discernment, a growth. Finally,
Trent said that confessions must be made to an authorized
priest. Again, we must remember the origins of the kind of
confessions Trent is talking about. It started, we recall with

monks praying with other monks who were not necessarily priests. Even in scripture no mention is made that the confession of one's sins must be made to a minister of the church, only to one's "brother."

After Trent, a whole literature was devoted to the question of which confessions were necessary and which were considered merely devotional. Private confessions developed into the high art of spiritual direction as they originally started out. There was constant, ongoing dialogue over many years between penitent and his pastor or spiritual director and we read of many lives of the saints in the seventeenth to nineteenth centuries which were nourished by this penitential direction. What caused the collapse of this practice was the breakdown of the small parish and the growth of large, urban or suburban parishes of modern times. Personal knowledge, time, and opportunity with one's pastor were no longer feasible. So confession receded as the place of spiritual direction; it was shortened and all that was left was a stranger, meeting anonymously with some unknown priest in a dark box anxious only to get absolution. This is what has broken down in our times and has been the cause of the revision of the rites.[4]

We must now close with a word about how penance became an intruder among the sacraments of initiation. This happened when, as we have seen, the elements of the initiation rite were rearranged; that is, when confirmation and the eucharist were separated from the water-baptism. Eventually, confirmation (in the West) settled somewhere near the age of puberty. The eucharist moved along a wide variety of ages until it was decided to be given at the age of seven by Pius X in 1910. Meanwhile as we have just examined, penance was in no particular place in its development throughout the centuries. But two things we do know: penance was in no way originally connected with the three sacrament initiation system and that in no way was it connected with children. Yet, in our time, it is connected with both: it is customarily received before communion and children were required to receive it before their first communion. Thus, until very recently, the order of the sacraments was: baptism, penance, communion, and confirmation instead of the original way we learned them in our catechism: baptism, confirmation, eucharist, penance. What happened? How did this sacrament manage to intrude itself into the broken-down initiation rite?

First of all, the association of penance with the eucharist probably was established in that famous decree of the Fourth Lateran Council of 1215. During this era, participation in the sacraments was at a very low ebb and the bishops here and there had noted with dismay that the people were not receiving communion even on Holy Thursday, the "birthday" of the eucharist. Yet they wanted all to receive communion often unless, of course, prevented by serious sin. So the Fourth Lateran Council promulgated this decree:

> All the faithful of either sex shall, after attaining years of discretion, faithfully confess their sins to their own priest, at least once a year, and shall, according to capacity, perform the penance imposed on them; they shall also reverently receive the sacrament of holy eucharist at least at Easter, unless on the advice of their own priest, for some reasonable cause, they defer doing so for a time.

Since this council had mentioned the two sacraments side by side, the connection was made. Both in theory and in practice penance intruded itself before communion. The Council of Trent in the sixteenth century tried to dispel any necessary connection between the two sacraments but was not successful.

Meanwhile, there was a wide span concerning the age in which people started receiving the eucharist, and the "years of discretion" mentioned at the Lateran Council was officially interpreted as seven—showing the strong influence of the Roman law of the Emperor Justinian—but in practice ran the range from twelve to fifteen. Likewise, in an independent development, the sacrament of penance was never a part of children's lives. We have absolutely no unambiguous evidence of children ever going to confession or being absolved before puberty for the first twelve hundred years of the church's history. However, with this "years of discretion" debate, sooner or later the two sacraments would meet. The reasoning would be that if one were "discretionary" enough to receive the one sacrament, then, automatically, he was discretionary enough to receive the other. This actually happened with Pope Pius X's decree of 1910. He was reacting to the late age of the first reception of communion, especially to the rigorist Jansenist heresy which had pushed the age to twelve or more. Pius X settled the age for first eucharist at seven. He further stated that the reception of communion is in no way dependent on confession. The only connection is an accidental one: should the person be in mortal sin, he would first be obliged to confess. With no mortal sin, even the accidental connection is removed. A child of seven could not commit mortal sin and therefore did not need confession beforehand. Nevertheless, in practice the sacraments were joined, and the average Catholic was raised on the assumption that every child would first confess before receiving his first communion. Again, the fact is that this is not required even in the church's canon law—although the child, if he requests penance, cannot be denied it.

In any case, penance became, quite by accident, an "intrusion" in the fractured initiation rite. Moreover, its own development ran the gamut of emphases throughout the centuries: from "penance" pointing up the external works as a sign of sincerity (early stage), to "confession," stressing a repeatable, private, one-to-one encounter (medieval stage), to "absolution" representing a more juridical exchange between two anonymous people alone in the dark (post-Trent stage to modern times). Because each one of these terms described but one partial aspect of the whole conversion act, a new word has been revived in our day: reconciliation. The new rites of penance are geared to stress this word, not as a one-time act, but as a lifetime process.

NOTES FOR CHAPTER 12

1. Quoted in *Moral Teaching in the Primitive Church* by Francis X. Murphy, C.S.S.R. (Paulist Press, 1968).

2. Quoted in *The Faith of Our Early Fathers* by William A. Jurgens (Liturgical Press, 1970), p. 130.

3. Quoted in "The New Rite of Penance" by Doris Donnelly, *Sign* (April 1976), p. 20. For a fuller background on this lady, as well as a fascinating insight into St. Jerome himself, see *Jerome* by J.N.D. Kelly (Harper and Row, 1976).

4. Actually, spiritual direction is not necessarily associated with the sacrament of reconciliation (penance). In the first centuries where the Christian communities were quite small, the local bishop could give spiritual guidance to the whole congregation in his Sunday homilies. Later, as membership grew, the priests simply followed the general pattern of their bishops. It was the rise of monasticism that brought individual personal spiritual direction to the fore and it was therefore the monks who gradually connected it with the new private penance. The parish priests were not prepared to do so and so they gladly turned the people over to the monks. Hence the tradition and reputation (to this day) of the religious as spiritual directors. Venerable Bede's *History of the English Church and People* is replete with examples of such spiritual director monks. After the thirteenth century people tended to go beyond the monks for spiritual guidance. Thus was ushered in the great lay mystics, men and women, to whom the people flocked. This is the age of Thomas a Kempis, Meister Eckhart, Henry Suso, Richard Rolle, Juliana of Norwich, Walter Hilton and the anonymous author of the famous *Cloud of Unknowing*. Note that the parish priests were still not involved even in the sacrament of reconciliation, although around the time of the Reformation and the Council of Trent they were urged to undertake spiritual direction in connection with this sacrament. Canon law added its force (canons 886–888) but with little success. Today's new rite once more encourages parish priests to take up this task within the comfortable context of the revision. (This summary is indebted to Rev. Gordon E. Truitt).

13

Penance and Process

1

We have sketched the development of the sacrament of reconciliation from public, community penance to private, interior confession. The words "penance" and "confession" are significant because they pinpoint the emphasis of the centuries. At one time the weight was on proving one's sincerity, healing the community, and so doing penances. At another time the weight was on individual sorrow and personal self-accusation and so this accusation, this confessing, became important, especially when the number, kind, and circumstances of mortal sin were demanded. But in this development from penance to confession something was lost. We hinted at this in the last chapter. Now we must take time to explore the matter further.

First we might recall that the emphasis on doing penance was squarely based on the early concept of community. We saw how baptism was such a definitive step into that community of Christian believers. We saw further how the community was not passive at baptism, but promised its fidelity, its assistance, its support, its very name and honor to the newly baptized candidate. This fidelity, we saw, was at the heart of the refusal to ever rebaptize. How could God renege his gracious love represented by an outreaching community? Man could deny God but God could not deny him. Hence no rebaptism, no second act of love from a God who could and would never recall his first act. Therefore we saw that public penance derived from community

cohesion. Those sins which were openly scandalous and detract-
ing to the Christian community demanded repentance. More.
They demanded sorrow demonstrated by a long and arduous
process called penance. In other words, a strong sense of community necessarily evoked a strong sense of the social concept of
sin. A close-knit fervent church had no choice but to confront a
public sinner in its midst. This is why the community which
called the sinner to task prayed, fasted, and felt responsibility for
him as he went through his public penance. There was no
thought in the early church that the Christian sinner would ever
work out things by himself or herself. Hardly. No more than the
ear could say that it did not recognize the eye (1 Corinthians 12).
Public canonical penance was rare, an embarrassment, but obviously deeply rooted in a sense of community cohesion.

But this public canonical penance was superseded by the private Irish confession. We might observe now that, as much as
anything else, such a development could take place only within a
weakened sense of community. In other words, once a confront-
ing and sensitive community disappeared, once a sense of community identity and cohesion was lost, then the only realm left
was the personal, the private conscience. Slowly, all of the social
aspects of sin and repentance dried up. The emphasis grew
towards the individual, and all of the remaining official community aspects of confrontation and support fell on the priest. He it
was who gave absolution, removed guilt, and reentered the penitent into the community in a private, secret ritual.

The implications of this sort of process is that the sacrament of
penance has little social relevance but caters rather to the individual inner conscience. Matters of the world and politics and
justice would get submerged in the private conflicts within a
person, especially in the sexual area. A self-centered morality
would grow, and eventually going to confession really meant a
form of reconciliation with *one's self*, relieving one's personal
guilt—not, as the old public penances implied, reconciliation
with one's brother. Nor was there much emphasis on God himself as a most reconciling Father who in many ways, in a variety
of situations throughout history, reached out to man:

A useful contrast is provided by a glance at the Baltimore Catechism No. 2, in which the character of the sacrament as a manifestation of God's love and mercy is virtually swallowed up by concern over making a "good," i.e., technically correct, confession. The Catechism has fifty-five questions on the sacrament of penance, only one of which remotely touches on the history of salvation and then only by reference to Christ's institution of the sacrament. None of the other signs (usually more vivid and appealing) by which God throughout history has manifested his love for sinners is mentioned at all. Of the fifty-five questions, forty-five are concerned with the acts of the penitent in the confessional or immediately before or after the confession.[1]

The net result of all this self-interest has been the sudden and painful recognition in the last fifteen years of how poorly developed the Catholic social conscience was and how unprepared Catholics were, as a people, to take issue with racism, hunger, and justice.

A second development is also evident from the shift from public penance to private confession. The confessional box became, with all due reverence, a cheap way of forgiveness. This is to say, that the whole sacrament was wrenched from the *process*. Going to confession replaced *doing* penance; it became a one-shot encounter which often substituted for the virtue of doing penance all the time. It preempted all those other ancient and necessary steps of reconciliation with one's brother, works of charity, prayer, fasting, and all the other aspects of true repentance. The monks in their monasteries who started the private confession did not have this problem. The monastic life by its very nature presented a penitential life in its entirety. The monks were alert to sin and its effects. They invented their "chapter of faults" by which they openly admitted their sins and their failure to be less than perfect. Their spiritual direction which promoted the sacrament of penance was well within a context of an ongoing process of repentance. The trouble came when the monks took this contextualized process and introduced it to the outside world. There, apart from the rhythms of penitence and good works, apart from the overall pattern of spiritual growth, the sacrament of penance tended to become an isolated ritual. Soon, what was in reality an exceptional sacrament designed to be a high point of a lifetime of spiritual striving and reconciliation became the norm, especially through the work of the medieval scholastics in their endless search for the "essence" of the sacrament and its matter and form. The sacramental ritual replaced the virtue. It became an easy and quick and repeatable way of remitting sins and so a substitute for prayers, fasting, almsgiving, charities, and the whole complex of actions that formed the context of Christian reconciliation. In the monastery what was a built-in "penitential catechumenate" was simply not there in external society.

Finally, since external society did not make the connection between the practice of the virtue of penance and the sacrament as did the monks, there increased the notion of a double standard. The monks and the clergy and other religious were thought to have a particular and special road to heaven. They were not permitted public penance, as we have seen, and the penalties and penances were different for them. These distinctions, plus the monastic penitential life in general, fostered the idea that two types of morality existed: the maximum for the religious and the minimum for the laity. All in all, the rise of private confession and its subsequent development into a kind of personal self-affirmation has proven to be so narrow that we have seen its collapse in our day; and even though some scholars think that the Irish monks had in mind to revive the sacrament of penance itself and did not intend its subsequent direction[2] nevertheless its lack of communal dimensions has brought it to a state of nonuse today.

2

In an effort to restore some balance, the church promulgated a new Rite of Penance in December of 1973. However, before we examine this New Order we must take time here to mention that its success or lack of it will depend heavily on two factors: (1) context and (2) community. First, context. Any new ritual will have to be rescued from isolation and prevented from the reductionism of its predecessors. The sacrament of penance must be diffused within the virtue of penance. Preachers and teachers will have to emphasize the sacrament of the new rite as but one experience in the ongoing process of conversion. There must be a return to the catechesis that puts into perspective some of the traditions we have mentioned before. For instance, there must be a renewed interest in the eucharist as the place of forgiveness. These days some are less happy with the term mortal sin and are looking for a term that will cover matters not so light as to be classified as venial and not so final and determinate as to be called mortal (deadly, killing any relationship between God and self). They often refer to these "serious" venial sins as grave. Surely the eucharist would forgive all venial sins and even these grave sins. The eucharist should be the first thought instead of confession which is so fixed in the popular mind, especially since Pius X moved the communion age to seven and the confession-communion connection has been difficult to dislodge ever since.

Secondly, in accord with Our Lord's injunction, we must also be reconciled to our brother and indeed we must do this first before coming to the altar. We have placed too much weight on the clergy, on the priest confessors, and have made them the sole centers of reconciliation. We ought to return to the old lay confessions even if they are not regarded as sacramental. We have seen that that is how it all started out. Monks and laity went to other monks who were not priests for discernment and prayer. We have seen the scriptures on this point, "Hence, declare your sins to one another, and pray for one another, that you may find healing" (James 5:16), and again, "Anyone who sees his brother sinning, if the sin is not deadly, should petition to God, and thus life will be given to the sinner" (1 John 5:16). Again, "If your brother should commit some wrong against you, go and point out his fault, but keep it between the two of you. If he listens to you, you have won your brother over" (Matthew 18:15). In connection with this, it is worth noting that the new rite of penance does in fact stress that all the members of the church, not simply the clergy, are partners in the ministry of reconciliation. The new rite frankly says, "Communal celebration shows more clearly the ecclesial nature of penance. The faithful listen together to the word of God which proclaims his mercy and invites them to conversion, at the same time they examine the conformity of their lives with that word of God and *help each other through common prayer.*"[3] In fact, the lay penitent is seen as a concelebrant of the sacrament of penance in the new rite. "Thus the faithful Christian, as he experiences and proclaims the mercy of God in his life, *celebrates with the priest* the liturgy by which the church continually renews itself."[4] Finally, we must not neglect the time-honored works of charity: almsgiving, prayer, and fasting.

There must be a great deal of catechesis that restores to the community a keen sense of cohesion, identity, and relationship. There must be a renewed sense that we are God's community and that we have a word and a ritual which marks us out as a reconciling assembly. Yet, in actual practice, this is not the reality, and it will be difficult to gather a sense of community concerning reconciliation when people really don't feel a part of their parishes to begin with. To invite people to a community reconciliation when they have no sense of community is going to meet with indifference and puzzlement. Therefore, prior to any catechesis on reconciliation, we must awake in the average parish the notion that we are all constantly summoned by God's word and that we bear responsibility for one another, that we are indeed engaged in a never ending process of conversion all the time. We must stop confining the forgiveness of sins to merely private, isolated sacramental times. On the contrary, the ideal should be that the celebration of the sacrament by the community is but the high point or peak of the many reconciling actions that have gone on before.

The actual celebration of the sacrament of penance within a community must stand in the same relationship as the act of sex in a good marriage. The sex act gains its integrity and meaning only as a summary of all the small motions, minor acts of love and consideration that go on all the time. Masters and Johnson tell us that the sexual act is basically meaningless without the context of love and mutual regard and consideration. So, too, the saints have told us that an isolated sacramental act without the context of inner repentance, mutual good works and fraternal love is likewise meaningless. It is this lack of context that has been at the basis of the old Protestant scandal that Catholics can do anything they want and then just run into confession and get absolution. No, we must restore to the church in general and the parish in particular a spirit of the virtue of penance such as the medieval church had in its Lenten practices, pilgrimages, penitential sermons, parish missions, ways of the cross, etc. These were all designed to promote the community sense that all were indeed moving towards that final reconciliation in heaven. Karl Rahner expresses it this way:

> The dogmatic theologian must clearly emphasize that he would be stunting theology ... if he maintained ... that the process of penance (as metanoia) ... is limited to the reception of the sacrament of penance, in the sense of individual confession. The following can be just as much salvific events of metanoia, provided that they are recognized as God's work and are experienced as God-given, as the grace of forgiveness and the bestowal of life: genuine acts of self-criticism, of "revision of life," of the avowal of guilt, of the plea for pardon, of the rejection of social conventionalisms and institutionalisms with which one has up to now identified oneself to one's own advantage; the admission of a social self-manifesting "movement" which one has up to then tried to obstruct out of indolence or egoism; a readiness to confront the harsh truths in one's own existence.... To this extent the (individual and collective) elimination of cliché-ridden and stagnant forms of what is really meant by penance is to be regarded as a legitimate process which is itself a part of *metanoia*.[5]

Next, in reference to community, we have a long way to go to recapture a sense of sin as a social, community-vibrating reality.

Sins may be secret but they are never private. Any virtue or vice of the individual Christian either raises or lowers the general moral tone of the church. This is what the early church was so sensitive to. Yet we are so unaware of the communal dimensions of sin. As we saw before, the isolated practice of private confessions has dulled our minds to our relationships with others in the believing community. We have told our little secret sins while "neglecting the weightier matters of the law, justice, and mercy and good faith" (Matthew 23:23). We need to be taught that just as one family member can bring disgrace or glory upon all who bear his name, so can the Christian. We need to stress the acts of forgiveness between spouses, parents and children, family groups and parish members. In a word, this is the *process* of penitence of which we spoke. It is these everyday incarnations of reconciliation that will make the sacrament credible and meaningful. Once more the sacrament of penance and the virtue of penance should individually and communally be interplaying rhythms of the Christian life.

We see efforts at this because the new Rite of Penance promulgated in 1973 attempts to diffuse the focus on the priest alone. For one thing, the term commonly used in the new rite is reconciliation. It implies a more personal touch, a wider scope of God and community. Secondly, the new rite has prayers, scriptural readings, hymns which involve both priest and penitent. It is basically a shared celebration and the priest can claim the old title of physician of souls in that the new rite denotes a caring interaction which should lead, in the words of the new rite, to "diagnose the ills of souls and offer suitable remedies."[6] All will therefore depend on the attitudes of the confessor and the penitent *celebrating together* God's gracious mercy.

However, if the focus has been spread away from the priest's absolution to the whole procedure, we must come back to consider the priest's role to begin with. We have spoken of lay confession, and the eucharist as forgiving, and the works of charity. We said that the sacramental celebration should be the peak of all the ongoing elements of the process. But when in fact we

do come to the sacramental celebration itself, the priest is important. He is the representative of the bishop who is the father of
the community. He is a living commentary of the fact that we are
seeking peace and forgiveness with the church as well as with
God. The priest is the community's figure, the community's official reconciler. He is also a judge even though that term is not
especially congenial to the modern mind. He is judging in the
sense that he is testing the penitent's sincerity, repentance, and
motivations. More than ever, he may even decide, if the penitent
is serious about the process of conversion, to delay absolution
until the penitent has further examined his motives and really
means his sorrow and purpose of amendment. In all this the
priest remains as judge, not in the old sense of passing a sentence, but in the original sense of discernment and discretion.
We confess before the priest precisely on the grounds of community, precisely because of the old "pax ecclesiae," the peace of
the church.

We may also digress here to reflect on the old matter of grant-
ing faculties. As most Catholics know, a priest can celebrate the
sacrament of penance only if he has been granted permission,
jurisdiction, and faculties to do so by the bishop. Some may see
in this an anachronism to be done away with. Yet, it has value.
The priest is standing in for the bishop, and the bishop's primacy should be upheld for there is a long and ancient tradition
of his role in the discipline of reconciliation. Well before the
second century there is evidence that the bishop was the one who
decided what penance should be imposed according to the severity of the sin and he was the one who officially reconciled the
penitent at the end of the penitential process. In the *Apostolic
Tradition* of Hippolytus, written around the year 215, we have a
record of the prayer for the consecration of a bishop which
includes these words: "O God, Father of our Lord Jesus
Christ ... grant upon this thy servant whom thou hast chosen
for the episcopate, to feed thy holy flock ... that by the high
priestly Spirit he may have authority to forgive sins according to
thy command, assign lots according to thy bidding, to loose

every bond according to the authority thou gavest to the apostles . . ."[7] Therefore the fact that the parish priest needs faculties from him reflects the theory that he is a surrogate for the bishop and that therefore it is indeed "through the ministry of the church" that one is forgiven. The bishop as a member of the college of the universal church should be symbolically present in reconciliation as he is symbolically present in the initiation rite of baptism through the chrism.

Perhaps any misgiving about the priest is not so much that he indeed is officially representing the church and that his faculties do emphasize this, but that he has been elevated into power. He has the "keys" of the kingdom of heaven and therefore that puts him in a position of authority. We come to him begging, picturing him miser-like with God's grace. "There is little sense, however, that the keys in question are instruments of shared joy. There is not that delicious anticipation of unlocking to someone the treasure that we ourselves have found and do not seem to give delightful access to the secret beyond the door. Instead, the theological tradition links them unbearably to the question of who's-in-charge-here."[8]

We must learn that it's not a question of who's-in-charge, but of the church's representative celebrating with the people the communal sacrament of reconciliation. However, all this may still be academic for we need not stress the obvious point that in actual practice in all the sacraments the bishop's presence is not perceived nor appreciated. For the sacraments to recover their ecclesial dimensions we must first do something about the superstructures that pass for dioceses and parishes.

Finally, a corollary to the notion of community we have been exploring is the old theological problem of integrity; that is, the insistence of the Council of Trent that all mortal sins must be confessed as to kind and number and circumstance and that, moreover, this is by order of God's will. We will comment later that perhaps this has to be more accurately explained, but for the moment we would define it as tied in with the priest and the community aspect of the church. If one is truly sorry for his sins and wishes to be reinstated into the Christian family, he will want to confront the church's minister and episcopal representative. He will want to present himself and, in the psychology of guilt and repentance, tell all. There is a great value in this, and perhaps it is the value, after all, that is really consecrated in Trent's words. In any case, the importance of telling the kind, number, and extenuating circumstance of all mortal sins is basically related to the concept of community.

3

The new Rite of Penance promulgated in 1973 and made operative in Lent of 1976 has three types of reconciliation plus one nonsacramental approach. The first approach is the traditional private one-to-one confession, but with changes. Now there is a word of welcome from the priest to the penitent and an opening prayer that is really the first word in an ongoing dialogue. This is followed by an optional reading of scripture either by the priest or the penitent. There are some options to choose from. Now comes the general accusation of sins, followed by some form of an act of contrition (some ten options are offered in addition to the traditional one or one in the penitent's own words). Then the priest gives some penance, usually suited to the confession, and then pronounces the words of absolution. They are changed from the old "I absolve you from your sins in the name of the Father, etc." to the following, "May God, the Father of mercies who reconciled the world to himself through the death and resurrection of his Son, and poured out the Holy Spirit for the forgiveness of sin, grant you pardon and peace through the ministry of the church, and I absolve you in the name of the Father and of the Son and of the Holy Spirit, Amen."

The priest says these words while extending his hand or hands over the penitent. This is an ancient symbol of reconciliation and a sign of the Spirit's activity. After this there is a prayer of thanksgiving and the dismissal. This first approach, while it does not do away with the confessional box (only some four hundred years old) does imply more of a confessional room situation. This is deduced by the reading of scripture which would require some light and room to read and the imposition of hands which would require a face to face situation, although not demand it. Most parishes will design a room which accommodates both a screen situation for those penitents who wish to remain anonymous and an open situation for those who want to sit down for a face-to-face dialogue.

Notice that the new formula stresses more of the communal aspect of sin with its reference to the church. There has been some regret expressed that the phrase did not say "*with* the church," rather than through it, and so stress the community aspect. Also some have objected to the retention of the declarative ending, "And I absolve you. . . ." They would have wished a better transition with what went before. Perhaps something like, "And I, as representative of the Christian community and in its name, absolve you. . . ." or a more petitionary form as of old with the stress on praise. In any case, this first approach requires a more careful preparation and a slightly longer time. It precludes a hasty encounter and gives more emphasis to the old discernment and praise motif.

The second approach recommended and given by the new rite is the communal confession which many parishes have been using for years. Basically, it is the private one-to-one confession in a community setting. It also represents the novelty that for the first time in history the two traditions of public and private confession are united in one ritual. The format is essentially a common reading of scripture, reflection, prayers, and homily. Some time within this setting private confessions are celebrated. Those in the congregation who have only venial sin need not, of course, approach the confessor; but those in mortal sin must if they are to receive sacramental absolution. There remains the current speculation whether serious venial sins—grave sins—need to be brought to the confessor. The value of the communal confession is that it brings together a significant number of people and provides the opportunity for the understanding that sin truly does affect the Christian community and that the community so gathered does have a chance to display this truth. The drawback is that there is still the demand for the private confession to the priest. In a large crowd, penitents will be required to be brief and perhaps confine themselves to some basic mortal sin thereby frustrating the dialogue and time which the first approach holds up as ideal.

There is the danger that this type may become too popular for the time being and preempt the necessary first approach which does give the time for spiritual direction and discernment. It may become a too easy routine to fulfill a yearly Easter duty. There are already some signs that it is waning here and there. But used discreetly this communal confession can be a help towards the growth of community and social consciousness.

The third approach is general confession or absolution. This is a gathering of many people who, presuming inner repentance and genuine sorrow, receive absolution without speaking their confession. This is basically an emergency situation at present. Such would be the case where many soldiers are going into battle, or with people in a hospital ward whose confessions could be easily overheard, or with people who without this opportunity, would be deprived of the eucharist or penance for a long period of time. Canon lawyers interpret this "long time" as short as three days, and even one day. However, it must be noted that, according to the present norms, there is still a serious obligation after the general absolution within a reasonable time to actually share in a one-to-one verbal confession of sins.

This is still a rather restricted situation, quite uncommon, but there are those who see legitimate extensions forthcoming. One writer, for example, says, "The situation is indeed such, in many parishes at least, that if we would like the faithful by and large to avail themselves frequently of the grace of this sacrament, we shall have to choose between rather hurried individual confessions, thus undermining the integrity of that form of reconciliation, or regular communal celebrations with general absolution."[9] In fact, a survey in *Worship* magazine shows these extensions:

> The French bishops, in November, 1973, specified that general absolution was justified when there is not a sufficient number of confessors, when there is a large gathering of penitents, such as would be found on the occasion of a pilgrimage or on the eve of a great feast, and also in cases involving great numbers of children from Catholic schools or catechism classes. In 1972 the Archbishop of Montreal permitted general absolution in parishes and schools during the two weeks preceding Christmas. . . . The Archbishop of Campinas (Brazil) has permitted general absolution at Christmas, during Lent and Holy Week. . . . The bishops of Chile and those of Columbia as well have determined that, due to the serious shortage of priests, general absolution should be regularly employed. In November, 1973, the Archbishop of Mexico City declared that general absolution was justified on Sundays and holy days, at Lenten services, as well as for the various groups. . . .[10]

In any case, it will be up to the national hierarchies to expand any use of the General Absolution.

Finally, added to the new rite are several nonsacramental services which are designed to dispose individuals and congregations to a better and deeper penitence and a more fruitful use of the actual sacrament.

4

We might close this chapter with some observations. First, regardless of whatever happens to the sacrament of reconciliation in actual experience, we should try once more to place it in context. It must be related to baptism and to the eucharist. Baptism, because there was the place of definitive conversion and penance is truly a "second" baptism. The eucharist because, as we have seen, it is the sacrament which celebrates those very acts by which we are saved, and the sacrament of reconciliation is but its emphatic moment. This is to say that, while we admit that the eucharist is the primary sacrament of reconciliation, "in penance the church deals with the concrete fact of sin in its members, assists them in their conscious conversion, and leads them to reconciliation in a way which it cannot do in the eucharist. . . . [In other words] while the eucharist celebrates the totality of God's saving action in Christ and thus is *the* sacrament of reconciliation, penance celebrates a particular aspect of this mystery. Here the church reconciles itself with those estranged from the fellowship signified in its eucharist or who need special help in the ongoing process of conversion."[11]

This brings up a very practical and direct question: May we then ever approach the eucharist, presuming genuine sorrow and sincere motivation, and have even our grave sins forgiven? The answer, from everything that we have investigated in the long tradition of the eucharist, is yes. But there are practical problems. One is that perhaps, as a discipline, the famous triad should still exclude one from such a direct approach: practical apostasy or denial of the faith, murder, and adultery (including the technical adultery of divorce and remarriage?) since such matters—and some others—would be well known to the community at large. Sacramental confession should be demanded here in deference to the community. Other grave sins, less community-shattering, could be brought directly to the eucharist. Secondly, the danger of abuse is real. People should not always choose to approach the eucharist directly without also moving towards sacramental confession. As we have indicated above this specification is both needed and demanded by the nature of the liturgy and a sense of community: to proclaim and to advertise God's gracious mercy and the church as a reconciling assembly. There simply must be certain points in every Catholic's life when he or she does in fact made a public acknowledgment of his sinfulness and a public celebration of God's forgiveness. It would seem therefore that the present discipline of demanding sacra-confession of *every* grave sin before approaching the eucharist has to be resolved, not in the light of theory (for that seems to be clear) but in the light of practical pastoral theology.

Secondly, the sacrament of penance, while not disparaging the confession of devotion, should be replaced as a more rare thing. This is not meant to cause scandal and advise against the use of the sacrament. Rather it is a plea for a more generous use of all the other ways God has given to us. Fraternal correction, "lay" confession, almsgiving, prayer, and fasting, and the community eucharist should be much more encouraged as the place and time for forgiveness. The sacrament itself should be reserved for peak moments and in cases of genuine mortal sin. And such peak moments should never lose their basic meaning of praise. God already forgives us at the moment of genuine conversion and sorrow. The external sacramental rite is meant to advertise not only one's sinfulness but God's unspeakable mercy to the rest of the community. We should never forget that all the sacraments are liturgy, public praises to a merciful God. As we said earlier, every sacrament is but an extension of the original Pentecostal experience, and to have once more received the Spirit is always the cause for rejoicing and praising God.

Thirdly, the church should clarify and make more precise the insistence on integrity, that is, the necessity by divine law, of confessing all mortal sins according to kind, number, and significant circumstance. We have already discussed that in itself there is something to be said for the notion of integrity. If one presents himself to the church it is to "tell all" and on this score alone it is justified. Yet, the "divine law" notion must be made more flexible for in fact, as we have seen, this has not always been in effect. The first centuries do not give a clear indication of all mortal sins being confessed so exactly. Trent itself made exceptions for mutes and deaf people and the church dispenses the demand for integrity in missionary countries (see the directives of the Congregation for the Evangelization of Peoples). We recall, too, that in baptism *all* sins are forgiven whatever, even mortal sins, and there is no spelling out there of the sins as to kind and number and circumstance. Nor ought we to forget the Eastern traditions which forgive sins at the eucharist with no mention of exactness.

Vatican II's Decree on Ecumenism says of the Eastern churches:

> These churches, although separated from us, yet possess true sacraments, above all—by apostolic succession—the priesthood and the eucharist, whereby they are still joined to us in closest intimacy. Therefore, some worship in common, given suitable circumstances and the approval of church authority, is not merely possible but is encouraged. . . . Everyone should realize that it is of supreme importance to understand, venerate, preserve, and foster the rich liturgical and spiritual heritage of the Eastern churches in order to faithfully preserve the fullness of Christian tradition. . . . What has already been said about legitimate variety we are pleased to apply to differences in theological expressions of doctrine. . . . With regard to the authentic theological traditions of the Orientals, we must recognize that they are admirably rooted in Holy Scripture, and fostered and given expression in liturgical life, are nourished by the living tradition of the apostles and by the works of the Fathers and spiritual writers of the East. . . ."[12]

If indeed the Western Catholic church recognizes as legitimate the sacramental and liturgical traditions of the Eastern churches, then it must apply this as well to the sacrament of penance which, in their tradition, does not always and invariably demand integrity.

Moreover, we should note that in the Council of Trent's deliberations the law of integrity was not intended to apply to each and every case and even the necessity by divine law to confess all was a *conditioned* necessity. "What is often forgotten is that the necessity in question was seen as conditional. This was explicitly recalled in the debates over and over. . . . Trent asserted the obligatory character of such confession and made no effort to determine when circumstances called for it by God's will and when they did not."[13] In other words, Trent did not intend to extend the law of integrity to each and every private confession and gave us no guidelines as to when it did not. So Trent did in fact leave other options open without spelling them out. There is more room for variety than we think. "The Council of Trent is done no service if it is made to answer the question regarding the situations in which integral confession takes precedence over other values that are to be realized in conversion. If it is pastorally desirable to have a variety of forms of confession and absolution, the Tridentine decree cannot be used as an argument to the contrary."[14] What all this means on the practical level is that people should have more freedom to seek forgiveness in all of the legitimate ways open to them and that obligations should not be multiplied where a person, truly contrite and repentant, seeks reconciliation from God and the church whether in a one-to-one encounter with the priest-confessor or in a communal situation or in a form of general absolution.

Fourthly, the hierarchy will have to come to terms with its priests and recognize that not all of them are temperamentally suited to be confessors, celebrators of the sacrament of reconciliation (any more than all of them should be baptizers). In other words, faculties allowing any particular priest to be the surrogate of the community father (the bishop) will have to be extended more discreetly. Ultimately the success or failure of the new rite will be the attitudes of both priest and penitent.[15]

Finally, as we shall stress again in our last chapter of this book, the whole question of the new rite of penance is basically a question of spirituality. Revisions are not just for the sake of novelty. They are for the sake of bringing us all into a deeper relationship with Christ. The less we see the new rite of reconciliation (and all the rites) in this light the more we shall become merely preoccupied with the ritual fringes and niceties and still be in the dark.

NOTES FOR CHAPTER 13

1. Ralph Keifer and Frederick McManus, "Understanding the Document," *The Rite of Penance: Commentaries 1* (The Liturgical Conference, 1975), p. 6.

2. Paul Palmer, "What Must We Confess," *The Priest* (November 1975), p. 42.

3. The Rite of Penance, no. 22.

4. The Rite of Penance, no. 11. Again, we stress that the tradition of lay confessions is a strong one and even until the thirteenth century the opinion persisted that in emergencies, if no priest were available, confession to a layman was not without merit. This may be due to the fact that, prior to this time, no really satisfactory theory had been worked out to answer these questions: To what extent is the actual process of the forgiveness of sin by God tied to the priest's role of judgment? Can priest-confessors actually free people from their sins or only tell them that God in fact has promised forgiveness to all who sincerely repent? This is to say, is the priest's absolution merely declaratory? Is such a power to absolve sin limited exclusively to ordained ministers or can one in emergency situations obtain forgiveness by confessing to another member of the church, namely, a lay Christian? To what extent is one really bound to confess to an ordained priest? These were frequent and legitimate questions discussed by the theologians and the canonists of the twelfth century. To mention one, for example, St. Albert the Great, teacher of Thomas Aquinas, speaks of the power of freeing another from sins by lay persons of especial holiness and in emergencies by all laypersons. All in all, throughout the thirteenth century there still remained a solid opinion that some kind of positive value attached to lay confessions. As far as we know it was the theologian Duns Scotus who first challenged this sentiment. See Bernard Cooke, *Ministry to Word and Sacraments* (Fortress Press, 1976), pp. 467–476.

5. Karl Rahner, *Christian at the Crossroads* (Seabury Press, 1975), p. 76.

6. The Rite of Penance, no. 10.

7. Quoted in Johannes Quasten, *Patrology*, vol. 2 (Newman Press, 1965), p. 188. See also B. Poschmann, *Penance and the Anointing of the Sick* (Herder and Herder, 1964), pp. 19–52.

8. George McCauley, *America* (April 3, 1976), p. 282.

9. A. T. in *Worship* 48, no. 9 (November 1974), p. 551.

10. Ibid., p. 553. See also Karl Rahner, "Communal Penance

Services and Individual Confession," *Theology Digest* 21, no. 2 (Summer 1973).

11. The first sentence is from James Dallen's article, "Eucharist and Penance" (*Worship* 50, no. 4 [July 1976] pp. 324 ff). The second sentence is from a resolution which he quotes from the participants in the special study of the exact relationship between these two sacraments.

12. Decree on Ecumenism, nos. 15–17, tr. Austin Flannery, O.P. (Costello Publishing Co., 1975), pp. 464, 467.

13. Carl Peter, "Integral Confession and the Council of Trent," in *Sacramental Reconciliation*, ed. Edward Schillebeeckx, *Concilium* 61 (Herder and Herder, 1971), p. 107.

14. Ibid. See also John Gallen, "General Sacramental Absolution: Pastoral Remarks on Pastoral Norms," *Theological Studies* 34, no. 1 (March 1973), p. 114.

15. See the advice of Thomas Hennessy in "From Confessor-Judge to Confessor-Counselor," *New Catholic World* (Fall 1974). Also see Regis A. Duffy's "Concelebration of Penance and a Therapeutic Model," *Worship* 48, no. 5 (May 1974).

14

The Forgotten Sacrament

1

There is no question that Jesus is healer. The gospels are filled with the stories of cures he effected. But the important notion in such stories is that Jesus never cured a body for its own sake. He was rather concerned for the whole man. So Jesus multiplies the loaves and the fishes, heals the blind man, raises Lazarus from the dead—but such marvels were not wrought for their own sakes. After all, the people would get hungry again, the blind man would get old and his sight would deteriorate and Lazarus would die again. On the surface, then, such cures have no meaning if left to themselves. But on a deeper level they do have a profound meaning. Jesus is the real bread from heaven, he is the real light, he is the real life. "I am the way and the truth and the life." Such cures ultimately have meaning only in that they promote the salvation of the whole person, his faith in Jesus and his surrender to God's will as found in Jesus. In short, the cures are grounded in faith and are meant to lead to a higher truth and a final meaning which is Christ and the salvation he came to bring.

This is why there is what scholars call a "messianic secret" in Mark's gospel. After some stunning bodily cures, Jesus goes and hides, the very thing we would not expect him to do if he were anxious to draw attention. He does an outstanding, public deed and says in effect, "but don't tell anyone about this." But it is likely that Jesus did this because he feared to become known simply as a healer of bodies, a kind of wandering magician. Since he was far more concerned about the whole man, about persons, not just their twisted or deformed appendages, he played down his curative miracles. He was savior, not doctor.

Moreover, as a biblical Jew, Jesus knew that man is a unit. It would take the philosophical Greeks of another age to split what the Jews could not and make man into body and soul. Since man is a whole, Jesus ministered to that "whole" person; and part of that whole mentality was the connection between sin and sickness. As we saw in the rites of initiation, spiritual powers are everywhere present to the people and human beings live daily in the powerful tensions of good and evil. Sickness and death are part of those evils and impinge on our daily lives. Not that we are personally sinful, the proof of which is some affliction. Rather we are part of that spirit world which seeks us, both for good and for ill. We are a part of that world in which wickedness is present and demonstrates itself not only in the persistent television reports of war, greed, avarice, and abuse of power, but in many other ways—including the evil configurations of sickness and death.

In other words, sickness and sin are related. Again, not that any particular person is personally guilty of sin and *therefore* is sick. Jesus put that to rest (John 9). Rather sickness is a sign of a deeper, more general evil abroad in the world. Sickness is an inescapable symptom of man's need for deliverance. It is this ultimate evil which could bring everlasting death that Jesus has overcome. That is why countless times in the gospels Jesus' cures demand faith, and he himself refers to sin in the context of healing. That is why when we come to look at Jesus in his healing ministry in his church and in his church's actions (the sacraments) we must keep the focus on the main theme that Jesus is savior. Particularly the Sacrament of the Sick we must view from the perspective of this overall savingness and ultimate victory in Christ. Every healing, therefore, and every use of Christ's sacrament of the sick must basically be a call to conversion and faith and a fuller sharing in the Easter mysteries first encountered in baptism and now, in this time, place, and circumstance, encountered most poignantly once again in its dramatic fullness and ultimate implications. Only incidentally would any sacrament such as that of the sick be a call to bodily healing. Every anointing is a sign of the coming of the kingdom.

It was in this sense—of proclaiming the kingdom—that healing continued in the early church. When Peter, for example, cured the crippled man at the Temple Gate he was quick to point out, "Why do you stare at us as if we had made this man walk by some power or holiness of our own? . . . It is in (Jesus') name, and trust in his name, that has strengthened the limbs of this man. . . . Such *faith* has given him perfect health, as all of you can observe" (Acts 3: 11–16). The point of the cure was faith, and faith in Jesus as saving from sin which is why Peter added, "*Therefore*, reform your lives! Turn to God that your sins may be wiped away!"

These motifs of proclamation, faith, kingdom are also found in the gospels. The evangelists record Jesus sending out his disciples two by two to preach repentance and acceptance of the gospel. He also gives them a share in his powers. Mark adds these words, "With that they went off, preaching the need of repentance." His next sentence shows the traditional understanding of the whole view of life: that all evils (including sickness) are not isolated but are part of an overall network of sin. He adds, "They expelled many demons, anointed the sick with oil, and worked many cures" (Mark 6:11). This is certainly no indication of any sacrament of the sick, but it does foreshadow the ministry of healing, as related to sin, repentance, and faith, that would be the essence of that sacrament.

The real indication of a special "mysterion" (sacramental mystery) connected with oil and the sick comes from the famous quotation of St. James:

Is there anyone sick among you? He should ask for the presbyters of the church. They in turn are to pray over him, anointing him with oil in the name of the Lord. This prayer uttered in faith will reclaim the one who is ill and the Lord will restore him to health. If he has committed any sins, forgiveness will be his (James 5: 13–15).

James probably understands that bodily healing will take place, but the spiritual healing is included as well. His text also indicates that it is a question here of a serious illness, since the sick person does not go to the presbyters or priests but has to send for them. Moreover, since these presbyters are officials of the church, it is not a question of some group of charismatic healers, but rather the regular and normal institutional anointing of the sick. The sick, notice, not necessarily the dying. As the United States Bishops' Commentary puts it: "A balanced exegesis of James would suggest neither a purely eschatological spiritual healing (salvation in the life to come, the future resurrection of the dead), or simply a bodily-medicinal effect in the manner of faith healing. This rite touches upon the salvific situation of the sick person: his religious powerlessness and the threat that sickness poses to his faith and trust in God. As a result, the sick Christian shall be raised up from this weakness and saved from the obstacle that sickness constitutes towards his salvation."[1]

2

Interestingly, after James' rather clear testimony, we find little commentary about this sacrament for almost seven hundred years—and what is there in these centuries is not always so clear. Actually, in the case of this particular sacrament, we might expect this. Any sacrament for the sick could not be expected to get the attention of the more "major" sacraments of baptism and eucharist. Besides, since no one could program who was going to be ill or seriously ill or be near death, the community was hardly poised on a grand scale for the use of this sacrament in any public and constant way. In other words, this sacrament is by its nature an individual one, or at least confined to a private, individual time of personal sickness. Therefore, it was not the subject of any massive public discussion or writing. And in what sparse writing we do have, because of James' mention of sin, it is not always easy to disentangle talk about some kind of penance and the sacrament of the sick.

What references do we have? We have a first century tablet, recently discovered, which shows that St. James' directive was being carried out. We have our old friend Hippolytus who describes the bishop's consecrating of the oil at the end of the canon of the Mass with this prayer, "O God, who does sanctify this oil, as you grant to all who are anointed and receive of it the blessing by which you did anoint kings and prophets, so grant that it may give strength to all that taste of it and health to all who use it." This prayer implies that the sick person either took the oil internally or used it externally on his body. There is an early fifth-century letter by Pope Innocent I which declares that indeed St. James is referring to a genuine sacrament of the sick, and as we might expect (if we recall that he was the one who said only bishops can confirm) the oil used must be blessed by the bishop, although priests may also administer this rite. But then he adds a revealing bit of information: "Now there is no doubt that these words (of James) are to be understood of the faithful who are sick, and who can be anointed with the holy oil of chrism, which has been prepared by the bishop, and which not only priests *but all Christians* may use for anointing, when their own needs or those of their family demand."[2]

Yes, it has clearly been established that laymen and women conferred this sacrament. There are two reflections that might help us to assimilate this. First, lay conferral is true of some of the other sacraments if we think about it. For example, the ministry of baptism, originally reserved to the bishop, a presbyter, or a deacon was extended very early to laymen and, later on, to laywomen and eventually even to non-Christians. Then, too, we might recall that confirmation was originally reserved to the bishop and was extended in the East as a matter of course to the priests and in the West, by exception, to them also. It is also on record that some popes permitted priest-abbots to ordain their subjects to the diaconate and to the priesthood. Therefore ordinary priests can, by indult, confirm and ordain. The point is that some sacraments which we associate exclusively with one ministerial office have been given to those of "lesser" office.

Secondly, the oil used in the sacrament of the sick, as we can deduce from Hippolytus' account, constituted, like the eucharist, a "permanent" sacrament. In the eucharist, after the bishop's consecration the bread and wine were the body and blood of Christ, no matter who handled them afterwards. So, too, the oil, after its consecration, was permanently holy, no matter who handled it. As the people brought home the eucharist so too they brought home the oil; and just as they communicated themselves when they wished, so too they anointed themselves or members of their family. It is very much akin to our more prominent use of extraordinary ministers who give out communion to the congregation or the sick. Today we are used to laypersons doing this. So it was with the oil. Laypersons took it and used it and thus conferred the sacrament of the sick. As we shall see, this lay conferral disappeared in the ninth century, and later was forbidden by Trent. The reason it disappeared was that the sacrament of the sick became associated with the dying and the sacrament of penance. Then it no longer stood apart but had moved into clerical preserve. The priest had to be there to hear the confession of the dying person, and it was an easy step to include the anointing, which came to be seen as entrance into glory, as part of the clerical preparation for death.

The next clearest reference we have is from Venerable Bede of England who lived in the eighth century. He confirms that we have in St. James the institution of the sacrament of the sick and sees the priest's role as predominant although he admits to lay anointing. It is, however, in Charlemagne's liturgical reforms of the eighth and ninth centuries that we see a distinct change of emphasis and minister. The oldest extant complete rite for anointing that we have is from a Carolingian ritual dating from about the year 815. We must remember that this was the time, influenced by those monks from Bede's England and Ireland, when a renewal of priestly piety was going on. The result was not only the establishment (in the West) of the bishop as the ordinary minister of confirmation, but also the priest as the ordinary minister of the sacrament of anointing. Next, a view of the sacrament which had been growing for a while came in full force. This was the view that saw anointing not primarily for the sick but for the dying. This was the sacrament which prepared one for the afterlife. Because the anointing became associated with death, then it was easily pulled into the orbit of the eucharist and penance at the deathbed scene. The order began as penance, anointing, and Final Eucharist (Viaticum) and soon became penance, Final Eucharist, and anointing. This made the anointing the last of the three, the one given in deathly extremes, the *extreme unction.*

One of the reasons that the sacrament shifted in emphasis from that of the sick to that of the dying (although the Eastern church kept the focus on the sick) is the theoretical one of how a physical result (bodily health) could issue from a sacramental, supernatural cause. Sacraments specifically deal in the realm of grace and not with material cause and effect. Besides, if we made bodily health the aim of the sacrament, and if the sacraments always effect the grace they contain (presuming proper dispositions), then why aren't more people physically healed? To overcome this problem, it was decided that the sacrament, after all, does *not* have bodily health as its chief aim, but spiritual health in the sense of the forgiveness of sins. However, there were already two sacraments around for that very purpose: baptism and penance. Therefore, a step further said that this sacrament forgave the remnants of sin, the residue, any last ill effects that would prevent full purification. It was thus an easy step to regard this "last remnant" tidying up as the immediate preparation for death, for glory.

We see the sin association predominating in the new formula that was used when it was determined to anoint the five senses. That formula, in use until the revision of 1972 says, "By this holy anointing may God forgive you whatever sins you have committed by the use of your sense of sight, hearing, etc." Basically, the ceremony came from the baptismal anointing with appropriate references to the sick. Many parts of the body were anointed and the number of anointing varied from time to time. The back of the neck, the throat, the loins, the ailing part of the body, etc., before the anointings settled on the five senses. Likewise, in Charlemagne's reforms, the rite could be repeated for seven days. The sick person could also be clothed in white garments, carried to the local church where he was sprinkled with holy water and then ashes were placed on his head and chest. The Seven Penitential Psalms were recited over him, and then he was anointed with some fifteen or more anointings. Then the sick man recited the Creed and the Our Father (borrowed from the baptismal rite). The priest would give him the kiss of peace and communion and promised to visit him should he still be alive in seven days. In time the ceremony grew uncomfortably long and tedious and clamored for some simplification.

3

Because the anointing was now theologically and popularly associated with dying and death and was relegated to the last of a threefold approach to this finality (penance, eucharist preceding it), it soon lost its appeal and its use. For one thing, the layperson's role no longer existed. He had no active part in the anointing anymore. He was the passive recipient of something he used to do as well. Secondly, who wanted to be bothered with or take part in a sacrament given only when death was practically certain? If the anointing was now presented as the vehicle to carry one into the afterlife, the ordinary Christian did not want much to do with it. Then, too, there grew up the popular notion that if one did in fact recover from death's door he was obliged to live out the rest of his life in penitence; for example, he could not get married or had to renounce it. Anointing became out of sight, out of mind until one was forced to deal with it. It became the forgotten sacrament.

But the dying association stuck. Peter Lombard of the twelfth century took this view and was among the first to call this sacrament extreme unction. Succeeding theologians followed suit. The sixteenth century Council of Trent tried to pull matters back into proper perspective, although it was not forceful enough in breaking the connection of death with this sacrament. It said, "this anointing is to be used for the sick, but especially for those who are dangerously ill as seem to be at the point of departing this life." This statement is a fudging of the issue, but it is trying to bring the focus back on the sickness. Trent also said that the priest is the proper minister of this sacrament, but did not mean to exclude the laity. "Accordingly, when Trent equates the presbyters of the text of James with her own presbyters, or priests, and concludes that priests alone are the 'proper' ministers of the sacrament, she is defending the propriety of her present practice and not denying the validity of a practice almost equally old of lay anointing, where there was a felt need."[3] Trent's teaching and the popular association of this sacrament with dying and death remained in force until Vatican II. Then this Council left no ambiguity as to the meaning of anointing: "Extreme Unction, which may also and more fittingly be called 'anointing of the sick,' is not a sacrament for those only who are at the point of death. Hence as soon as anyone of the faithful *begins* to be in danger of death from sickness or old age, the appropriate time for him to receive this sacrament has certainly arrived."[4]

Finally, a whole new rite was issued on December 7, 1972, and implemented in January of 1974. New emphases are noted. For one thing the new rite of anointing avoids such terms as "extreme unction" and "last rites." The term used is the Sacrament of the Sick. Moreover, the whole thrust has been considerably widened to include, not merely the actual anointing, but the whole ministry to the sick. An attempt is made to draw in everyone again: the family, friends of the sick one, and the

parish community. It is recognized that basically sickness is dealing with alienation and fragmentation. The sick person is truly
cut off from the normal rhythms and people of everyday life. He
can accordingly become quite preoccupied with self, find the
time heavy, himself lonely, unable to pray, depressed. His
"wholeness" is dissipated, scattered, fragmented. The sacrament
is designed to restore that wholeness, to help the person to grow
spiritually *through* the sickness, to have in mind what Jesus had in
mind: the whole person is to be saved, made better, holier, enter
more deeply into the mystery of Christ's own suffering, death,
and resurrection. Even the emphasis on sin is weakened. This is
saved for the proper sacrament of penance. Viaticum has been
restored as the legitimate last sacrament. Once more, we notice
in the new rite a mention of baptism and a renewal of the baptismal vows. After all, it is baptism, as we have seen, which
plunges us in principle into the passion, death, and resurrection
of Jesus and every eucharist is a fulfillment of that process. Now,
during sickness, and near death, the final eucharist has a special
significance. More than ever it brings to perfection what baptism
meant all along. That is why the two are mentioned together in
the new rite.

The sick person himself should be active in the rite. In fact he
is the one who is urged to request the sacrament, not have someone else do it for him. The five senses are no longer anointed,
only the forehead and the upturned hands. The wording has
been changed to a more positive tone. Pope Paul VI gives us the
approach when he writes, "The sacrament of anointing of the
sick is administered to those who are dangerously ill by anointing them on the forehead and hands with blessed olive oil or,
according to circumstance, with another plant oil and saying
these words: Through this holy anointing, may the Lord in his
mercy and love help you with the grace of the Holy Spirit
(Amen). May the Lord who frees you from sin save you and raise
you up (Amen)."

Finally, the community is urged to be quite involved. This
means not only the family and friends, but the parish. Communal anointings are encouraged at the parish church within

Mass so that the community at large may be sensitized to the needs of the sick and their basic isolation. The community is there to provide both encouragement and meaning especially in our society which is preoccupied with the technology of sick care. The community is present at church or at the hospital among the tubes, monitors, tanks, and closed circuit television to remind the patient of his humanness; to urge him to freely join himself to Jesus' sufferings and perhaps even his last moments in anticipation of the everlasting salvation Jesus came to bring to all. The laity can be involved, not only by sharing in the cere-monies, by engaging in the healing ministry, but also by bringing the eucharist to the sick as well.

Although the term "serious sickness" has been broadened to include persons about to undergo major surgery, sick children of an age to know what is going on, and mental illnesses as well, the element of death has not been forgotten. The new rite pro-vides ceremonies and prayers for those who are indeed dying and will die shortly. In a sense, even the funeral arrangements are considered an extension of the church's healing ministry: the final celebration of the community of the now completed pro-cess of salvation; the undercurrent of deep sorrow at human loss and yet a certain joy that the final rebirth has taken place. As most people know, even the Mass of Christian Burial tries to strike this more positive note; and certainly while not designed to be casual or indifferent to the human grief, it seeks to be a summation of what was started in the initiation rites, a ritualizing of those old words of Paul's, "Are you not aware that we who were baptized into Christ Jesus were baptized into his death? Through baptism into his death we were buried with him so that, just as Christ was raised from the dead by the glory of the Father, we too might live a new life" (Romans 6:3).

Amen.

NOTES FOR CHAPTER 14

1. *Commentary on the Sacrament of the Sick* (The Catholic Con-ference), p. 18. For a fuller pastoral discussion see the cassettes

by Charles W. Gusmer, "Rite of Anointing: Pastoral Care of the Sick" (NCR Cassettes, 1974).

2. Epistle, 25.8, 11. PL 20, 561.

3. Paul Palmer, "Who Can Anoint the Sick?" *Worship* 48, no. 2 (February 1973), p. 91.

4. Constitution on the Sacred Liturgy, no. 73.

15

From There to Here

1

Now that we have seen our five sacraments, something of their history and development, it is time to take note of an insistent, recurring theme connected with them. In every sacrament we have investigated we see a marked return to community preparation and participation. Moreover, within this renewed emphasis, the role of parents is specifically mentioned over and over again. For the average Catholic this emphasis may run the gamut from pleasant surprise to sheer dismay. Both the surprise and the dismay are rooted in our immediate past history. We were told to keep our hands off religious education. We left such sophisticated dealings up to the professionals: the clergy and religious. Now, suddenly, everyone is telling us that it's our job as parents to take up the task and that our hands should very definitely be "on." Most people not only have some anxiety about their ability to take up this task, but when they in fact take up the textbooks, their anxiety is increased a hundredfold. What do we have here? Where is the old question and answer Baltimore catechism? Do we really need all those pictures and large print? Doses, large or small, of psychology and sociology, are apparent. There are plenty of suggestions for classroom "celebrations" called paraliturgies. Being asked to be more (passively) present in the five sacraments is one thing. Being coaxed and encouraged to actually be active and even to share the teaching is another. To be required (even if this is technically illegal) to attend parent preparation classes is the last straw. So, to round out our discussion of the five sacraments, let us review, however briefly, the history of religious education and see where we in fact do fit in.[1]

Obviously, the very first instruction and exhortation to the new Christian faith came from Jesus and, after his death and resurrection, from his apostles. They excitedly made their proclamation to religious, biblically orientated Jews. Their message was direct, moving, and simple: "Men of Israel, listen to me! Jesus the Nazarene was a man whom God sent to you with miracles, wonders and signs as his credentials. . . . He was delivered up by the set purpose and plan of God; you even made use of pagans to crucify and kill him. God freed him from death's bitter pangs, however, and raised him up again. . . . This is the Jesus God raised up, and we are his witnesses. . . . You must reform and be baptized, each one of you, in the name of Jesus Christ, that your sins may be forgiven; then you will receive the gift of the Holy Spirit" (Acts 2: 22–39). So spoke St. Peter on that Pentecost day and on that day some three thousand were baptized. This was the first catechism instruction made to adults and its content was basic: faith, repentance, and baptism.

The need for a neat statement such as Peter's gave rise to set formulas such as our Apostles' Creed. Although this creed was not put together in its present form until the sixth century, it nevertheless organically grew out of the basic statements and professions connected with Christian initiation. There was, after all, some use in a concise profession of faith. From the time of the apostles on, it was the Christian practice (as we have seen) to require some explicit statement of faith in Jesus. It wasn't long before set wordings established themselves and, once established, promoted elaborations known as creeds. We sense very early creedal and liturgical formulas in scripture itself. The eunuch baptized by the deacon Philip confesses, "I believe that Jesus Christ is the Son of God" (Acts 8:37). The early Christian secret sign, the acrostic "Fish" whose Greek first letters stood for "Jesus Christ, Son of God, Savior" testifies also to a primitive creed. St. Paul's epistles have several creedal formulas which are clearly liturgical. The very introduction of the trinitarian formula used at initiation and recorded in the gospels, gives the basic outline for a more developed creed later on. In other words, all of this testifies to catechesis as a prerequisite for conversion from the earliest times.

Meanwhile, the simple and profound message of Christianity did catch on amazingly. As the gospel spread beyond the Jews to the Gentiles, some new approaches had to be tried. Why? Because the message and shape of the original revelation was Jewish: its vocabulary, images, and figures. How would a Greek or a Spaniard understand Jewish categories and descriptions? A clever teacher could adapt to his Gentile audience, but still the basic thought patterns, the impulse, the genius would always be biblical Judaism. So the next step was to educate and "soften up" the Gentiles. The next step, as we have already seen, was the invention of the catechumenate. We saw that this was a three year program of spiritual, doctrinal, and moral training and preparation. It was an attempt to educate interested candidates and their families in the gospel.

This civilized effort was suddenly brought to a halt, however, in the fifth and following centuries. This was the time when the crude, unlettered Franco-Germanic barbarians invaded and overran Europe. These hordes wrought terrible destruction. Still, for all of their vandalism they did not wish to eradicate the superior Roman culture. They wished to copy it. Since the civil administration had collapsed, the church filled the vacuum and took on the enormous task of both civilizing and converting the barbarian. Missionaries of every kind took up the challenge. Often however, in the press of numbers and mass conversions, little instruction was given and follow-up was slow. Missionaries were often content that the barbarian knew the Creed and the Our Father, and they built their catecheses around these two points.

But there had to be more than oral instruction to these illiterate barbarians, at least in the form of simple and straight doctrine. So there began to grow up an "atmosphere" of what can be called a Christian culture. There were, for example, those edifying stories of the lives of the saints. Pope Gregory the Great (d. 604) wrote a marvelous collection of saints' stories and legends thereby providing an important spurt to the cult of the saints so popular in the Middle Ages. Then in time there developed the many feast days, pictures, statues, and shrines which dotted the lands. The later cathedrals were often called sermons in stone since they provided many sculptures of the biblical stories. In a word, "catechism" was absorbed through many implicit and explicit cultural inputs.

As pervasive as these cultural instructions might be, there were serious defects. One defect was the problem of language. No one, except the clergy, was literate enough to understand the official Latin. With the language being an obstacle, the liturgy, so basically a teaching tool, was ineffective. People became passive spectators. Another defect was a too heavy reliance on externals and memory aids. This reliance forced some religious truths into some very artificial and stilted categories. We saw this already in the medieval fondness for numbers which spawned the seven sacraments, the seven petitions to the Lord's Prayer, the seven gifts of the Holy Spirit, and the seven capital sins. This "forcing" distorted the natural unity of the faith. Often the line between faith and magic was crossed. Externals were too much relied on. There are many recorded abuses concerning indulgences, relics, and pilgrimages. The eucharist sometimes degenerated into a magic talisman. Mass lost its central attraction. Fetish and faith intermingled and the medieval soul was capable of the most primitive superstition and the most exalted spirituality.

Notice that so far in our quick scan of the way things were catechetically the first fifteen hundred years we have said nothing about the role of children. The reason for this is very simple. Children *had* no role. There was no formal teaching of children as such. The church simply followed its natural Jewish and Roman heritage. In the old Jewish system, children were forbidden to attend the synagogue. The idea was that the father attended the synagogue, learned from the rabbi and then naturally transmitted the faith to his children. In Roman law, the father of the family had absolute control over his children. He decided whether they should live or die, how they should be educated, what jobs they should do, and whom they should marry. Both these traditions forced Christianity into the same basically sensible position. The Christian faith was essentially an adult religion and as the parents went, so would go the children. It was taken for granted that the parents would do the task aided by the culture, the liturgy and feast days, and the cult of the saints. Every guild, for example, had its patron saint. Local inns were named after biblical personages. Hospitals were often dedicated to the Holy Spirit. Even the emperor was crowned in a religious ceremony. The "Christian atmosphere" was highly supportive to parents. This is why it was reasonable to place all the burden on them and the sponsors. That is why sponsors for baptism had to undergo an examination to see if they, as adults, knew the faith well enough. They were examined on the two catechetical staples: the Creed and the Our Father. This explains why such sponsors, even up to our own day, had to know and even memorize these two prayers. We still see the remnant of this practice in the requirement, in some dioceses, that sponsors must get a letter or notation of worthiness from their pastors.

Because of the parent-to-child thrust, parents were constantly exhorted in the Middle Ages to teach their children. Pope Gregory the Great is on record as urging his bishops to teach the parents so that they in turn might catechize their children. A typical reminder of the times (seventh century) comes from a certain St. Eligius who writes, "Know by memory the Symbol (Creed) and the Lord's Prayer, and teach them to your children. Instruct and admonish the children whom you have received as newborn from the baptismal font, to live ever in the fear of God. Know that you have taken an oath on their behalf before God."[2] After thirteen centuries these words still find echoes in the pronouncements of Vatican II.

There were then, in the Middle Ages, no schools, no formal

catechism classes for children. We do read of certain schools arising under Charlemagne in the eighth century, schools which were attached to cathedrals and monasteries. But such schools lasted only a few decades and were really the preserve of the very few and practically restricted to boys preparing for the clerical state. Even when the old feudal system was breaking up and society was changing and towns were arising, new orders appeared on the scene. Such were the Dominicans and the Franciscans, and they went out to meet the needs of adults in those stressful times. They revived the art of preaching and went out to a new class of urban workers with their message.

2

The turning point, the dramatic shift from catechizing adults to formally catechizing children came in the sixteenth century. We might say that the father of the catechism is Martin Luther. It was he who saw in the century's-old invention of printing a most effective and inexpensive way of propagating his ideas. His pamphlets were enormously popular. It was a short step to conceive of a book for the people: first for his new Lutheran pastors and teachers and then one specifically for the people and finally one even for children. This book, the catechism, was put out in 1529. Soon a shorter catechism, with questions and answers, was published and given directly to *children*. Reflecting his new approaches Luther divided his catechism into the Commandments, the Creed, and the Sacraments. But the important point is that he started something. He not only introduced a catechism for children, but in time the logical outcome of this decision would be to have this catechism learned, not in the home, but in the classroom. Luther started another trend, unchallenged for many centuries: the children were to memorize their answers and give them back by rote.

The Roman Catholics were stunned by Luther's printing successes. They had no choice but to follow suit. Actually, there were other compelling reasons to do this. We had mentioned the loss of the people's ability to understand Latin and a liturgy which had become truly mystifying and overloaded with externalism and superstition. A catechism might be a good remedy for these ills. Further, a catechism would fulfill a great need in those crises times: a clear, concise question and answer book to combat the new Lutheran religion. So the first Catholic catechism was published in Augsburg in 1530, the year after Luther's. The most popular catechism of all time was published by St. Peter Canisius in 1555, and he put out a children's edition (note) in 1559. By 1686 there were over four hundred editions of the catechism and as late as the 1920's the "Canisius" catechism was still being used in Germany. Another very popular catechism was that of St. Robert Bellarmine, whose work was translated into sixty different languages because it was the one most widely used in the missions. Finally, we must note that the Council of Trent itself in 1563 decreed a new missal, a breviary, an index of forbidden books, and a catechism to be prepared for the use of adults and of children. Three years later such a catechism was indeed printed. It never became popular although it was an excellent work. The reason was that it was overshadowed by the catechisms of Canisius and Bellarmine.

As the centuries after Trent moved on and the church lost control of society, and indeed as nations arose and became more secular, then a new shift took place. In the phrase of the times the secular rulers were very enlightened. They promoted universal education and, as children of their times, they felt that some moral education was imperative. They were not so much interested in doctrinal purity as in moral control. In any case, they insisted that therefore religion be taught in the new schools and become a part of the curriculum. This was of some advantage to organized religion in those troubled times. It gave the teaching some shape and some definition. However, the liabilities soon outweighed the gains. For one thing, religion was effectively moved out of the home into the classroom. Secondly, it became just another subject. Learning the information rather than living the formation was more important. Thirdly, since the catechism was inserted into the classroom, the tendency grew to segregate religion from daily life and ultimately reduce it to one more subject to be gotten through and graded. Finally, marks for religion did their own mischief for they merely indicated the pupil's informational knowledge, not his practice.

Now for our purposes we must pause to note the radical change that has taken place in the religious instruction and formation of the children and the family. First of all, the Council of Trent, in responding to the crisis of the times, deliberately and consciously shifted perspective. It gave direct impetus to something entirely new in Christianity: the formal instruction of children. Secondly, the catechisms it fostered were in general superior works, scholarly, concise, and understandably orthodox. However, because of the times in which they were written they were defensively weighted. They overstressed points under attack. Then, too, they reflected the new teaching methodology of the time. A few centuries before the Greek Aristotle had been discovered in the West. His precise analytical method was very influential and made itself felt not only in late medieval theology but, as a result, in the catechism based on it. The result was a truly logical and well organized catechism, but one which became less and less historical, biblical, and narration orientated. Thirdly, the new emphasis on teaching children eventually created a mentality which let adults slip into second place, to become religiously passive while the professional clergy and religious took over in the classrooms.

Our own United States' experience has fostered these results. Secularism was still increasing. Because of religious pluralism and anti-Catholic bigotry, public schools were considered less and less satisfactory in transmitting moral, religious values. Alternates were sought out. The Protestant tradition generally turned to the Sunday bible classes. The Catholics began setting up their own school system, one that was not tax-supported but supported by its members. In 1884 the United States bishops, meeting at the Council of Baltimore decreed that every parish should set up its own parochial school where formal religious instruction and a religious atmosphere were to be part and parcel of the general curriculum. As expected, anti-Catholic resistence continued to be quite vocal and strong. They succeeded (to this very day) in preventing any state or federal assistance to millions of the country's citizens, but the Supreme Court, in the noted Oregon case of 1925, did uphold the right of Catholic parents to send their children to private religious schools. Still, even with the rapid growth of the parochial school system, many Catholic children continued to attend the public schools.

The famous Baltimore catechism had its origin in the general concern of the hierarchy for the faith of its children. It was first published in 1885, but interestingly, its title page carries a bit of minor misinformation. It states that the catechism "was prepared and enjoined by the order of the Third Plenary Council of Baltimore." Strictly speaking this was not accurate. The Baltimore catechism was actually written in about a week's time by a certain Monsignor Januarius de Consilio. It never had the official approval of the Baltimore Council, although later certainly Carnal Gibbons gave it his approval. What had happened was that the bishops had asked for advice among their peers concerning a local American catechism. Several European models were considered. A committee was further appointed to prepare a draft model. One of the bishops gave this project to Msgr. de Consilio. He quickly prepared a draft which was immediately published without really getting all of the bishops' collective official approval. As we pointed out, however, Cardinal Gibbons gave his approval and soon this "Baltimore" catechism became the most widely used catechism in America. It was revised in 1941 and is still used in some places today.

Meanwhile, several factors were working once more to turn the whole catechetical scene around. For one thing, modern educational theories were being expounded. Everyone was rethinking the process and the methods of education in general. Newer psychological insights were being examined. It would be too much to ask to have religious education exempted from this general scrutiny. There had always been some dissatisfaction with the classroom situation and with the narrow formula kind of religious learning. There was a need to get back to a more rounded approach, one that involved more of life and more of the church's liturgical life. So in 1900 a Catechetical Movement was formed. After World War I, which brought a lull in religious rethinking, the old rote memorization came under attack. Catechetical Congresses began to be held. Global strategies were plotted. Then, just as many new approaches were being tried, Vatican II came along and further reshifted emphases. It, of course, upheld the traditional role of the parents but also made a great deal (as we have seen) of the family's and the community's role in the celebration of the liturgy (including, naturally, the sacraments). It was to be expected that, in all of the new insights, mistakes would be made and catechisms would be tried, discarded, and revised with great rapidity. To bring some stability into the catechetical scene the United States bishops issued a booklet called *To Teach as Jesus Did* in 1973. It outlined the general principle of doctrine and morals that would guide catechetics. Another publication followed called *Basic Teaching for Catholic Religious Education* and the title told it all. A year later a massive project to publish a national Catechetical Directory was launched and is still being prepared at this writing.

3

Now all of this has a great deal to do with the subject of this book. The role of parents has come full circle. Once more the teaching and the liturgy are being designed to involve the parents and the community heavily. A far more comprehensive catechesis is envisioned with the burden coming down emphatically on the role of the parents:

Since parents have given children life, they are bound by the most serious obligation to educate their offspring and therefore must be recognized as the primary and principal educators. This role in education is so important that only with difficulty can it be supplied when it is lacking. . . . It is particularly in the Christian family, enriched by the grace and office of the sacrament of matrimony, that children should be taught from their early years to have a knowledge of God according to the faith received in baptism, to worship him, and to love their neighbor.[3]

The parents' faith and practice is being put on the line and made normative. The church is seeing itself as assisting the parents rather than the other way around.

The irony is, of course, that precisely at the time the responsibility is being placed on the parents, the parents are receiving the least support themselves. The breakup of family life is commonplace, divorces have passed the million mark per year. These are bad enough. What is worse is the lack of shared values and community support. Pluralism, individual whims, the humanistic banalities from the mass media undermine authority and morality. As one writer put it, "If anything should be put forward in the church's proclamation, it should be the understanding that to live by the gospel is to live in a state of deviancy from many of the values most dearly held in our culture."[4] Mobility is high, neighborhoods have disintegrated and even the Catholic church (at least in its actual parish expression) presents a bewildering pluralism on every conceivable moral, liturgical, and doctrinal subject. Still, for all of this, the final transmission of the faith, the "success" of belief will continue to depend on faith-filled families and the support that such families receive to fulfill their tasks. The modern catechetical effort has tried to keep this in mind. It has gone back to the older tradition where Christianity was seen basically as an adult faith passed informally on to children the way all values are passed on: by a comfortable daily living out of the gospel in the home and in the assembly of fellow believers celebrating with dignity, joy, and vigor those saving mysteries of God in Christ.

"In the assembly of fellow believers" brings us to our final point. Parents in isolation cannot do the catechetical task well.

Nor, apparently, can a once-a-week CCD class. Andrew Greeley's findings are: "The NORC research would indicate that the various forms of nonparochial school religious instruction which have become popular in the Catholic church in the last ten years are not an adequate substitute for parochial schools. In most cases they seem to have practically no effect at all"[5] But even the parochial schools fall short if parish life is lacking. Moreover, as has often been said, since Christianity is not so much information as formation, then the parish does in fact assume larger catechetical importance, and of all the many things a parish does, its celebration of the sacraments can be the most catechizing of all.

The sacraments celebrated within a community setting are valuable teaching moments. Baptisms, anointings of the sick, weddings, funerals, and, above all, Christian initiation, within the public and regularly scheduled weekend community masses are most effective. Not only the words, but the doing, the actions, the movements, the people all emit a sense of what is going on. Grandparents to children are caught up in the audio-visual action of the sacraments celebrated within the public Mass liturgy; and, along with the whole congregation, they become in effect collective sponsors for the various candidates. Add to this the obvious gladness of the occasion, the genuine applause of the congregation plus some public refreshments afterwards and you have catechizing at its best: by osmosis. In fact, what we are describing here is a return to the original method of early times. The truism of our survey has returned: through faith-filled activity in the parish community the children learn.[6]

NOTES FOR CHAPTER 15

1. I am grateful to Bishop Raymond Lucker who graciously loaned me his dissertation on the history and development of catechetics.

2. PL 87, 527.

3. Declaration on Christian Education, no. 3.

4. Ralph Keifer, *Commonweal* (September 27, 1974), p. 520.

5. *Origins,* April 8, 1976, p. 672.

6. See articles such as "The Restoration of the Catechumenate as a Norm for Catechesis," by Thomas P. Ivory, *The Living Light* 13, no. 2 (Summer 1976); also, "The Revised Adult Initiation and Its Challenge to Religious Education," by Charles W. Gusmer, *The Living Light* 13 (Spring 1976).

A Pastoral Epilog

We have taken our five sacraments and examined them from the historical point of view. We have traced their development throughout the ages down to our own times, when all of them have been revised. Now we close with some personal reflections—very hesitant and uncertain—on several of the practicalities that beset the man in the parish, whether pastor or layperson.

The first practicality is that old, tired word, community. Still, overused as this word may be today, community is the context of every sacrament. Community is presupposed quite explicitly in both Vatican II's decrees and in the introductions to the revisions of the sacramental rites. We have already taken note of its most forceful expression in the new rite for the initiation of adults. First, we notice that the initiation of adults in this public manner is definitely presented as theologically normative. That is, even though in practice the baptism of infants will continue to predominate, the public, graduated steps of adult initiation is the norm. It calls for a restoration of the catechumenate and the restoration of Lent as the final time of preparation for the baptism that takes place on the Easter vigil. The directive says, "The initiation of catechumens takes place step by step in the midst of the community of the faithful. Together with the catechumens, the faithful reflect upon the value of the paschal mystery, renew their own conversion, and by their example, lead the catechumens to obey the Holy Spirit more generously." And, again another directive reminds us that the "initiation of adults is the concern and the business of all the baptized."[1]

All this bears out our contention in the first chapters of this book that the sacraments are not isolated signs, performed by an isolated individual for an isolated individual. Sacraments are actions of celebrating community and are truly brought into being as such. There is a lovely phrase that describes the church as "Jesus assembled." That says it all when we come to a discussion and understanding of the sacraments. "Jesus assembled"—the believing community—*is* the sign of the reality which is God's grace. The believing and worshiping community are themselves the primary sacrament because they are the church which is in turn the sign of Christ.

The implication of the sacraments as being legitimate only as community celebrations of the mysteries of salvation is truly staggering. This is so especially in reference to the sacraments of initiation which have in fact become *the* public event of the local and universal church with its rhythms of Lent and Easter. It implies a totally different concept of the church from most people's who tend to look only at the external, institutional structure of the church or who see it as a service center to dispense the sacraments at the individual's (or pastor's) convenience. It implies a church that is communitarian, engaging a variety of ministries, bound by the living word of the scripture and nourished by a common eucharist. It implies familiarity, relationship, unity, and a deep sense of fellowship.

Alas, some parishes simply are not that by any stretch of the imagination. It's not that all parishes, like all other institutions, suffer from excessive mobility, the distraction and competition of the mass media, and the shrinking number of people interested in even attending church. It's that some parishes are impersonal, overlarge, poorly staffed, and working on different priorities, such as reducing the debt or running a spiritual service station which opens weekends, and closes during the week. But even this is not the ultimate practical, pastoral problem for the survival and proclamation of the sacraments. The ultimate problem is the lack of clear-cut leadership and understanding that parish life is supposed to be precisely as the revised sacramental rites imply. The problem is that there has not been any massive, consistent, national program to help parishes and the clergy that staff them to realize this. Of all of the important items on the bishop's national agenda, never has the parish come up for a full-time study. One thinks (with gratitude) of the unprecedented catechesis which accompanied the new rite of penance. Never has so much print, lecture, and workshop tackled a single topic with such national determination and thoroughness. One wishes that someday a similar effort would be made on behalf of the parish.

The point is, the average Catholic identifies, rightly or wrongly, his parish with the "church universal." Christ is truly localized for him at his parish level. The comings and goings of bishops and synods do not immediately grab him. He is grabbed at the level of his marital needs, his family needs, his economic needs, his spiritual needs in his parish. Or he is not. Sacramental celebrations where there is no community are a picture without a frame. They lack the essential context which would make them truly communal, redemptive signs of God's gracious activity. It would seem to me that as we talk sacraments, as we teach revisions, as we catechize, we must first of all look to the foundation on which all this rests: the believing community. If that is less than it should be, the sacraments will always be less than they should be.

It is hard to resist a further pastoral footnote to this matter of community. It is the conviction that if sacraments basically depend on parish community, then the parishes in turn depend on the leadership—in this case, the bishops. The need for pastoral bishops—ones with "feel" for people, for parish life, for community problems, for family stresses is paramount. Bishops untouched by life, fresh out of the seminary positions or from a series of antiseptic administrative offices can hardly find parishes a priority of their ministry. One yearns for the bishop-pastors of the early centuries: people like Basil, Gregory, Augustine, Ambrose, Chrysostom, Cyril, all of whom were bishops and pastors and who therefore were able to combine the most lofty theologizing with the most basic good pastoral sense. That's why it was with a great deal of personal satisfaction that I read the address of Bishop Albert Ottenweller to the National Conference of Catholic Bishops meeting in Washington in November of 1975:

I feel very honored to be able to present to this body of bishops a concern of mine for the future of the church. I will try to be brief and to the point. From the outset I must admit that I have a prejudice in favor of priests who are in pastoral ministry.

I see the parish as the key to renewal in the church. I am not a theologian, nor a scripture scholar. For more than thirty years I have worked as a parish priest. I see myself as a journeyman pastor experienced in dealing with people and problems at the grassroots.

I think a pastor's expertise is taking theory, theological principles, and making them work on the level of where people are. I think this was Martin Luther King's genius—he drew the principles of civil rights out of the textbook, Jesus' teaching from the gospels, and took them down to a crowded basement of a Baptist Church in Selma, Alabama, and brought them to birth in people there; and they marched through the streets, and theory became a *movement*.

I think priests do this in parishes. Under the guidance of the Holy Spirit the bishops at the Second Vatican Council saw a vision of what the church of our time ought to be. But that vision must be brought to life in the churches and in the market place. It is one thing to formulate guidelines for the new rite of penance—it is quite another thing to put those guidelines to work so that ordinary Catholic people may celebrate penance as a deep and satisfying experience.

This said, I would like to propose that a study be made of the model parish as presently structured compared to the other possible models. I think restructuring is critical because parish priests are finding it extremely difficult if not impossible to bring the directives of the Second Vatican Council to life in their parishes (especially the large parishes) as those parishes are now constituted.

I will not take up your time going over the problem of

declining Mass attendance, alienation of youth, lack of communication, etc., that beset large parishes in this day. They are
only too well known. I would like to mention, however, the
frustration of pastors and others working in parish ministry.

I see talented priests avoiding parish work in favor of the
specialties such as campus ministry, counseling, religious education, etc. I see pastors of larger parishes transferred to
smaller parishes, having breakdowns, just waiting around for
retirement. I believe that a substantial part of the problem lies
in this fact that, at least, the large parishes are not fitted for
the job the council is asking them to do. To coin a phrase—
we're trying to put new wine into the old bottles.

What do I mean by restructuring the parish? Mostly when
we talk about models we think in terms of church in general.
Instead of talking about the institutional *church,* and *church* as
a community I would like to speak of the *parish* as institution
and the *parish* as community. For our purposes I would like to
define institution in this way: *Institution* is a grouping of
people organized to put out a product, or deliver a service.
For example, at General Motors people are organized as
workers, sales people, etc. to produce and market au-
tomobiles. In an institution the product is important not the
person.

I would define community as a group of people banded
together not to put out a product or to deliver a service, but to
grow in relation to one another. Example: the family. A family
does not put out a product or deliver a service. Members are
responsible for each other. They care for each other and in
loving relationships they grow as persons.

Now let's refer these ideas to the parish situation. A parish is
an institution. And this must not be minimized. A parish de-
livers services. It educates, cares for the poor, helps the missions, etc. But a parish is also a community. Members of a
parish have a need and a right to be like an extended family,
to know each other, care for each other and so grow in the
love of God and of one another. My contention is that right
now, organizationally, parishes are very heavy on institution
and very light on community.

For example, suppose in the parish we are worried about

our religious education program. It is not effective. Young people are not showing up. How do we meet the problem? Institutionally we must put out a better product. We will improve CCD teacher training. We'll buy the best film strips we can find. Perhaps we'll even invest in a director of religious education. We'll give it one more try. After all this effort, maybe, children stay away in even greater numbers than before. Why? They are hungry for community, but we keep giving them institution. We emphasize product more than person.

The movements that seem spiritually alive and appealing are such groups as cursillo, marriage encounter, charismatic prayer groups, comunidades de base—groups that are person and growth oriented. It seems very odd that in most cases parishioners must go outside the parish structure to be a part of one of these movements.

My proposal is that parish structure be studied to find a model more adaptable to our times and to the vision of the council.

Both the crisis and the challenge it seems to me lie in the parish. We can strengthen commissions, conferences and departments on both national and diocesan levels, but unless their programs are able to be absorbed and implemented on the parish level, not much is accomplished.

I know a pastor who reads it like this. He says, "I feel like there is a big funnel above me. All kinds of programs are dumped into it from the top: the new rite of penance, bicentennial observance, Holy Year, fight against abortion—and he listed some more—and they come down through the narrow end of that funnel right on my head."

It seems to me that beautiful programs have been developed for use in parishes. I call them secondary programs. Many of them, ideal as they are, never see the light of day, or at most only dimly, because the primary structure of the parish is faulty. It is not adapted to do the job we ask of it.

If we can say with Pope Paul, "The church is a mystery," we also can say, "The parish is a mystery." It is a reality imbued with the presence of God.

It lies, therefore, within the very nature of the parish to be

always open to new and greater exploration. It is my proposal
that the structure of the parish be explored so that it truly can
be God's little flock.[2]

Indeed, if the mysteries of salvation are to be manifest we do
need to look to new structures in the parish. We shall have to
learn to live with pastorless parishes and parishes administered
by total team ministries which include religious and laity. The
challenges are great, but it is my conviction that we cannot talk
sacraments unless we first talk parish and its task of bringing
people into a relationship with one another on many other levels.

The second practicality that poses a most difficult pastoral
problem is the conversionist mentality of the sacraments. They
all loftily speak of sincere faith, of genuine conversion, of *metanoia*. Parents are preached to, candidates are admonished—
yet, in practice we really don't know how to handle the situation
where conversion or faith are not evident. In practice, it means
that we have much ambivalence about either refusing or post-
poning any of the sacraments or instituting on our own any kind
of catechumenate. We don't want to play God; we don't want to
sit in judgment on another's conscience and, above all, we don't
want to be accused of being elitist. Besides, who knows? The
sacrament may actually "take" someday.

Yet, as often as we parish priests in fact do not refuse, so much
more often we are dismayed over what we have called the millions of baptized pagans. Again, like the parish problem, the
local problem is aggravated by the fact that the parish priest has
to make these decisions alone. There is no open policy. Demands
on parents, for example, vary from diocese to diocese and parish
to parish. For every one priest who hesitates to scatter the sacraments indiscriminately, there are hundreds of others who put
trust in the "objective" grace of the sacraments. For every one
who worries about cheapening the sacraments, there are hundreds more who will gamble freely with them. The tension between elitist "purity" and assembly-line magic is a real one.

Parishes need help in knowing which way to go if the sacraments are to mean anything.[3]

Moreover, as we suggested earlier, we have to come to terms with *adult* conversion. We have already seen that the new rite of the initiation for adults presupposes adult conversion as normative. But generally we don't know what to do with such adults who are sincerely converted to the Lord. We are either suspicious of them, embarrassed by them and so take them secretly aside for instructions, try to reroute them into religious life or breathe a sigh of relief when they latch onto the local cursillo or charismatic movements. A simple, open, bold, genuine adult convert threatens us all too much. Yet, as the new rite suggests, we have to give *this* experience priority and have a parish sense of awe at least equivalent to the emotional atmosphere with which we surround first communion and confirmation. And this includes those adolescents and adults, already initiated into faith, who have had a "second" conversion. We must invent some parish paraliturgical service that gives them a public platform to declare their deeper commitment to Jesus. This must be before the local parish community. We must not relegate them to a private fringe group.

A third practicality is the need to discover a genuine American liturgy. If, as Bernard Lonergan says, theology mediates between a current cultural matrix and the meaning and role of religion in that matrix, then the liturgy, especially the sacramental liturgies, are in prime position to express this mediation. The tension, however, is to keep the sacramental tradition traditional enough so that it expresses ancient truth and current enough so that it speaks to the culture. Our present sacramental liturgies may fulfill neither role. They may be so ancient as to be meaningless today or so contemporary as to be faddist. It would seem that the genius of all of us Americans, not just the hierarchy, must be tapped to come somewhere in between.

A fourth practicality is one we have already mentioned: the return to a sense of the sacred (wonder) in all of creation. It is only with this rediscovered sense that the sacraments will be "expanded" to include a wider ministry. As Father Kenneth Smits says,

> This means a respect for *all* life, sacraments that celebrate *all* of human growth, from birth to death, and Christian initiation as a sacred celebration which encompasses all that human birth means to all concerned, and it is not limited to removing an invisible stain on an invisible soul. It also means anointing of the sick and the wider ministry associated with it that embraces all of sickness and the human condition of the sick person. This means rites of reconciliation that deal with the dividedness of the human condition, personal, familial or societal, internal or external. It means rites of Christian marriage that envelop all of the celebration and are not just a ritual to perform before the celebration begins. And it means ordering in Christian life that celebrates the whole reality of Christian ministry, in all the diverse forms that are needed in the contemporary and future Church, both men and women, permanent and temporary, new and old. We need better and fuller liturgical signs, as well as the development of liturgical forms to celebrate many lesser occasions of life, so that the totality of human living, not just isolated moments which seem to be the chosen preserve of grace, can be recognized and celebrated. All creation, even though laden by sin, is from God, and all creation has been initially grasped by Christ in his redemptive action. We are the inheritors of this great promise of both creation and salvation. It would seem that a large field is open here for rediscovering Christ in our American culture and heritage. The agony and pain of the paschal mystery would always be there, but resting upon the solid foundation of the incarnation. . . .[4]

Fifthly, we must worry about making the sacraments an internal matter only. This means that as the community celebrates the sacraments and as the sacraments create the community, then the result should be a greater catholicity. In other words, the sacraments are related to evangelization. They are related to the six million members of the Jewish community in America, the seventy-one million members of the Protestant community and the ninety million Americans who have no religious affiliation whatever—not to mention the nominal members of our own forty-eight million Catholics. And, it is not just a question of reaching out to these people to "convert" them, but a reaching out to them to promote justice.

To put it another way, the making of a just society is the task of a morally committed Christian community. After all, through a series of encyclicals, beginning with *Rerum Novarum,* we Catholics have been urged not merely to alleviate the results of poverty and injustice, but to focus on eliminating their causes. Unless the average parish community is related to the world problems, it will wind up, even with the best of sacramental liturgies, as a self-serving system alienating the young and suffocating the old. We must remember that "what Catholicism provides as Catholicism . . . is a definition of community that includes all the people, the fostering of an ethic that affirms life, the sponsoring of programs that provide for the development of peoples, the celebration of eucharist that is transforming for everybody, and a community without walls marked by Christian love that is for the poor."[5] We must not forget that if the Good News is indeed to bring the good news to the poor then we must be prepared to deliver when the poor respond.

There is caution, of course, as we talk here essentially of the connection between a sacramental Christian community and social justice. The caution comes from the sterile experiences of the Protestants at the turn of this century and the Catholics of the 1960s who engaged in a one-sided activism. Their failures show us that more than a mere worthy social goal is required. That "something" is a spiritual dynamic which the sacraments can help create. That something must be a "journey inward that constantly fuels the journey outward." Social justice begins and ends with the Spirit. Without that core spirituality, celebrated in and from the sacraments, all is reduced to an empty and ultimately bankrupt humanism.

More than this I cannot say for it is beyond the scope of this book to discuss the matters of evangelization and social justice. All that I wish to emphasize is that any parish worth its sacramental salt must constantly investigate itself to see that its aims are not self-serving; that indeed the very nature of such a parish is to witness for justice and sometimes against the prevailing unjust culture. "When the church is in step with the times it's dead. Whoever marries the spirit of the times will be a widow," says Pastor Richard Neuhaus. This advice does not imply the angry pulpit harangue that is so unfair and offensive to decent parishioners. It means rather that a rhythmic sacramental life, by its very nature, not only sees most of the world in poverty and political bondage, but feels the compulsion of the Spirit, celebrated in common prayer and sacraments, to do something about them. "The love of Christ urges us on," says St. Paul.

The final practicality is the ideal of spirituality. The sacraments ultimately deal with the Spirit of God who first loved us, who takes the initiative and who asks our human response under his impulse. It would seem that a whole area of prayer, of faith, of living a committed life has to be explored first. These are the "stuff" with which the sacraments deal. Perhaps the grassroots return to spirituality, prayer, and meditation in the past years is telling us that we have jettisoned too much of our Catholic tradition; that the wisdom of the mystics, the insights of the Fathers, the living word of scripture, the coming to terms with Christ by saints of every age have to be sounded again. And even the native genius of popular devotions must be taken more seriously.

We complained in the first chapter about the sacraments being taken out of context, of being reduced to isolated moments apart from the community mysteries. All that this epilog is saying is to beware of the danger reappearing. To understand the sacraments is very valuable, but to place them in a living context of a believing and celebrating community is more valuable. And more challenging. All of the sacramental directives, revisions, and rubrics in the world will go unfulfilled without a living community. And for one who must necessarily be biased, having been a parish priest for over twenty years, I would say that in practice that means the revival and support of the parish.

NOTES FOR A PASTORAL EPILOG

1. The Rite of Christian Initiation of Adults, nos. 4 and 41. See Roger Beraudy, "The New Rite for Adult Baptism," *Theology Digest* 24, no. 1 (Spring 1976), p. 57.

2. *Origins* 5, no. 25, p. 394ff.

3. See "Too Strict About the Sacraments These Days?" by Rev. James Callancin in *Today's Parish* (October 1975), p. 37. For the Protestant difficulties in this area see "To March or Not to March" by Francine du Plessix Gray, *New York Times Magazine* (June 27, 1976), p. 7ff.

4. Kenneth Smits, "Liturgical Reform in Cultural Perspective," *Worship* 50, no. 2 (March 1976), p. 109.

5. Marie Augusta Neal, S.N.D., "How Americans Look at Religion Today," *New Catholic World* 219, no. 1312 (July/August 1976). The entire excellent issue is devoted to evangelization.